# READING TO LEARN

## SOLVING PROBLEMS IN THE TEACHING OF LITERACY
### Cathy Collins Block, Series Editor

# READING TO LEARN

## Lessons from
## Exemplary Fourth-Grade Classrooms

Richard L. Allington
Peter H. Johnston

Foreword by Michael Pressley
Afterword by Gerald G. Duffy

THE GUILFORD PRESS
New York   London

© 2002 The Guilford Press
A Division of Guilford Publications, Inc.
72 Spring Street, New York, NY 10012
www.guilford.com

Printed in the United States of America

This book is printed on acid-free paper.

Last digit is print number:  9  8  7  6  5  4  3  2  1

Library of Congress Cataloging-in-Publication Data is available from the Publisher.

ISBN 1-57230-763-3 (cloth)—ISBN 1-57230-762-5 (pbk.)

*To Ms. Unser, friend and unfailing colleague*

# About the Authors

**Richard L. Allington, PhD,** is the Irving and Rose Fien Distinguished Professor of Education at the University of Florida. He currently serves on the editorial boards of *Reading Research Quarterly, Remedial and Special Education*, the *Journal of Literacy Research*, and the *Elementary School Journal*. He has previously served on the editorial boards of the *Review of Educational Research* and the *Journal of Educational Psychology*. Dr. Allington has published several books, including *Classrooms That Work: They Can All Read and Write* and *Schools That Work: Where Children Read and Writer* both coauthored with Patricia M. Cunningham, *No Quick Fix: Rethinking Literacy Programs in America's Elementary Schools* with Sean Walmsley, and *Learning to Read: Lessons from Exemplary First-Grade Classrooms* with Michael Pressley and others. His latest book is *What Really Matters for Struggling Readers: Designing Research-Based Programs*, published by Allyn & Bacon.

**Peter H. Johnston, PhD,** is a Professor in the Reading Department at the University at Albany–SUNY and a senior researcher for the National Research Center on English Learning and Achievement. He currently serves on the editorial boards of *Reading Research Quarterly*, the *Journal of Literacy Research*, the *Elementary School Journal*, and *Literacy, Teaching and Learning*. Dr. Johnston chaired the International Reading Association (IRA) and National Council of Teachers of English (NCTE) Joint Task Force on Assessment that produced the position monograph *Standards for the Assessment of Reading and Writing*. He is also author of *Constructive Evaluation of Literate Activity, Reading Comprehension Assessment: A Cognitive Basis, Running Records: A Self-Tutoring Guide,* and *Knowing Literacy*. His research has received awards from the IRA and from the Educational Press Association.

# Preface and Acknowledgments

This book represents the efforts of a large and dedicated group of colleagues. Peter Johnston and I asked Michael Pressley to write the Foreword because it was Mike who initiated this line of research and who codirected the first-grade exemplary teacher component (Pressley, Allington, Wharton-McDonald, Block, & Morrow, 2001). While Mike left the University at Albany to take a position at the University of Notre Dame after data collection was completed for the first-grade project, he has continued his involvement with the research team. For that I am most grateful, and because of this involvement it seemed most appropriate that Mike write the Foreword to this book.

Peter Johnston accepted my invitation to codirect the fourth-grade exemplary teacher component after Mike's departure. Peter and I had codirected an earlier longitudinal project studying teacher change (Johnston, Allington, Guice, & Brooks, 1998) and I thought that after a year of sabbatical leave in New Zealand, he would feel guilty enough to accept this new responsibility. Unbeknownst to either of us at the time, I would also depart the University at Albany after the fourth-grade data had been collected and the preliminary analyses begun. This left Peter in charge of a large-scale project, one with rapidly depleting resources. While I have attempted to assist Peter in the completion of this project, that is easier said than done from 1,200 miles away. But the project is nearing completion, and Peter is still speaking to me. For that and for his dedication to this effort, I am forever grateful.

Our colleagues in the Department of Reading at the University at Albany have all contributed in one or more ways to the execution of this study. Anne McGill-Franzen, RoseMarie Weber, Sean Walmsley, Jim Collins, Ginny Goatley, and Sherry Guice all helped us think through the complexity of this undertaking. This study was improved because of their assistance and expertise.

Four colleagues at other universities—Ruth Wharton-McDonald at the University of New Hampshire, Gay Ivey at James Madison University, Lesley Morrow at Rutgers University, and Cathy Collins Block at Texas Christian University—worked with us in designing the study, completing the data collection, and analyzing, interpreting, and presenting the results. We could not have attempted such a large-scale effort without their assistance and expertise. Additionally, Nancy Farnan, Marcie Cox, and Helen Foster James of San Diego State University helped us locate exemplary teachers and with the data collection.

A number of graduate research assistants conducted many of the classroom observations and executed much of the associated data reduction and analyses. In many cases these folks gave several years of their lives to this research project. Jeni Pollack Day, Kim Boothroyd, Greg Brooks, Steven Powers, Haley Woodside-Jiron, John Cronin, Melissa Cedeno, Susan Leyden, Jean Veltema, and Paula Costello all deserve special recognition for the insights they offered about effective teaching and for their extraordinary efforts to make this project a success.

Thirty fourth-grade teachers allowed us into their classrooms and their lives over a 2-year period. They trusted us and were interested enough in this project to put up with strangers wandering around their rooms and their lives. This book would not exist were it not for their willingness to take the risks associated with such an effort. We have attempted to capture the classrooms of six of these teachers in the case studies included in this book. Some of the remaining 24 classrooms have been featured in other work we have published (e.g., Allington & Johnston, in press; Johnston, Woodside-Jiron, & Day, 2001). Each and every one of these teachers influenced our thinking about effective fourth-grade teaching. Thank you for your patience, insight, and genuine friendliness. Thank you also for what you offer all those fourth graders whom you have taught and have yet to teach.

I must also note that this project would never have left the gate, as they say, were it not for the leadership of Judith Langer and Arthur Applebee, the codirectors of the National Research Center on English Learning and Achievement. Without their support and encouragement (and gentle explanations why such-and-such paperwork must be completed), this project would never have begun, much less have been completed. Funding for this project was provided by the Research and Development Centers Program (Grant No. R305A6005) as administered by the Office of Educational Research and Improvement, U.S. Department of Education. Without such funding, it is unlikely that a study of this scope could have been undertaken. However, the contents of this book do not necessarily represent the positions or policies of the sponsor.

Finally, I must briefly explain why this book is dedicated to Mary Unser. Ms. Unser is the senior member of the Department of Reading at the University at Albany–SUNY. She arrived there as the departmental secretary just a few months before I did, almost 30 years ago. Her unending supply of good humor, her patience with me and other faculty, her helpfulness to the graduate students enrolled in the department's programs, and her unwavering "How can I help?" attitude made my long career at the university a delightful experience. I miss her down here in Gainesville. As for her role in this project: Imagine the numbers of things that need to be attended to when you have two senior faculty and an armful of research assistants traveling to four states. Just imagine. And yet, somehow, we all got through it, and Ms. Unser was always there on Monday, smiling and asking for the travel expense receipts.

RICHARD L. ALLINGTON

# Foreword

## Michael Pressley

You are about to read an important book. It is an honor to have played a small part in it. When the National Research Center on English Learning and Achievement (CELA) was proposed, I worked with the SUNY–Albany group to develop a proposal to study elementary-level classrooms where literacy instruction was producing high engagement and achievement. Shortly after the funding of the Center, Dick Allington, Cathy Collins Block, Lesley Mandel Morrow, Ruth Wharton-McDonald and I set off on the first leg of that research venture, studying grade-1 classrooms in New York, California, Texas, New Jersey, and Wisconsin. We gained a clear understanding of how effective grade-1 classrooms differed from more typical ones and wrote a book-length summary of our findings (*Learning to Read: Lessons from Exemplary First-Grade Classrooms* by Pressley, Allington, et al., 2001; see also Pressley, Wharton-McDonald, et al., 2001).

That research experience continues to shape my reactions to many of the positions being advanced by policymakers and researchers about how to improve beginning literacy instruction in the United States. Parents and teachers are confronted daily by claims that beginning literacy will improve rapidly if there is more standardized testing or teacher-proof phonics curricula put in place. Standardized tests will leverage the curriculum in the directions covered on the tests. One prominent area covered on such tests is the reading of words in isolation; thus teaching of phonics will increase, which mediates word-level reading, especially if states are only willing to subsidize grade-1 curricular materials that are heavy in phonics. Although my perspective is that it makes sense to give grade-1 teachers excellent materials to do their job—including excellent phonics kits—there is no way that tests or materials of any sort will guarantee excellent beginning literacy instruction.

The problem with the policymakers' confidence in tests and materials is obvious in light of the Pressley, Allington, et al. (2001) analyses: Grade-1 classrooms where literacy achievement is high differ in many ways from grade-1 classrooms where growth in reading and writing competencies are less certain. Excellent first-grade teachers have high expectations of their students and emphasize reading and writing with great variety in the delivery of the instruction (i.e., from whole group to small group to individual lessons) and the content of the instruction (i.e., from phonics lessons to author studies and writing of class big books). Much of the instruction involves scaffolding, which requires the teacher to perceive the instructional needs of a child as he or she carries out the task of the moment, offering just enough instruction to sustain the student's progress with the task. Ironically, not much of what some policymakers mandate is needed in grade-1 classrooms is evident in the effective grade-1 settings that we studied. That is, effective grade-1 teachers do not confine their instruction to the areas stressed in standardized tests. Moreover, although they teach word-level skills, phonics is woven into their curriculum rather than dominating it. Contrary to the policymakers' perspectives, it is the *teacher* who makes the difference in classrooms where beginning literacy achievement is high.

After the completion of the data collection for the grade-1 study, Dick Allington, Peter Johnston, and their associates (all of whom contributed to this volume) set out to conduct a comparable analysis at the grade-4 level. Because I was seriously ill at the time, I was not able to participate in that leg of the research journey. I have watched at a distance as the work moved forward, recognizing that the study was impressive in its scope: carried out in five states, with 10 days of observation per classroom and interviews of teachers accompanying the observations. Social scientific work is abundant in this book!

The results of this impressive analysis of grade-4 teaching are summarized and illustrated by detailed case studies of the excellent teachers observed. The components of excellent grade-4 literacy instruction are complex but again driven by an outstanding teacher. Effective fourth-grade teachers are caring, enthusiastic, and confident that they can teach children to read. They create classrooms that are language-rich, with much discussion about reading and writing between teacher and children as well as between children. They use a variety of curricular materials, with students reading many different genres. Although they plan their instruction well, they also take advantage of teachable moments by providing many apt mini-lessons in response to student needs throughout the school day. Reading and writing are often connected with social studies, science, or even current events, which effectively integrates the various content areas and the school day. Rather than worrying about how their students will perform on a standardized test, they focus on their efforts and areas of improvement. They are keenly aware that their students all have unique developmental trajectories, and they are determined to foster the development of each and every student in their care. Successful fourth-grade teachers are models of literacy who demonstrate by their actions that reading and writing are important.

Excellent fourth-grade classrooms are constructivist, with students and teachers working *together*. The direct transmission of knowledge from teachers to students—which is the approach that policymakers seem to embrace—is *not* emphasized in these rich environments. Rather, students are expected to construct and communicate their own interpretations of what is being read.

Excellent grade-4 teachers sustain their excellence despite considerable state testing pressure and requirements that they follow uniform curriculum guidelines very closely. The teachers showcased in this volume know that literacy involves far more than the competencies captured by contemporary standardized achievement tests. Clearly, a complete understanding of literacy progress in individual students requires the testing community to develop assessments that tap students' abilities to interpret and reflect on what they read as well as students' motivations to read and write. In reading this volume, I feel a sense of sorrow that so much of what these excellent teachers do will not be captured by existing accountability measures. When it becomes possible to measure literacy competence more broadly, the types of classroom environments described in this book can serve as inspiring models for the profession.

This book provides a more complete understanding of excellent fourth-grade instruction than any other resource now available. The case studies, especially, offer rich witness to the workings of excellent classrooms where achievement is high, where students are always reading the "good stuff" and composing their own awesome stories and books. In short, this is a book that every fourth-grade teacher should read, as should anyone interested in improving literacy instruction in the middle and upper elementary grades.

The U.S. Department of Education, Office of Educational Research and Improvement, sponsored the research summarized in this volume. I think they got the full value of their investment, although I am also keenly aware that recent documents related to literacy instruction issued by federal agencies have ignored qualitative analyses such as the one reported here. The National Reading Panel (2000) explicitly excluded ethnographies, despite the recommendations of at least one member of the panel (Joanne Yatvin) that ethnographies should be included in a report claiming to summarize the scientific evidence related to beginning reading instruction. Ethnographies are the best approach I know of for revealing how the many elements of instruction can be interwoven to produce teaching that is much more than the separate parts. The National Reading Panel, however, favored experimental studies that focused on individual literacy instructional practices. Although such work definitely is important, it does not accomplish what the ethnographies reported in this volume and elsewhere accomplish, which is to identify how the individual components of reading instruction can be orchestrated and to provide the raw data for constructing theories of complex instruction.

The authors of this volume have created a theory of what creates excellent grade-4 literacy instruction that is grounded in the realities of the fourth-grade classrooms from across the nation that were studied. Every one of these classrooms had its own personality, and the mixes of instruction are anything but cookie-cutter replicates across sites. The teachers in these classrooms invent their instruction to accommodate the children they teach and to reflect the practices that they have found helpful with their students. This book invites teachers to be inventive. The theory summarizes the consistencies across classrooms—consistencies that can be manifested in many different ways, depending on the teacher and the classroom community being served.

The qualitative work summarized in this volume took years to compile. Given the amount of effort to carry out this task, I doubt that there will be anything like a comprehensive follow-up to this research. Unfortunately, efforts such as the National Reading Panel (2000) have favored research that is replicated repeatedly, in contrast to more ambitious and novel studies, such as this one, which look at literacy in ways that have not predominated in the literature. Great science is not achieved solely by the replication efforts favored by the National Reading Panel but by work that cuts new edges, identifying new directions that are potentially profitable research areas in which to illuminate a phenomenon (Pressley, in press). Although I do not believe the study summarized in this book will be replicated *in toto*, the work reported in this volume will stimulate many to study fourth-grade teaching more completely. I look forward to that work, for much needs to be known about how literacy can be developed in the middle elementary grades.

In their important book *Surpassing Ourselves*, Carl Bereiter and Marlene Scardamalia (1993) propose that experts become experts by their determination to improve continually. One of the most important points made in this book, *Reading to Learn*, is that the excellent fourth-grade teachers profiled are not satisfied with their teaching. They are motivated to do better, just as the excellent first-grade teachers studied by Pressley, Allington, et al. (2001) were motivated to do better. Fourth-grade teachers who have this passion—to become an expert fourth-grade teacher—should read this book and think about how the teaching described might be adapted for use in their own classrooms. The study reported in this volume is scientific educational research that has high potential to inspire changes that would make grade 4 a much better experience for 9- and 10-year-olds. Great fourth-grade teachers are looking for the kind of insights and inspiration that are in the pages of this book.

I close by relating a story about my brother, who is an engineer in the defense industry. He recently told me about how members of Congress make suggestions to leading aerospace engineers about how projects, such as the anti-missile, should be designed. He concluded the story by remarking, "No one in Congress is capable of making meaningful technical recommendations to the caliber of engineer who works on these projects. They can be helpful in working with us to figure out the best way to pay for what needs to be done, but they can't be helpful in the design of the projects." Ain't it the truth!

What Congressperson would be able to teach fourth grade like the teachers in this book, or design such instruction for others? The Congress can be helpful, however, in (1) figuring out how to provide the funds so that more folks can acquire the education and training that would enable them to become excellent teachers, and (2) ensuring optimal student–teacher ratios and materials that would facilitate quality instruction. Policymakers need to submit to a hard examination of their consciences about which roles they are qualified to play in the efforts to improve literacy instruction in this country, and which roles are better left to experienced educators and educational researchers.

**Michael Pressley, PhD,** is the Notre Dame Professor of Catholic Education and a Professor of Psychology. He is a leading expert in elementary literacy instruction.

# Contents

## PART III

## WHAT HAVE WE LEARNED ABOUT GOOD
## FOURTH-GRADE TEACHING?

# PART I

## What Do We Know and Need to Know about Good Fourth-Grade Teaching?

# 1

## Teaching Fourth Grade in the 21st Century

"I am well aware that there is no one best, ideal way of teaching . . . when you get right down to it, it's not the method or philosophy that's most important, it's the teacher, her knowledge, her relationship with students, that's always been primary" (Routman, 1996, p. 163).

Michael Bazeley of the *San Jose Mercury News* wrote recently (May 29, 2000) that one district-mandated reading program "is helping bury a notion central to public education for decades—that the classroom revolves around the teacher as a trained professional in control of what happens and when."

"Standardized practice is malpractice when viewed from a perspective of professional accountability. Professional teachers should be allowed to focus on doing the right things rather than on doing things right" (Darling-Hamond, 1997, p. 66).

Csikszentmihalyi notes that both surgeons and slave laborers work. "But the surgeon has a chance to learn new things each day, and every day he learns that he is in control and that he can perform complicated tasks. The laborer is forced to repeat the same exhausting motions, and what he learns is most about his own helplessness" (Csikszentmihalyi, 1990, p. 144).

Good teaching is always a passionate and personal accomplishment. The good news is that a recent national survey of new teachers concluded, "Their passion for teaching is striking. It is . . . underappreciated and a valuable asset that money can't buy" (Public Agenda, 2000, p. 1). The bad news is that, at the same time these results were released, at least one journalist (quoted above) and two nationally syndicated columnists (Raspberry, 2000; Sowell, 2000) were characterizing teachers as simple-minded and noting that, because of this, it seemed that explicit instructional mandates were the only way to improve teaching. And, most recently, four teachers wrote about their experiences with curriculum mandates—mandates of very differing natures but mandates on how to teach nonetheless—in a themed issue of *Primary Voices* (July, 2001). One common theme they expressed was the difficulty of remaining focused on children in the face of "one size fits all" instructional mandates. Yet all reported that it was their focus on the daily small successes of individual students that fostered their passion for teaching and fueled their continuing quest for self-improvement.

Good teaching is complicated as well as passionate. Good teachers describe their work in ways very similar to Csikszentmihalyi's (1990) description of surgeons' work, quoted above. They talk about their need to continually improve their ability to offer high-quality instruction—even after 15–20 years or more of experience (Day, 2000); they talk about creating instruction that best meets the needs of *individual* students. Hardly ever do these teachers talk about "best" methods or curriculum materials. Instead, as Duffy (1997) notes, "the best literacy instruction is provided by independent, enterprising, entrepreneurial teachers who view instructional models as ideas to be adapted rather than tenets to be followed" (p. 351).

Good teachers work much like the surgeon who operated on RLA a few years ago. Upon finding a rare and much more complicated situation after the initial diagnosis and incisions were made, this surgeon quickly modified the planned procedure, consulted with several epidemiologists, and successfully solved the medical problem. Thankfully, the surgeon did not adhere to a predetermined procedure but instead drew upon his expertise, and that of others, to implement a medical procedure that was personalized to the patient's specific, and unexpected, needs. The expert teachers we have observed do the same sort of on-the-spot decision-making hundreds of times each day.

Political enthusiasm abounds at this time for "solving" the problem of low-achieving students in America's schools through mandated curricular and instructional reforms. For instance, in 1998 Congress passed the Comprehensive School Reform Demonstration Act. This federal legislation provided funding for schools that would elect to implement one of several "proven programs." The American Federation of Teachers touted three "proven programs" to their members and encouraged the adoption of one of them. In each case, these programs offered preplanned curriculum packages as well as mandated restructuring of the school day. Today, thousands of schools are now using these programs, even though, at best, there is minimal and often manufactured "proof" of their success (Coles, 2000; Pogrow, 2000; Schweinhart & Weikart, 1997; Taylor, 1998; Venezky, 1998) but solid evidence that most teachers adapt even the most directive programs in ways they deem beneficial to their students (Datnow & Castellano, 2000).

One question no one seems to ask about the various curricular and instructional mandates and "proven programs" is whether they foster the development of teacher expertise. In other words, do teachers become more expert teachers as a result of these mandates and programs? Do they assist teachers in making better instructional decisions hundreds of times each day? Do they foster the development of teaching excellence? And, relatedly, we might ask: Does it even *matter* whether teachers become more expert at their job?

This last question seems an odd one because expertise in a profession is usually related to performance: We search out medical specialists for their specific expertise; we select financial planners who have expertise in the areas that our specific situation demands; we assume our insurance agents and even our landscapers have the expertise necessary to address the needs our particular situation presents. But when it comes to teaching, many policymakers and pundits seem largely antagonistic to the idea that teacher expertise matters to any significant degree.

Naysayers notwithstanding, teacher expertise seems to be one of the critical factors in achieving high levels of student academic performance. As Darling-Hammond (1999) has recently demonstrated, the quality of a state's teaching force (measured in various ways) is a much more powerful predictor of student achievement levels than other factors, including student demographic characteristics and measures of school resources. Teacher quality accounted for 40–60%

of the variance in the National Assessment of Educational Progress (NAEP) achievement for fourth- and eighth-grade reading and math. These results echo the findings of achievement studies in Texas and Alabama (Ferguson, 1991; Ferguson & Ladd, 1996). In both of these large-scale analyses, money invested staffing schools with more qualified teachers produced larger achievement gains than any other educational investment.

Interestingly, the Darling-Hammond (1999) analyses showed that *none* of the highest achieving states had implemented extensive state-mandated "high stakes" testing systems, whereas most of the lower achieving states had fairly extensive state testing systems with high stakes for students as well as schools. In addition, higher-achieving states had higher standards for becoming a teacher, more extensive professional development requirements, and fewer noncredentialed teachers in the workforce.

In our experience, state curriculum and instruction mandates are also popular among those who view testing as a primary solution to the "achievement problem." Unfortunately, as Darling-Hammond (1997) notes, "increasingly prescriptive policies created through the political process in the name of public accountability are reducing even further the schools' responsiveness to the needs of students and the desires of parents" (p. 65). Of even greater concern, such mandates are a significant factor in the loss of both new teachers and some of the profession's most effective teachers; as professional autonomy is increasingly restricted, many teachers leave the profession for occupations where their expertise and autonomy are respected. Policies that reduce the numbers of expert teachers would seem an odd strategy for attempting to improve educational outcomes.

A recent federal report on the status of the teaching profession (Dozier & Bertotti, 2000) notes that, in recent years, fewer than half of the college graduates who are licensed as teachers have applied for teaching positions. Almost half who do elect to teach leave the profession within the first 5 years of their career. In this study teachers reported that (1) the disregard of their expertise, (2) micromanagement of their teaching, and (3) the failure to be consulted on issues that affected their classroom work were among the most common reasons for the professional dissatisfaction that led them to seek different careers.

McNeil (2000) offers a dismaying longitudinal case study of the impact of state educational reform initiatives in one large Texas school district. She documents how "standardized" teaching was mandated and monitored through the use of checklists, required daily lesson plans, and specific curriculum materials. Some test scores rose after these reforms. However, both student retention in grade and the proportion of children identified as pupils with disabilities also rose dramatically. Therefore, it is difficult to know whether achievement actually improved or whether fewer lower-achieving students sat for the tests (Allington & McGill-Franzen, 1992). What we do know is that after nearly 15 years of such reforms, fewer than half of the students graduate in almost three-quarters of the district's high schools, ranking the district among the worst in the nation in graduation rate (Johnston, 2001).

McNeil (2000) argues that the "teacher proofing" emphasis of the state and district mandated reforms undermined high quality teaching and

> made schools exceedingly comfortable for mediocre teachers who like to teach routine lessons according to a standard sequence and format, who like working as de-skilled laborers not having to think about their work. The [reforms] made being a Texas public school teacher extremely uncomfortable for those who know their subjects well, who teach in ways that engage their students, who want their teaching to reflect their own continued learning. (p 187)

In a similar vein, Duffy and Hoffman (1999) argue that current policy mandates typically ignore the fact that research links improved reading achievement to teachers who use methods and materials thoughtfully, not to the methods or the materials alone. A half century of methods and material studies have demonstrated their relative inefficacy for improving teaching or learning (e.g., Bond & Dykstra, 1967; House, Glass, McLean, & Walker, 1978; Knapp, 1995). Obviously, the effectiveness of good teachers is enhanced by a rich supply of appropriate curriculum materials. So, too, these teachers enhance student learning when their teaching reflects the sort of instructional moves that have been identified as generally effective. The complicated part of teaching effectively is selecting and organizing the curriculum materials and selecting the appropriate instructional moves that meet the needs of the learners encountered in the classroom. Accomplishing this "fit" requires a particular expertise that cannot be packaged by "experts" at some far-off university or publishing house.

Because children differ on virtually every dimension, standardized instruction is the equivalent of educational malpractice (Darling-Hammond,1997). Comparative studies of the effects of different curricula routinely produce larger within-curriculum variability than between-curriculum variability. In other words, the difference between the most effective implementation of curriculum A and the least effective implementation of curriculum A is always larger than the average difference between curriculum A and curriculum B (e.g., Bond & Dykstra, 1967; House et al., 1978). *Teacher quality matters much more than curriculum materials.* Research has replicated this fundamental finding for roughly the roughly 30 years. But even with this consistent research record, many policymakers at all levels continue to invest their confidence, mistakenly, in the power of mandated methods and materials, programs and packages, to "solve" the "achievement problem."

Furthermore, Darling-Hammond (1999) points out that investments in improving teacher expertise return, dollar for dollar, far larger gains in achievement than do investments in tests, materials, or programs. We would agree and also note that for almost all of the 19 or so "textbook adoption" states (e.g., Mississippi, Louisiana, California, Texas, Florida, South Carolina, etc.), student achievement on the NAEP ranks in the lower half of the distribution of states. In other words, even though some states spend enormous sums of money in an attempt to control teaching through textbook mandates, achievement in these states lags behind those states that leave such decisions up to local officials, typically teams of teachers.

The views of parents and the general public seem more closely aligned with the research findings than with the views of policymakers. Rose and Gallup (2000) summarize the results of the annual polling of American attitudes towards education: "The public's belief in the importance of qualified, competent teachers is strong" (p. 50). When asked to rate the desirability of a selection of school reform strategies, more than twice as many respondents rated increasing the supply of good teachers as more important than any of the other strategies. For example, 52% rated improving teacher quality as the most promising strategy, compared to 17% in favor of more rigorous standards and 10% for eliminating social promotion.

The public, it seems, understands the need for high-quality teacher preparation and ongoing professional development. Unfortunately, control of education has moved steadily away from the local community and local educational leaders. Increasingly, mandates from state and federal education agencies constrain local decision making. As the authority moves further and further from the classroom and community, less and less attention is given to the available educational research or the preferences of consumers (parents, local taxpayers, and students).

The recent passage of federal legislation that will significantly increase the amount of achievement testing for students seems another example of policymakers misunderstanding the nature of effective teaching—and another example of shifting the nexus of authority out of the classroom and into bureaucratic offices located far away. Secretary of Education Rod Paige (April 27, 2001) told members of the Education Writers Association that such testing was needed because

> at the community level, tests of student achievement help us to define success in terms of student performance—not spending. To focus on the outputs of our system, not the inputs. At the classroom level, testing also helps teachers. *Tests tell us which kids need extra help, and what kind of help fits each child.* (emphasis added)

Perhaps Secretary Paige is unfamiliar with the limits of current standardized achievement tests, for there are no tests that can accomplish either of the goals he sets forth in the final sentence. *None.* Just reading the technical manuals that accompany any standardized group achievement test will disabuse one of such notions. These tests are not reliable measures of *individual* achievement. As noted in the recent report of the National Academy of Science (Heubert & Hauser, 1999), the results of these tests should not be used in high-stakes decisions (e.g., high school graduation, retention in grade, special education placements, and so on). In any event, any teacher can tell you which students are having difficulty in his or her class. It is not more testing that is needed to identify the children who would benefit from instructional support.

In addition, the standardized achievement tests mandated by Congress wholly lack the sophistication necessary to provide useful information about what kind of assistance different pupils might need. In fact, few tests of any sort—even individually administered achievement and diagnostic tests—can provide useful information unless the results are interpreted by someone with significant expertise. In other words, it is curricular and instructional expertise that leads to reliable interpretation of test performances and classroom accomplishments. As far as we know, providing teachers with test results does not increase either level of expertise.

The two broadest and most common educational reform initiatives—curricular mandates and achievement testing—seem to arise from a fundamental disregard for the importance of teacher expertise. Both seem to ignore a significant body of research on the nature of good teaching and good teachers. We won't speculate as to why.

## SHIFTING THE FOCUS OF EDUCATIONAL RESEARCH AND EDUCATIONAL REFORM

There is much emphasis today on "effective" schools and "effective" teachers, with *effectiveness* defined primarily, if not exclusively, by student performance on group administered standardized achievement tests. Attempting to define effective teaching based on student test scores raises a number of problematic aspects, including the following:

- The limitations of current assessments as reliable indicators of student achievement (Linn, 2000).
- The potential for assessments to narrow the curriculum such that important aspects of literate accomplishment are ignored (Johnston, 1998).
- The documented use of various strategies (referral to special education, retention in grade, use of test preparation materials, suspension of students from school during the testing period, and so on) that raise reported test scores while not improving actual achievement (Allington, 2000).

Given that even the National Academy of Science (Heubert & Hauser, 1999) has argued against the use of standardized achievement tests for making decisions about individual students and teachers, one might speculate as to why this use of tests has become so politically popular. Sergiovanni (2000) suggests that "it is much easier to nail down what an effective school [or teacher] is than to struggle with a broader definition of a good school [or teacher] . . . maybe that's why policy makers avoid trying" (pp. 93–94).

If commercial curricular materials and packaged educational reform initiatives are unlikely sources of accomplished teaching, and if achievement tests are impoverished and unreliable estimates of instructional needs and teaching efficacy, where does this leave us? Thirty-five years ago, Bond and Dyskstra (1967) concluded their national comparative study of curriculum materials with the admonition that "future research might well center on teacher and learning situation characteristics rather than methods and materials" (p. 123). Over the past two decades educational researchers have taken this advice to heart. As a result we know a great deal about the nature of effective classroom teaching (typically evaluated based on student achievement test data in quantitative studies and achievement documentation in qualitative studies). However, this research does not provide anything like an architect's blueprint for conducting lessons. Rather, the research—both quantitative and qualitative studies—offers us something akin to an impressionist's renderings of what good teaching looks like.

While much of the research has focused on identifying the nature of effective teaching, few studies have observed expert teachers to describe how they currently teach, what factors shaped their teaching style, what their students learn, and how they view their teaching and student learning. The study of experts has much to recommend it (Chi, Glaser, & Farr, 1988; Csikszentmihalyi, 1990). We have found it surprising that good teaching, expert teaching, has so often been ignored by educational researchers.

Perhaps good teaching has been ignored because in recent years, the field has focused on the school as the unit of analysis in studying educational outcomes. Indeed, research on effective schools (Edmonds, 1979; Postlewaite & Ross, 1992) is reported to have shaped educational reform efforts in thousands schools (Pressley, 1998). But effective schools are those schools that are staffed with many good teachers. It is impossible to imagine a "good" school staffed with mediocre teachers. Nonetheless, policymakers and educational researchers alike have largely ignored the potential of focusing on teachers and the art of teaching for deriving improved understandings of the nature and sources of effective teaching.

Perhaps good teaching has been ignored because defining "good" teaching, as Sergiovanni (2000) argues, is a bit more complicated than it first seems. Parents and students seem to know who the good teachers are. Parents, especially middle-class parents, attempt to manipulate teacher assignments in the hope of having their children assigned to the classrooms of those good teachers. So just what is it that parents value in teachers? It seems to us that parents want teachers who care about their child, who treat their child fairly, who create "safe" classrooms where children's differences are accepted and treated as the norm—and, of course, they want teachers who effectively develop their child's academic proficiencies.

Policymakers and researchers, however, have more often focused on that final characteristic in defining good teaching as indicated by achievement tests. While the development of academic proficiencies in children is a primary purpose of schooling, parents want more than just that, as does society (Johnston, 1999; Sacks, 2000). Currently, these other desired outcomes of schooling have taken a backseat to the development of academic proficiencies, as reflected in the now ubiquitous state curriculum standards and state achievement tests. Thus "effective" teachers are more often defined as those teachers who generate larger than average test score gains from their students (Sanders, 1998). Even shelving the problems with testing for the moment, are teachers identified in this manner as "effective" always *good* teachers?

Consider, for example, what happens when we ask teachers and parents (including members of the school board) what attributes all students leaving an elementary school might ideally demonstrate. Narrow the focus even more by asking this group to identify which attributes are desirable in children as readers. Figure 1.1 displays the results of one such exercise in a Northeastern school district (Walmsley & Allington, 1995). Although *achievement* was one of the attributes targeted as desirable by the members of this community, there were other attributes as well (and we can imagine additional ones beyond those noted, such as self-regulation, perspective taking, curiosity, confidence, and imagination). In our experience, there is little disagreement among the various participants in exercises of this sort. They want children to be able to read well, and they want all children to be readers—to routinely engage in voluntary reading. They want children to be exposed to a range of literary material, including some of the classic works. They want children to have favorite books, favorite authors, and favorite genres. They want children to be able to discuss the books they have read—to be able to articulate what they liked or disliked about the book. They want their children to know how to use literacy to accomplish their desires, their goals. Only one of these attributes is measured routinely in most schools— and in the most limited manner (Johnston, 1998).

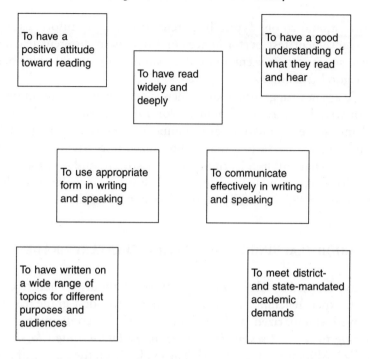

**FIGURE 1.1.** Language arts attributes that teachers in the Adams–Cheshire Regional School District expect of all children by the end of grade 6. From Walmsley and Allington (1995, p. 38). Copyright 1995 by Teachers College, Columbia University. All rights reserved.

How do parents and others assess whether a school is a "good" school—one that develops most, if not all, of these desired attributes? By and large, they seem to rely on their personal experiences with their children, grandchildren, nieces and nephews, and any other children with whom they routinely come into contact. According to Rose and Gallup (2000), most parents of school-age children believe that their child's teachers are doing a good job, generally, of meeting their expectations. Parents are far more likely to award their child's school a grade of A or B than they are to award those grades to schools generally, and they know a lot about the school their child attends. What they know about other schools is more likely acquired from the media, not from experience. And the media primarily report on test score comparisons.

We know less about how parents identify good teachers—what sources of information they use, what characteristics they deem most important, and so on. Typically, parents do not have information on the achievement test performances of students in different teachers' rooms, so test scores seem an unlikely source of parental judgements about good teaching.

We are not suggesting that academic achievement is an unimportant or trivial feature of schooling. Nor are we contending that good academic student outcomes are unimportant in ascertaining teacher quality. But we are stating that standardized tests trivialize the complexity of what children learn in good classrooms and that too exclusive a focus on standardized test scores leads to trivialized teaching (Johnston, 1998), especially among less expert teachers.

## GOOD TEACHING IN THE UPPER ELEMENTARY GRADES

We have learned much in the past few years about the nature of effective, expert teaching. The research on effective first-grade teaching was well summarized and documented in the companion book, *Learning to Read: Lessons from Exemplary First-Grade Classrooms* (Pressley, Allington, et al., 2001). The evidence on the nature of good primary-grade teaching presented there is well supported by other recent studies (e.g., Taylor, Pearson, Clark, & Walpole, 2000). Whereas much attention has been paid to research on early literacy instruction, both historically and recently far less attention and research have focused on the effective teaching of reading in the upper elementary grades. However, stimulated by various federal initiatives, individual states have created achievement benchmarks that reflect the new goal: all students attaining thoughtful literacy. This new standard actually represents two challenges. First is the challenge to educate all children well. For most of the past century schools in the United States were organized to educate only some children well (Allington & Cunningham, 2002); schools set different goals for different children. The traditional three reading group model in elementary schools and the three-track high school were the result of this differentiated education model. Second, in most schools the focus traditionally has been on developing basic literacy, not thoughtful literacy. Basic literacy requires the ability to read and recall and to write neatly and spell correctly. Thoughtful literacy, in contrast, is characterized by the ability to read, write, and think in the complex and critical ways needed in a postindustrial democratic society. Such proficiencies include and exceed the basic literacy goals of the past (Johnston, 1999; Langer, 1995a).

Fourth-grade achievement has been a popular political target perhaps because the national achievement assessments and state-by-state comparisons begin the fourth grade. Thus we see state policies such as the "fourth-grade guarantee"—all fourth graders required to attain a specified level of reading proficiency on some new state-sponsored assessment to be promoted to the fifth grade. Considerable media attention is devoted to publicly ranking schools based on fourth grade assessment results. Some states even reward teachers whose students perform well on the chosen assessments, increasing the stakes considerably.

Most assessment pressure is focused on reading, but there is substantial variation among states in how reading proficiency is assessed. Some state assessments apply a narrow focus, while others attempt to provide a broader standard of reading ability. No state assessments evaluate students' *thoughtful* literacy, although some provide estimates of students' learning that moves in that direction. However, Bob Linn (2000) captured the current state of assessment well when he noted that, "I am led to conclude that in most cases the instruments and technology have not been up to the demands that have been placed on them by high-stakes accountability" (p. 14). Nonetheless, we need to continue to ask what it is that students learn in different classrooms *about* reading and writing, and what it is they learn *through* reading and writing.

In most U.S. elementary schools these days, fourth grade is the high-stakes teaching assignment—although this is not new; fourth grade has long been considered a critical point in the elementary school experience. Chall (1983) wrote of the "fourth-grade slump" as the point at which some children who had been previously successful begin to experience reading difficulties. It is at fourth grade that linguistic, cognitive, and conceptual demands of reading increase somewhat dramatically; there is a heavier use of textbooks and an expectation of greater independence in using reading and writing as tools for learning. The vocabulary encountered while reading is "less conversational," more often unfamiliar, with more specialized, technical vocabulary (e.g., *delta, plateau, basin*) sometimes representing abstract rather than concrete ideas (*gravity, freedom, representation, civilization*). In addition, the syntax of fourth-grade texts is more complex, more demanding—more adult-like. Finally, the level of reasoning also shifts, with a greater emphasis on inferential thinking and using prior knowledge of topics and texts to puzzle through "inconsiderate" texts (i.e., What stance is the author taking on industrial polluters? Is there another stance that others might take?).

Traditionally, reading has been seen as shifting from learning to read to reading to learn in fourth grade. It is in fourth grade that the focus on content subjects such as science and social studies shifts more to learning from textbooks. It is in fourth grade that these two subject areas also begin to focus on topics that students often had little prior knowledge of, or prior experience with (e.g., levers, water cycle, state history, geography). In other words, fourth grade has been the point where informational texts became central to the curriculum and where students were expected to begin to acquire information from those texts. Meeting this expectation is no small task; reading about unfamiliar topics in texts structured differently from the narratives that dominate primary-grade reading (Duke, 2000) presents new demands on the reader. Chall (1983) also notes a lack of clarity in the elementary upper grades about the role that trade books should play in learning content. That is, traditional textbooks often become the primary reading materials for science and social studies in fourth grade, and while some teachers continue to use historical fiction, biography, and other informational texts in these subjects, many do not. Fourth grade is also where students typically are introduced to "research" projects—usually reports, oral or written, or both. For all these reasons, fourth grade has been tabbed as the beginning of "traditional" school.

Despite all the recent attention focused on fourth grade, there has been relatively little research on the nature of instruction in fourth-grade classrooms. Although a number of such studies of primary-grade classrooms have been reported in recent years, only a few studies of fourth grade (or third or fifth grade) have appeared, and these typically have been small and local (e.g., Ladson-Billings, 1994; Pressley, Wharton-McDonald, Mistretta-Hampston, & Echevarria,1998; Sosniak & Stodolsky, 1993). Likewise, although educational reform activity has been directed towards enhancing early literacy instruction, few broad efforts to improve the quality of reading instruction in the upper elementary grades have been undertaken by any local, state, or federal education agency. Finally, although attention and funding have been funneled to literacy intervention in the early grades, far less of both has been targeted for better understanding how to meet the needs of students who struggle with literacy learning in the upper elementary grades.

## CONCLUSION

The nature of effective upper-grade elementary teaching is the focus of this book. More specifically, we focus on outstanding fourth-grade teachers and their classrooms. The next chapter reviews the available research on effective teaching—especially the teaching of reading—in upper-grade elementary classrooms. We close that chapter with a short synthesis of the key findings of those studies and a brief introduction to our own study of exemplary fourth-grade teachers. The middle chapters offer case studies of six fourth-grade classrooms we studied in four states. These chapters are our attempt to reveal the complexity of teaching fourth grade well. We close the book with three chapters that attempt to integrate our findings with the earlier research as well as extend that research in directions little studied. We asked Gerald Duffy to write the final chapter, an Afterword of sorts, in the hopes that his expert and independent eye would provide further insights on exemplary teaching and the development of such teachers.

# 2

## What Do We Know about Effective Fourth-Grade Teachers?[1]

What teachers know and understand about content and students shapes how judiciously they select from texts and other materials and how effectively they present material in class. Their skill in assessing their students' progress also depends upon how deeply they understand learning, and how well they can interpret students' discussions and written work. No other intervention can make the difference that a knowledgeable, skillful teacher can make in the learning process.

—NATIONAL COMMISSION ON TEACHING
AND AMERICA'S FUTURE (1997, p. 8)

Teaching fourth grade well in the 21st century is challenging because U.S. schools have been directed to achieve a new standard: *All* children will attain thoughtful literacy proficiencies. Because classroom instruction has been identified as the critical variable for fostering student achievement (Ferguson, 1991; National Commission on Teaching and America's Future, 1997; Snow, Barnes, Chandler, Goodman, & Hemphill, 1991), we set out to find out more about the nature of effective fourth-grade classroom teaching, with a focus on the development of students' thoughtful literacy attainment. Duffy

---

[1]Much of this chapter previously appeared in Allington and Johnston (2001). Copyright by the International Reading Association. All rights reserved.

and Hoffman (1999) argue that researchers should focus on developing better understanding of the complexity that characterizes classroom life, teacher expertise and decision making, teacher development across the career span, and in particular, how effective teachers manage to adjust instruction to meet the needs of individual students. We took their charge seriously. Until we can better articulate the nature and qualities of the instruction crafted by exemplary upper-grade elementary teachers, efforts to enhance the quality of the instruction at that level will be hindered.

In this chapter we begin by reviewing studies of effective upper-grade elementary teaching and then attempt to identify core constructs that were used to characterize effective teaching in those studies. We close the chapter with a brief rationale and design for the national study of effective fourth-grade teachers that we codirected.

## A REVIEW OF RESEARCH ON EFFECTIVE FOURTH-GRADE TEACHING

Our study was guided, in part, by that small body of studies on literacy learning in upper-grade elementary classrooms and especially by the few studies of exemplary upper-grade elementary teachers available in the literature. Because so much earlier research pointed to the relative inefficacy of curriculum materials in facilitating effective instruction, we were less interested in the studies that compared different curricula and more interested in those that attempted to delve into the complicated arena of good teaching, especially the teaching of reading, writing, and thinking. We attempted to locate studies of upper-grade elementary classroom teachers and their teaching, especially studies of effective classroom teaching of reading. Methodologically, these studies fell into three broad categories: Observational studies, interview studies, and survey research. Some studies combined methods, but typically one research method provided the principal data for each study.

### Observational Studies

The handful of observational studies of upper-grade elementary teaching support the earlier findings that instructional programs are relatively less important than the nature of the teacher and the teaching. Sosniak and Stodolsky (1993), for instance, studied four fourth-grade teachers in two schools in the same urban school district. Although both teachers worked with similar curriculum materials and operated under common achievement expectations, the researchers found that they did not teach "by the book," as is often suggested in the literature and imagined by administrators and policymakers. Indeed, for each teacher the role of the text varied from subject to subject. One teacher made heavy use of a basal reader during reading (88% of the time) but made little use of the social studies textbook (17% of the time). Another teacher relied less on the reading basal (31%) but more on the social studies basal (90%). Similarly, recitation as a reading activity ranged from 8–58% of the time, and reading workbook use from 8–34%. These teachers were in the same district, teaching at the same grade level, with the same materials.

Differences in teaching practice can, of course, translate into differences in student achievement. Over a 2-year period Snow and her colleagues (1991) observed second- and fourth-grade teachers who differed in effectiveness. The more effective teachers were characterized as:

- Providing explicit instruction.
- Using behavioral routines.
- Challenging and involving students.
- Creating a supportive, encouraging, and friendly classroom climate.
- Engaging in lots of constructive teacher–student exchanges.
- Offering a variety of reading materials.
- Scheduling frequent library visits.
- Crafting stimulating curricular activities.
- Asking many inferential questions.
- Displaying student work prominently.

These teachers produced dramatically superior student achievement. Placement in effective classrooms for consecutive years, led to high levels of achievement by all students. Even though these teachers taught in the same school district (and even in the same school), and used the same materials, they demonstrated tremendous variety in their application of the materials, in their instructional methods, and in classroom organizational plans (from open classrooms to traditional three-group organization).

These studies argue for a range of productive practices, with common foundational themes, rather than a rigid enforcement of particular programs and materials. In line with this view, Knapp (1995) reports on a 2-year study of high-poverty elementary classrooms in three states. The classrooms differed in instructional emphasis and, ultimately, in student achievement. Achievement in the "meaning-emphasis" classrooms was superior to that attained by students in "skills-emphasis" classrooms. The higher achieving classrooms were characterized by:

- Maximal opportunity to read.
- Reading and writing integrated with other subject areas.
- A focus on the ways of constructing meaning.
- Opportunity to discuss what was read.

In addition, Knapp noted that "the choice of textbooks by school or district does little by itself to make up for teachers' lack of experience with the approach contained in the textbook" (p. 174).

Consistent with these findings, researchers who observed teachers nominated as effective or exemplary report that the use of curriculum materials and instructional methods varied widely. For instance, Pressley and his colleagues (1998) found significant differences in the 10 fourth- and fifth-grade classrooms they studied in terms of the materials and methods used in teaching reading and writing. Common dimensions of instruction in these classrooms included:

- Use of diverse grouping patterns, including small group lessons and one-to-one conferences.
- Teaching of both higher-order and lower-level skills.
- Focus on vocabulary development.
- Use of diverse curriculum materials, with an emphasis on narrative literature.
- Frequent use of collaborative learning activities.
- Focus on developing student independence.
- Integrated literacy and content area instruction.

In this study 9 out of 10 teachers used trade books in theme-oriented curriculum units (often in a reading/writing workshop framework), whereas just one used a traditional basal reading series for reading instruction. Homework differed in emphasis from exploring engaging content to exercises on surface features of written text. Writing tasks differed substantially in breadth of genres selected and length of pieces written. Though breadth of reading genres also differed, there was an emphasis on narratives in all classrooms.

Ladson-Billings (1994) studied eight effective teachers of African American students; six of these taught in the upper elementary grades. She reports the following characteristics as typifying these successful teachers:

- Believe all children can succeed.
- See teaching as "pulling knowledge out" versus putting it in.
- View knowledge critically, as continually recreated and shared.
- Facilitate fluid teacher–student relationships that are equitable and extend beyond the classroom.
- Demonstrate connectedness with all students.
- Encourage students to learn collaboratively, to teach each other and be responsible for each other.
- Help students develop necessary skills.
- Seek excellence but take individual differences into account.

Each research team concluded that, although common themes could be identified, variation in materials and methods used characterized upper elementary teaching, even effective teaching.

## Interview Studies

Some researchers have used interviews to investigate the nature of effective elementary teaching, including teaching in the upper elementary grades. Ruddell (1997), for instance, summarizes his work on "influential" teachers—teachers nominated by former students as having had an enormous positive influence on their development. He reports that his interviews, surveys, and classroom observations portray these 95 teachers as:

- Using clearly formulated instructional strategies that provide opportunities for monitoring and give feedback to students.
- Having in-depth knowledge of reading and writing processes and how to teach them.
- Using internal sources of motivation frequently.
- Using external of motivation sparingly.

Ruddell also documents common personal characteristics of these influential teachers. They are:

- Warm, caring, flexible.
- Sensitive to individual needs and motivations.
- Set high demands and expectations.
- Enthusiastic about teaching.
- Create intellectual excitement.
- Consider alternative points of view.
- Attend to students' academic and personal problems.
- Make instruction personally relevant.
- Emphasize logical and strategy-oriented instruction, clear writing, critical thinking.

These teachers ranked establishing trust through personal contacts with students as one of the most important characteristics of their teaching, a finding that echoes Ladson-Billings' (1994) conclusions about effective teachers of African American students. Again, no particular instructional programs or materials were associated with influential teaching.

Some of the characteristics documented by Ruddell involve beliefs and theories about teaching and learning—the basis of instructional decision making. Other researchers have also documented these features. For example, Thomas and Barksdale-Ladd (1995) interviewed and then observed nine classroom teachers (grades 1–5) who were nominated as effective or outstanding. Their analyses identified nine common beliefs:

- All children can learn to read and write.
- Children learn to read and write by reading and writing.
- Modeling is the best way to teach literacy.
- Reading and writing are closely related and cannot be separated instructionally.
- Children learn from other children in cooperative environments.
- Print-rich environments are necessary for children to learn literacy.
- Children need daily shared reading, independent reading, and guided reading.
- Observing students is the only way to know who needs what teaching.

- Ownership is part of learning; making choices leads to taking responsibility.

All of these teachers planned their instruction based on their observations of their students; all had student portfolios, all engaged students in individual conferences on a regular basis; all had well-developed parent involvement programs; all integrated reading and writing with content area instruction; all were readers themselves. As with the other studies, a lack of reliance on particular instructional programs characterized these teachers' methods. They were more student-oriented than program-oriented.

Haberman (1995b) reports on a longitudinal study of effective urban teachers and provides a list of 14 characteristics that distinguished the more effective teachers. The first seven characteristics were documented in interviews over a 35-year period; the second seven were based on observation.

1. *Persistence.* The teachers believe that it is their responsibility to "find ways of engaging all their students in learning activities. . . . They persist in trying to meet the individual needs of the problem student, the talented, the handicapped, the frequently neglected student . . . persistence is reflected in an endless search for what works best with each student . . . teaching can never be 'good enough' since everyone should have learned more in any activity. . . . The basic stance of these teachers is never to give up trying to find a better way of doing things" (p. 779).

2. *Fostering learners and learning.* Effective urban teachers usually have a hobby or some other lifelong learning activity (e.g., opera, philately, a cause such as Save the Wolves, computers, and so on) that they often bring to the classroom. This engagement in self-initiated learning seems to be a prerequisite for stimulating learning in others. It also leads these teachers to open up the curriculum to more stimulating possibilities which, in turn, "frequently brings them into noncompliance with the extremely thick bureaucracies of urban schools" (p. 779). When challenged by their principals about nontraditional activities, they negotiate because "they see protecting and enhancing students' involvement in learning activities as their highest priority" (p. 779). Their focus on finding ways to engage students is a significant contrast to less effective teachers who focus on "covering the curriculum."

3. *Perspective.* These teachers conveyed a sense of the big picture—their long-term teaching goals in relationship to day-to-day practice. In other words, their instruction was not determined by the plethora of daily lesson activities recommended in the teacher manuals that accompany commercial curriculum materials.

4. *Responsible approach to "at-risk" students.* Haberman highlights this characteristic as the most powerful in distinguishing effective urban teachers from others. These teachers may cite poverty, violence, drugs, and other disruptive influences as contributing factors in low achievement, but they also cite irrelevant curricula, poor teaching, and bureaucratic schools as causes. These teachers believe that, regardless of the life conditions their students face, they as teachers bear a primary responsibility for sparking their students' desire to learn" (p. 780).

5. *Respect.* Effective urban teachers expect to find kids in their rooms whom they cannot love and kids who will not love them. But they also expect to be able to teach these kids. "They use terms such as caring, respect, and concern, and they enjoy the love and affection of students when it occurs naturally. But they do not regard it as a prerequisite for learning. . . . Genuine respect is the best way to describe the feeling [these] teachers have for their students" (p. 780).

6. *Burnout: Its causes and cures.* These teachers learn how to protect themselves from mindless, interfering bureaucracies. They figure out the minimum requirements for functioning in the system and how "to gain the widest discretion for themselves and their students without incurring the wrath of the system . . . they set up networks of like-minded teachers, or they teach in teams, or they simply find kindred spirits. They use these support systems as sources of emotional sustenance" (p. 780).

7. *Fallibility.* These teachers see mistakes and failure as an inevitable part of learning—their students' as well as their own.

8. *Teaching style.* These teachers tend to "coach" rather than engage in "directive teaching." In other words, their instructional interactions more often fostered students' independent application of developing skills and strategies as opposed to simply telling students what skill or strategy they should apply. Also, these teachers utilized a "watch me" approach to demonstrating a skill or strategy.

9. *Standards of success.* These effective urban teachers emphasize student effort and engagement over ability.

10. *Organizational ability.* They plan lessons and gather materials that engage students in learning.

11. *Emotional stamina.* They are able to persist in the face of violence, death, and other crises.

12. *Basis of rapport.* These teachers have an approach to student involvement that creates a classroom that is *their* classroom or *our* classroom, not *my* classroom; they work to develop a sense of community in the classroom.

13. *Readiness.* They expect a range of differences in students rather than expecting all students to be at the same educational point.

14. *Physical stamina.* They *know* that teaching is hard work.

Expanding to a more general model for teachers and other helping and human service professionals, Spencer and Spencer (1993) report a large-scale study of professional effectiveness that shows compatible findings. They employed the Behavioral Events Interview (BEI) to develop a "grounded theory" of job competencies by working backwards from the criterion of superior performance "to identify the characteristics of people who perform at these levels" (p. 135). Their "generic model" of effective teachers included the 14 competencies listed below (in descending order of importance).

1. *Impact and influence.* These people tailor their presentation and language to the audience, establish credibility, and use individual influence strategies, including humor, body language, and voice.

2. *Developing others.* They believe in students' potential and use innovative teaching methods to respond flexibly to individual needs, particularly "allowing students to use individualized ways to learn or to meet requirements" (p. 189).

3. *Interpersonal understanding.* These teachers take time to listen so that they are aware of students' moods and feelings as well as their backgrounds, interests, and needs.

4. *Self-confidence.* These teachers have confidence in their own abilities and judgments while taking responsibility for problems and failings. They are prepared to question and give suggestions to superiors.

5. *Self-control.* These teachers keep their own emotions from interfering with work and display stress-resistance and stamina.

6. *Other personal effectiveness competencies* include accurate self-assessment and learning from their mistakes. They genuinely like people and have positive expectations of others. The best teachers display "intrinsic enjoyment of their work and a strong commitment to the process of learning and to the mission of their school" (p 191).

7. *Professional expertise.* These teachers expand and use their professional knowledge.

8. *Customer service orientation.* They probe "to discover the student's underlying needs and match available or customized services to that need" (p. 193).

9. *Teamwork and cooperation.* Excellent teachers solicit input from their students and give credit to, and cooperate with, others. They have a "concern to help children and their desire to develop their own skills led teachers into mutually beneficial dialogue with other professionals" (p. 194).

10. *Analytical thinking.* These teachers make inferences, see causal relationships, and systematically analyze complex problems. In particular, these teachers "thought about the connections in the subject matter and how to get them across to students" (p. 195).

11. *Conceptual thinking.* Also noted was their ability to recognize patterns and diagnose situations. They "make connections between course work and their students' lives and . . . make complex material clear and vivid" (p. 195).

12. *Initiative.* Going beyond the basic job requirements and "tackling problems before they become urgent or inescapable" (p. 195) was another characteristic.

13. *Flexibility.* These teachers adapt their style and strategies to fit the circumstances. Indeed, the authors argue that "flexibility was critical for teachers . . . " (p. 196).

14. *Directiveness/assertiveness.* These teachers set limits, confront problem behavior, and say no when necessary. At the same time, "the best teachers have established boundaries so well that they don't focus on directiveness" (p. 196).

Once again, particular programs and materials are not mentioned in this list of characteristics. Instead, it is the beliefs, attitudes, and interpersonal and instructional skills of these effective teachers that dominate the conclusions of the interview studies.

## Survey Studies

Pressley and his colleagues surveyed a national sample of fifth-grade teachers nominated as effective (Pressley, Yokoi, Rankin, Wharton-McDonald, & Mistretta, 1997). Respondents reported that they:

- Planned extensive reading and writing as a central theme of instruction.
- Integrated reading and writing with content-area instruction.
- Utilized diverse grouping arrangements (including cooperative groups and conferencing).
- Taught both higher- and lower-order skills (often directly).
- Promoted student motivation for reading.
- Utilized diverse assessment tools to evaluate growth.

Pressley et al. (1997) noted that these upper-grade elementary classrooms were more diverse on many curricular and instructional dimensions than primary-grade classrooms. One aspect of this diversity was the range of curriculum materials these teachers routinely used: Much as Sosniak and Stodolsky (1993) found no clear pattern in the use of curricular materials distinguished exemplary teachers.

## Summary

Taken together, these various studies produce a dizzying array of features that might characterize good fourth-grade teachers and their teaching. Given that different researchers used different research methods and employed different lenses to study good teaching, the breadth of characteristics identified is not surprising. Each list contains a mixture of constructs—beliefs, behaviors, and propensities. A summary list (with some loss of detail) is presented in Table 2.1. Although a valuable start, such an uneven list is hard to capitalize on for several reasons. First, we cannot be sure that the various constructs we collapsed together represent, in fact, the same characteristics. Different researchers used different teacher selection, data collection, and analytical methods and often drew on different theoretical formulations of effective teaching. The richness of methodological variety can be seen as a potential strength of these studies, but that same richness makes synthesis complicated.

Second, given current sociocultural understandings of teaching

## TABLE 2.1. Summary of Features Associated with Exemplary Teachers

| | Studies[a] |
|---|---|
| **Personal characteristics** | |
| Emotional and physical stamina, stress-resistance, perseverance, and self-control. | H, SS |
| Warm, caring, flexible; concern for students personal as well as academic development. | R, H, L |
| Supportive, encouraging, and friendly. | S, SS, L |
| Enthusiastic, enjoy work. | H, R, SS |
| Genuinely like people and have positive expectations of them. | SS |
| A sense of agency (confidence)—the feeling that what one does makes a difference. | H, SS |
| Able to make accurate self-assessments. | SS |
| Continue to develop professional expertise. | SS, R |
| **Beliefs, attitudes, and expectations** | |
| Expect diversity and expect to be able to manage it. | H |
| All children can learn to read and write; believe in children's potential. | T, SS, H, R, L |
| View learning as a social endeavor. | T, L |
| View ownership as necessary for learning; believe that students need to make choices. | R, T |
| View mistakes as an opportunity to learn. | H, SS |
| Value modeling as important. | T, H |
| Value and give respect and trust. | H, R, L |
| **Instructional practices** | |
| Organized and effective planners. | H, R |
| Classroom routines; behavior, movement, lessons. | S, Pb |
| Utilize diverse instructional groupings. | Pa, Pb |
| Foster student ownership. | H, R, T |
| Provide students with ample opportunities for reading and writing. | K, S, Pa, Pb, T |
| Integrate reading writing and subjects. | K, T, Pa, Pb |
| Foster student self-regulation, independence, internal motivation. | Pb, R, H |
| Listen and observe to adapt instruction. | T, SS |
| Make high demands but sensitive to individual needs and motivations; challenge and involve all students. | R, S, L |
| Flexible response to individual needs and interests. | SS, H |
| Make instruction personally relevant and activities stimulating. | R, S |
| Provide explicit instruction, particularly of strategies. | H, S, Pa |
| Display student work along with other educational materials. | T, S |
| **Instructional talk** | |
| Offer many constructive teacher–student exchanges. | S |
| Value and facilitate discussion. | K |
| Value and encourage collaborative learning. | T, Pa, Pb, L |
| Emphasize strategic and critical thinking. | K, R, L |

[a]H, Haberman (1995); K, Knapp (1995); L, Ladson-Billings (1994); Pa, Pressley, Yokoi, Rankin, Wharton-McDonald, and Mistretta (1996); Pb, Pressley, Wharton-McDonald, Mistretta-Hampston, and Echevarria (1998); R, Ruddell (1997); S, Snow, Barnes, Chandler, Goodman, and Hemphill (1991); SS, Spencer and Spencer (1993); T, Thomas and Barksdale-Ladd (1995).

and learning, we find it odd that so little attention was given to class-room language in these studies. As Wilkinson and Silliman (2000) point out, "the language used by teachers and students determines what is learned and how learning takes place . . . [and] exerts a profound effect on students' development of language and literacy skills" (p. 337).

Third, we are inclined to ask, as does Lampert (1985), how exemplary teachers manage to teach, using *manage* in the sense that "a manager is one who is able to find a way to do something and that action and invention are fused together in the management process" (p. 193). The crucial question then becomes, what is the "something" they are trying to do—what conception of literacy teaching and learning guides these teachers' practice?—a question not adequately answered in these studies.

An additional concern is that some of the constructs introduced by these studies are of little practical help. For example, it has long been reported (and was repeated in these studies) that students in effective teachers' classrooms spend a lot of time engaged in academic work. Although appearing intuitively consistent with other descriptors, such constructs are of little help to novice teachers or those who work with them. By contrast, it would seem more useful to know that effective teachers foster such engagement through lessons that focus on meaning and its construction, and that part of doing so involves integrating reading, writing, and subject areas (e.g., Guthrie & Wigfield, 2000). Likewise, identifying how effective teachers *develop* "community" would seem of greater utility than reporting that a "sense of community" exists in effective teachers' classrooms. Similarly, if we put the personality characteristics of effective teachers in the foreground, then improving teaching becomes principally a matter of selecting teachers with "the right stuff"—perhaps useful at hiring time but of limited value in developing effective teachers. Nevertheless, the available research does provide us with substantive insights on the nature of truly effective upper-grade elementary teaching and the teachers who accomplish it.

Still, there is more to be learned. After all, the notion of exemplary teaching in fourth grade is fundamentally attached to assumptions about what we think teachers are supposed to be accomplishing. For example, if we want our teachers to create competitive children who possess stacks of knowledge and skills, that is one thing; if we want them to create collaborative, caring, independent learners with self-extending learning systems as well as a robust knowledge base, that is another. Teachers approach these different constructions of their practice differently, and children's voices, epistemologies, and relationships reflect their socialized experience (Johnston et al., 2001).

There are many important questions yet to ask. For example, why would it be significant that these teachers view fallibility as a normal and important part of teaching and learning (Haberman, 1995a)? Is this merely another item on a list, or is it part of a larger conceptual frame? Why is so much effective classroom activity characterized by the use of open tasks and student choice among assignment options? Why do these classrooms so commonly feature discussion and collaboration on academic work? Are these separate items on a list of characteristics or a reliable cluster of instructional dimensions linked to student engagement and achievement (Guthrie et al., 1996; Turner, 1995)? We believe that the study of expert teaching is a viable strategy for identifying the ingredients of (1) the effective teaching of reading and (2) ways to develop teachers to teach expertly.

Each of the studies of effective upper elementary teachers we have discussed offers important insights into expert and effective teaching in these grades. There is certainly convergence among the studies, although the convergence is considerably greater when conclusions are summarized conceptually rather than item-by-item. Indeed, it is our view that future research will gain the most leverage by seeking conceptual coherence in instructional analyses.

## OUR STUDY OF EXEMPLARY FOURTH-GRADE TEACHERS

Guided by the available research on effective upper-grade elementary teaching, we set out to gain a more differentiated understanding of effective fourth-grade literacy instruction. We hoped that this work would better inform both pre-service and in-service teacher development efforts. We were concerned that most previous studies of effective upper-grade elementary teaching had gathered information on relatively few teachers and their classrooms in limited geographic regions. It seemed important to broaden the sample of teachers because state educational contexts vary on many dimensions. For example, some states sponsor textbook adoptions and others do not; some states test basic skills, and others test a more thoughtful literacy; some states have limited their investments in teacher development, and others have focused their efforts in this area. We wanted to capitalize on the specificity of case studies while exploring the generality across diverse circumstances.

Consequently, our study involved classroom observations of, and interviews with, 30 fourth-grade teachers in five states (New York, New Jersey, New Hampshire, Texas, and California). The teachers were identified as exemplary through a multiple nomination process. We sought nominations from a number of educators in each locale. We asked for nominations of extraordinarily effective fourth-grade teachers who offered instruction that featured curricular integration at some level. Nominators were asked to identify teachers whose classrooms they knew well. In each state we then sought to locate fourth-grade classrooms that reflected the diversity of the educational efforts in that area.

Thus the schools in which the selected teachers taught were located in a variety of communities (rural, small city, large city, suburbs). They ranged in size from small schools with enrollments of approximately 300 students to larger schools with enrollments of 800–1,000 students. Most schools enrolled between 400 and 600 students. In over half of the schools, minority students represented at least 25% of the student body, and in a third of the schools, minority students represented over half of the student body. The schools served substantial numbers of children from lower-income families. In two-thirds of the schools more than one of five students received a free or reduced-price meal. In a quarter of the schools, three-quarters or more of the children qualified for such meals.

We observed in each teacher's classroom for at least 10 full days, composing field notes that attempted to capture both the structure of classroom activity (time allocated, groupings, movement, etc.) and the essence of the language environment (who talks, the nature and content of talk, etc.). Audio and video recordings of classroom activities allowed closer analysis of some lessons. Additional data were gathered (1) in two semistructured interviews with each teacher, along with multiple spontaneous (usually end-of-the-day) interviews, (2) in interviews with target children from each classroom, (3) in the form samples of student writing and reading logs provided by children, and (4) in end-of-year achievement test performances.

Although our sample of teachers had been nominated as "reputationally" effective, and although we had gathered voluminous sorts of evidence of these teachers' effectiveness, we still conducted a post hoc analysis of achievement test gains in the subset of classrooms where both third- and fourth-grade student achievement data were available. Not surprisingly, that analysis showed that student achievement gains outpaced expected levels of growth. These teachers did produce greater than expected levels of literacy growth as measured on standardized achievement tests (see the Appendix). However, as we point out later, literacy growth, especially as estimated on standardized tests, is not the only indicator of quality instruction and student achievement, and such estimates, in fact, are impoverished substitutes for more complex ways of estimating teacher effects on students' growth and achievement (Battistich, Watson, Solomon, Lewis, & Schaps, 1999; Falk, 2000; Johnston, 1999; Johnston et al., 2001).

Individual case studies for six of these exemplary teachers (three from New York and three from other states) follow in the next section of the book. These teachers represented a range in years of teaching experience (5–25) and ethnicity. Their classrooms represented a range of class sizes (19–33), student poverty levels (2–85% of students receiving free- or reduced-price lunches), ethnic mixes of students, instructional organization (from self-contained to departmentalized, from single grade to multigrade), and were located in various community types (urban core, urban fringe, small city, rural town, and suburban). In short, the case study teachers worked with a variety of students in communities that varied in substantial ways.

The case studies reveal both the similarities and the differences across these exemplary fourth-grade classrooms. Although our primary goal was to identify common characteristics of the teachers and their classrooms, we must note that . . . the variations we observed also convinced us that effective teaching can only be nurtured within a framework that celebrates the unique qualities and capacities of individual teachers.

# PART II

## What Do Good Classrooms Look and Feel Like?

# 3

# Inquiry and a Good Conversation

*"I Learn a Lot from Them"*

PETER H. JOHNSTON
JOAN BACKER[1]

One weekend in May, three ducklings—two brown and one yellow—were born in a lowly incubator in Joan Backer's fourth-grade classroom. A fourth—yellow—had joined them by Wednesday morning. Before the children trickled in, Joan was going through her morning ritual of planning the day's schedule on the white board. I teased her about why she bothered, for I had yet to see her follow the plans she routinely made. She explained that she needs a backup, even though she planned a discussion about the ducklings first thing, since they would draw the children's attention anyway—but "How can I tell how long the discussion will take?" This comment captures, in a nutshell, the essence of Joan's teaching. She planned her curriculum around the children's concerns, dragging the formal curriculum along

---

[1]This chapter is written from the perspective of the first author, a visitor to the classroom, to maintain a single voice throughout. However the chapter was jointly composed through discussion, interview, and response.

behind.[2] At first she protested that this was not a "normal" day because of the ducks but then noted, with some resignation that, really, no day is particularly normal. The students' interests have more influence on the day's learning than do common routines or state mandates.

Joan is approaching retirement while struggling with the housing and care of her elderly parents. The school in which she teaches is an urban public school that emphasizes literature and writing in a humanistic framework. Thirty percent of the students are eligible for free or reduced-price lunch; the racial composition of the school is 60% white, 10% African American, 20% Hispanic, and 10% Asian. The school has no playground, but the street outside is blocked to traffic during recess, weather permitting. The building, though old, is festooned with children's writing and artwork, along with a wide range of books and other literate and artistic objects. The teachers in the school have a book club discussion once a month that Joan views primarily as a source of ideas for her own teaching. All teachers and students (about 525) in the school are on a first-name basis.

Joan is a respected member of a talented faculty. She teaches inservice workshops for the district and has been involved in a nationally known writing project for a number of years. She is well connected to other teachers and her students' parents routinely come into the classroom before and after school to talk, as do her past students. As a professional, she is painfully reflective and never satisfied with her efforts. This year she has 27 students in a small classroom that has no desks, only round tables, a large rug, a couch, a rocking chair, and two computers. The children's imitation stained-glass work beautifies much of the huge and ancient windows that do little to keep out the noise of the city outside.

The organizing principle of Joan's teaching practice is inquiry. She constantly encourages inquiry into math, science, language, literacy, learning—the world. Indeed, although it is often possible to tell that a particular subject, like math or reading, is currently in progress, it is just as often not possible. Reading and writing are integrated and distributed throughout the curriculum. The observation and theorizing of science also turn up constantly. For example, Joan read aloud (with think-aloud modeling) "Sign of the Beaver" and "Red-

---

[2]Although the emphasis she placed on the children rather than the curriculum was a conscious one completely in line with her goals, it was, she said, something she would routinely "beat myself up about," feeling it perhaps made her not a good teacher.

bird," which were used as springboards for the social studies curriculum as well as literary discussion—each shift in focus expanding the children's ability to comprehend and think about things in a multidimensional manner. When the ducklings hatched in the classroom and the children wanted to name them, Joan reminded her students of "Sign of the Beaver" and how the Native Americans named children only after they had observed their characteristics. The students dutifully observed and then made a list of their observations, from which they named the ducklings—the objects of their study in science.

Homework commonly involves reading (planned by each group) and projects such as:

> "Find in these poems some pieces that you wish you had written."
> "Design an experiment to test your hypothesis about the ducklings' choice of land or water" (a question that arose from observation and discussion).
> "Work on testing your hypothesis about the most frequent upper case letter" (a question that arose when the students were planning of a handwriting lesson).

Joan favors "real" activities. For example, the students run an ice-cream business out of the classroom. After school they take turns selling ice cream from a cart, which provides math study through accounting, budgeting, and predicting sales for ordering; and composition practice when they write (and fax) letters to the company from whom they purchase their product. Studying the hatching and hatched ducklings provides grounds for further math (weighing, charting, graphing, predicting, classifying) as well as writing, reading, and research, particularly on the Internet. The children are quite competent at locating topics on the World Wide Web. On the first day of school after the ducklings' arrival, two pairs of children searched the Internet to find out how to care for the ducklings and to learn more about the peculiarities of their particular breeds. This use of the Internet not only required them to navigate the many screens they encountered along the way but to sort through documents for readability and relevance, so that they only printed out what the class would find useful.

Joan's choice of tasks not only emphasizes real problems and inquiry but collaborative solutions as well. It is common for the children to disagree with each other and with Joan, respectfully, and to provide the logic for their position. For example, in one discussion Laurel commented: "I disagree with Shelley because . . . and I agree with Jack and Gordon because he's not really sickly, and he was just born yesterday, so he might look sick because he only has one eye open. But the other duck only had one eye open too." This is the same kind of logical thought and audience awareness that they exercise in persuasive writing and critical reading.

On most days there is a clearly demarcated reading time when children either participate in group reading or read alone (they have one book for each format, and a journal for their thoughts). Once a week they engage in "buddy reading" time with a class of younger children. "Reading" includes reading and discussing books as well as writing relevant observations and experiences in their journals. However, much of the reading and writing is distributed functionally throughout other parts of the day. Journals are used to record observations of various kinds, including literary ones, and for writing drafts of poems or stories. Types of writing (written in a variety of different places) include: records of learning strategies used and "What I learned" (especially in math); letters (associated with the ice-cream business, science, class trips, etc.); plans and records of reading group activity; records of predictions and observations in science; notes made during read-aloud; essays, poems, and a host of other genres. Although relatively little writing is "big production," children do publish their work. Students enthusiastically verbalize their observations about authors' words and language choices— including the authors in Joan's class. When I asked these children, "Are there any good authors in this class?," they were not confused by the question, as children were in classes in which they are not treated as authors.

From this beginning sketch of Joan's classroom, we can draw out the principles from which she operates, using brief illustrations, before showing how it all fits together.

## JOAN'S GUIDING PRINCIPLES

### Inquiry

As noted, Joan organizes her class around inquiry. In a casual conversation one day, Joan commented that she was concerned that some of the students were still not asking a lot of questions. She cited Claude as an example and then observed that, actually, last week he *had* asked a question. Prior to taking a test, he asked, "How come they make these with 20 or 30 questions instead of just one?" She noted that although it was not an academic question, it was, nonetheless, a critical question. Raising this issue at all reveals just how much Joan values children's ability to ask their own questions and to take control of their inquiry. (In most classrooms the number of student questions is close to zero; Dillon, 1988.) But noticing a single example for a particular student and remembering it (nearly 2 weeks later) suggests how central inquiry is to Joan's teaching philosophy. An additional feature of Joan's style is that even though the behavior was not quite what she wanted, she responded to the positive side of it.

Joan fosters inquiry not only in "content areas" but extends on all levels. Reading and writing are commonly used in the service of inquiry. She even approaches spelling and the study of cursive writing through inquiry. For example, the "word for the day," selected by Joan or the students and written on a small chart along with its definition and pronunciation, became a source of inquiry in Joan's hand. On one occasion she covered up the day's word, *quagmire,* and asked the students to write it, as best they could, on pieces of cardboard using a marker, large enough for all to see. She then posted these on the board without names, and the students to analyze and categorize them. Some of the comments were as follows:

JOAN: What are you noticing?

STUDENT 1: Most people did a *qu* instead of a *kw.*

JOAN: Some did. Why did you write a *qu?*

STUDENT 2: I put a *u* 'cos you can't have a *q* without a *u.*

JOAN: How many of you thought of another word that starts the same? (*Most hands are raised.*) What else are you noticing? Any other patterns or things that surprise you?

Many observations are made of strategies used and patterns observed. Joan finishes by observing, "Well, it looks like we're in a quagmire now, so let's look at the word." They uncover the word. "Have any of you been in a quagmire? How did you know that?"

On one occasion Joan asked the students to help her plan a handwriting lesson. They decided they would need to work out which letters to start with. This led them to group letters by structure and to consider the letters most frequently used. Grouping the letters by structure required the students to attend to detailed characteristics of the letters in memorable ways. Since there was overlap among categories, there was also an incidental math experience of managing and representing set intersections. Deciding on the most frequent letter produced several possibilities, each with an accompanying logic, and a renewed attention to details of the organization of letters. Along the way, Joan commented that she was persuaded from her original selection by the logic of one of the students. Some students opted to pursue the matter for homework to satisfy their quest for an answer.

## The Process and the Partially Correct

I have already noted Joan's emphasis on the partially correct aspect of a child's performance rather than on the erroneous part. I would have to add that there was almost a complete absence of the words *no* and *wrong* in Joan's classroom. She routinely gave reflective, process-oriented responses, such as "That strategy is like the way we conserve words in poetry." There are two types of situations in which Joan's style of responding can be complicated. One is the type of situation when a child's response appears to come from "off the wall" while discussing a story or poem. Joan's handling of this challenge is exemplified by one such occasion in which she paused and said, "That's a very interesting way of thinking about it. I hadn't thought about it that way. I'll have to think about it some more." This response kept the class discussion moving, with the student still involved, and at the same time implied to the student "There are different ways to make sense of things, and I am interested in the sense you make because perhaps you see something that I don't."

The second situation in which it is difficult to avoid the "no" response is when a factual answer is flatly wrong—such as a "math fact." The incident that illustrates Joan's stance in these circumstances arose when the class was taking attendance. In Joan's room, attendance is taken by attaching a problem, or a poll, or some issue-raiser to each "present" response. In this case each student called on the next student and posed a problem associated with factors of six or primes. Three students answered their questions incorrectly, but the roll call continued uninterrupted, leaving the responses uncorrected. After the attendance had been taken, however, Joan mentioned two of the incorrect responses without attributing them, adding how surprised she was that they didn't catch them—thus drawing attention to her expected concern for self-monitoring. She then asked how many ways the students could do these problems and obtained half a dozen strategies for each. In the process she drew attention away from the error and towards the problem solving. One of the students noted the additional incorrect response, which Joan confessed she had missed (allowing that she, too, makes errors). Joan deliberately ignored the initial incorrect response with the intention of separating the problem from the person while drawing greater attention to the process and the sense of agency.

Joan routinely draws attention to the *process* underlying the activity. She often instructs students to "write down something you learned or a strategy you used," or asks, "Did anyone do it a different way?" And "Show us how you did that" is a staple of her teaching. When reading about ducks from an overhead transparency, the class came across the word *Moschata*. Joan asked, "How should I say that word?" The suggested pronunciations that flowed from the students were made into a chart on the flip chart, connecting the new word (Moschata) to the words the children used as analogies such as *school* to figure out the parts of it (using the /sk/ pronunciation found in *sch*ool as an analog for the pronunciation of the *sch* on Moschata).

Students were so confident that the process was the most important part that when they were sharing their answers and strategies for a math problem, they were able to say, as one student did, "Well, I got this wrong, but this is how I did it."

## Hearing a Community of Voices

Students' voices are valued in the classroom throughout the day. Their questions, predictions, and observations are taken seriously and accorded significance. Joan insists that children listen to each other, and she provides a clear model by listening carefully herself. Discussions are mostly propelled by students, and their observations are invited during read-alouds, written on post-its during silent reading, and validated with comments such as "suggestion taken," "interesting thought," "say more about that," and through restatements and summaries. Their observations and reflections are often written down by Joan and sometimes posted on the wall with names attached, so that they can be referred to as a partial class history. This strategy provides a sense of the significance of print and of their experiences, along with accountability for their statements. Joan also makes connections among students' observations and experiences.

Making sure all voices are heard is also part of building a strong learning community. The community spirit is fostered in this classroom by Joan's "random acts of kindness" wall, on which she and students can post any acts of kindness they observe in class. One such act involved decorating a new student teacher's journal with the children's self-portraits on post-its and proclaiming, "It's going to be great. A real family." Joan's notion of family includes being able to disagree civilly.

## Personalizing Instruction

The children's heights and class photos are taped on the door and their statements pepper the walls. When children come in at the beginning of the day, linger at lunch and recess, or work during class, Joan takes the time to engage them in individual and small group conversations through which she comes to know them as individuals. She creates class projects in which children represent themselves, encourages students to draw on their own experiences when interpreting literature, and assigns writing projects in which they share their personal experiences. Because of these efforts to personalize the classroom experience, Joan acquires a great deal of knowledge that informs her responses to her students. It is within this trusting context that students learn. There is no way in which a student could feel like a number in Joan's classroom. It is not merely that Joan knows each of the students so well, but that the children, too, know each other well.

## Valuing Language

Joan makes it clear that she values language. On her desk (crowded, with no chair) was Bill Moore's book *Words that Taste Good*. When reading aloud from a book, she might reread a line, as noted, and comment, for example, "Oh, I love that line." She treats students' language the same way. Comments such as "I like the way you put that, 'Full with fur,' " are common. For homework one day, she asked students to underline "I wish I had written" lines on a poetry sheet. The next day, when Joan was reading these poems to the class, the students begged to have their turn to read them aloud, and within a couple of minutes they were orchestrating readings in groups in which multiple voices read different lines. On the wall is a chart for children to classify the elements in the humorous poetry they have read. Categories so far include: playing with words, illustration, poking fun at behavior, mixed up words or actions.

Joan's interest in language was obviously contagious. On the first morning the children discovered they were "parents," Joan took the roll by asking them to give their name and a brief statement of their feelings. Jack used the expression "cute fluffballs," and Gordon responded that Jack's description reminded him of a phrase from a book by Sid Fleischman (1986): "They rolled out of his hands like little balls of sunshine." In the same conversation Aja created the descriptor "cutified." There was some discussion among the children about the authenticity of the word, but also support for its appropriateness, and Joan pointed out that "words are added to the dictionary every year." From these discussions of language, the children develop an interest in words and their sounds, structures, and meanings, and in the consequences of word choice.

## AN EXTENDED EXAMPLE

To show how Joan's philosophy plays out in her classroom, I will describe the first of several "duck discussions" that took place on a particular day—discussions that reveal, among other things, Joan's ability to stimulate her students in generating and sustaining deeply intellectual discussions and literate thinking. I am tempted to say that these discussions are made possible by a set of skills that Joan possesses, and to some degree that is true. But it may be more accurate to view them as manifestations of her fundamental interest in, and valuing of, what students have to say, and their collective questioning and willingness to investigate solutions to problems. For example, in keeping with Joan's attention to the students' questions, the previous night's homework included the assignment to "design an experiment to test the hypothesis that the ducklings prefer being in the water to being on land." Joan created this assignment in response to the students' observations of what happened when some of the ducklings were put in the water. The next day some of the students were given the opportunity, during class and recess, to set up their experiment and test their conflicting hypotheses. The test was a resounding success for a number of reasons, and it continued a discussion from earlier in the day—a discussion that I will now relate, annotating the places I believe are associated with significant learning. The example is lengthy in order to show the extent of engagement and commitment. Although the example is not explicitly related to developing literacy, I will show the ways in which this interaction expands children's literate development (summarized in Table 3.1 and indicated throughout the following analysis by parenthetical numbers).

The discussion begins with a concern for whether the latest

---

**TABLE 3.1. Significance of Conversational Interactions in Class Discussion**

1. Joan develops students' sense of authority—shows that she respects students and is deeply interested in what they have to say.
   1.1. Summarizes what students say and helps consolidate the discussion.
   1.2. Asks them to say more about an issue.
   1.3. Remembers what students said days ago.
   1.4. Encourages students to make connections with personal experience.
   1.5. Contributes as another member of the group rather than as the teacher.
   1.6. Accords significance to students' contributions (and boosts security).
   1.7. Reorganizes schedule around children's interests/issues.
   1.8. Does not close down digressions.
2. Students take control of the means of knowledge production.
   2.1. Encouraged to initiate investigations.
   2.2. Encouraged to make careful observations (across the curriculum) and distinguish between observations and interpretations.
   2.3. Taught to value collaborative development of ideas and respectful disagreement.
3. Multiple possibilities expected and encouraged.
4. Students encouraged to crosscheck and manage multiple sources of authority.
   4.1. Taught to remain open to correction.
   4.2. Taught to notice disjunctures and develop critical literacy.
5. Encouraged to predict, abstract, and theorize ("What if . . . ?").
6. Encouraged to make frequent connections to other discussions/subjects/experiences.
7. Builds democratic community.
   7.1. By modeling listening and respect, students learn to listening to and respect one another.
   7.2. Highlights and practices democratic processes.
8. Highlights a function of writing or connection to subject matter.
9. Invites consideration of language and conventions.
10. Recognizes the big issues and highlights them.
11. Focuses on what is done well or the part that is correct.
12. Gives plenty of time for reflection.
13. Collaborates with other teachers.

duckling to hatch in the classroom will be safe with the older duck-lings. The youngest has been kept separate because of this concern, but the students have resolved to run a test to see what will happen (2.1). The ensuing discussion suggests both the depth and signifi-cance of the literate engagements occurring.

Joan begins by asking that everyone "write what they think will happen" (5). She then invites the students to share what they have written, beginning with a weaker student, Laquesha. Laquesha's re-sponse is difficult to hear, both because it is quiet and because of the interested chatter, so Joan calls on Aja to restate it, which she does (7.1). The students then call on each other to comment and add their own proposals (7). Joan takes a brief poll to see where people stand on the matter and who is undecided. The split is about even.

Joan summarizes a comment by Clive to confirm what he said (1.1) and to make sure it is heard by all. She adds, "I hear you, and others, talking about *time*." She connects this point to the science teacher's discussion of "variables" (6), then connects it to Art's sug-gestion the previous day that it might be territorial behavior (1.3) and his question about *what* would happen *if* the tank were larger (5).

Aja suggests another possibility: that duckling behavior is like a gang and "if you're strong enough, you can be part of the gang—and they make fun of the geeky girls" (3, 1.4).

Joan puts the ducklings in the tank and the kids laugh— "They're scared!"

Joan asks, "Is that an observation or conjecture?" (2.2), then adds, "Jessie's writing down what she thinks, so she won't forget it" (8). Conversation and commentary abound. Joan notes, "Mia has written down a lot already."

The ducklings continue to peck one another occasionally. Clive proposes a new hypothesis: that the pecking is like monkeys' groom-ing behavior, suggesting that maybe it is not aggressive behavior after all (3). The conversation continues and includes the following com-ments:

"All the ducklings did it at the beginning" (2.2).

"Maybe it's not that bad—you just don't know" (3).

"Maybe they like to peck, and they are bored with pecking the food" (3).

"Nonetheless," Joan adds, "If I were it's mother, I'd want to take it out of there" (1.5).

Kane, a new and somewhat troubled boy, points out that "If he doesn't stay in their home, how will they get used to him?" Joan restates his question to bring it into focus for the class and, aware that Kane himself is in the process of fitting into the class, reminds the others that Kane was also the one who started them thinking about why the eggs lost weight instead of gaining it (1.6). Observations about which duckling is pecking which, and speculation about how color or species might be involved, flow freely (5). Joan urges the children to write down their observations and hypotheses so that they do not forget. She also points out that, as scientists, the difficult part is not getting so engrossed that you forget to keep notes (8).

Before school formally began this morning, students had posed the question, "Can the new duckling swim?" Now a container of water is brought forth and Joan puts the new duckling into it to answer the question. While the water level rises, Joan brings up the question of what to do with the remaining eggs, since 28 days have past and they are not likely to hatch. Some wonder why they did not hatch even though they were in the *same* incubator (4.2). Shelley tries to draw them back to the pecking question and asks *what* would happen *if* the two yellow ducklings were put together instead of the browns and the yellows (5). Joan acknowledges the importance of Shelley's question and notes how important it is to write down all the questions so that "we don't forget to go back and answer them" (8).

They continue to pursue the egg question. Daisy raises the problem of how they can know if the unhatched eggs are still alive. Joan says, "Say more about that" (1.2). Daisy elaborates and Jessie jumps in too (2.3, 7.1). Joan praises them: "This is wonderful! It is how you should be listening to each other" (7.1). Bogdan agrees with Daisy and distinguishes between eggs with small and large dark spots (observed in those already hatched). Aja proposes another procedure for distinguishing the viable from the nonviable eggs (3). Joan restates Aja's proposal to acknowledge, clarify, and verify it (1.1). Clive comments that it doesn't really matter because the next day the study will be over; the ducklings will be taken to the farm, and it will be the weekend (2.3). Chase agrees and provides a complicated argument along the lines of: "Let's say we were to. . . . And say we. . . . We wouldn't know whether they were going to be okay" (5). Lucy agrees, noting that "even if it came out very late, it might not be healthy" (5). She relates this to human babies, using herself as an example (6).

Joan again compliments them on the way they are listening to each other. The discussion resumes as Kane suggests that "*Maybe they're from a different bird*" (with a longer gestation period) (3). Shelley disagrees with Lucy, then Joan brings the discussion together with, "It seems like a couple of things are coming up here. What are the big issues? Help me think this through" (1.5).

Jack notes that even when the brown spots are on the eggs, they don't hatch for at least another day. Art disagrees: "The reason I disagree with you, Jack, is because when we did the candling for number seven [egg], it was clear" (2.3). Joan asks, "How many think we should crack number seven?" She counts 20 votes, notes that there are some abstentions, and decides to crack it. She then moves to the other eggs—those that have grown but are not fully developed. There is a smaller majority here, so she decides they should open them but first she cautions her students: "If you don't think you want to be part of that, if it's not something you can handle, you don't have to. Okay, we've already had the discussion. Do we crack all or some of the eggs?" The vote is eight in favor of all, and 14 for some. She notes: "This is how you go about making a large decision with a lot of parts. You take it in parts. Discussion is now open on how to decide which ones" (7.2).

There is some discussion, and Joan remarks that "I can see how thoughtful you're being about the creature inside the egg and if it has a chance of survival" (10, 11). She suggests that they could switch science and do it tomorrow (1.7), but that if the eggs are dead, the bacteria will have made them smell even stronger by then—a reference to an earlier discussion of "decomposers" (6). She brings it to a vote, and the students unanimously support doing the dissection today (7.2).

Joan then brings them back to the issue of deciding which eggs to dissect—which again elicits more points of view. Along the way Jack notices that Joan has written *develop* on the chart paper and asks whether it is supposed to have an *e* at the end. She responds, "No, but thanks for noticing and thinking" (1.8, 11). A couple of other students catch her up on her use of *she* when referring to the new duckling (4.1). The discussion presses on, tensions around giving the unhatched ducklings a chance vivid in the students' faces, and both the logic and futility of waiting thoroughly analyzed. In the process, Joan reminds them of the time that it took for the other eggs to hatch even after they had darkened (6). Daisy suggests the "floating test" as a way to determine which eggs are likely to hatch (3). Art agrees. Then Jack summarizes the arguments that have been made by Gary and Art, adds the time factor, and argues that there is no chance that they will hatch before the end of Friday (1.1). Clive wonders whether the eggs might be upside down so that the pip holes can't be seen (3,5). Shelley admits "I'm confused. Didn't someone say that only the ducklings were going back to the farm? The eggs aren't going anyway" (4.2). Gary argues that they can't be alive for the reasons already given, so there is no point in waiting, but concedes that sampling would be better.

Joan observes, "This takes me back to last Friday and egg number eight. Jack could feel it moving." She quotes what he said at the time, and then quotes Shelley, who could hear it inside (1.3) "If we were to hold each one and listen, could we check? Just digest that question for a minute" (12). Clive proposes that Joan's suggestion is one of several possible tests that have come up, including "candling, like x-rays." He notes that the tests involve different senses and can be used as checks on one another (4). Lucy agrees and suggests that they test the eggs this way and crack them today "if we don't hear or see anything. Is that reasonable?" They vote and unanimously agree.[3] The dissection will take place later in the day, with the science teacher in the classroom leading the surgery (1.7, 13).

That settled, they return to the original problem of the swimming experiment. One of the students comments that the duckling is cold, but Joan reminds him "That's an assumption." Meanwhile the duck is held upside down and they speculate about the size and significance of the dark spot underneath—whether it has to do with sex organs and whether they "do number one and number two out of the same part" (5, 1.8).

Joan puts the young duckling in the water and notes "I don't see any writing going on" (8). This duck tries to get out of the water. Joan takes it out, puts it in the box, and places the brown ducks in the water. They dive and splash and create pandemonium. The two yellow ones on land get on fine without the brown ones, they notice, and again speculate about the significance of species. Unprompted, Lucy and Gary retrieve the list of duck species to check their observations (4). Others notice the effects of water on the down of the ducklings and draw conclusions about oil and its distribution on the

---

[3]Joan comments to me as an aside, that that is what she beats herself up about: Why hadn't she come up with that idea and saved time?

down. One student notes that the book says ducklings do not initially have oil, that the mother helps bring out the oil in the babies. These ducklings, they point out, have no mother (4.2).

The conversation from which this portion was excerpted has taken about an hour and a quarter, and most of the students have been involved for most of the time. There have been many disagreements, but they have remained respectful. However, the noise level has begun to rise. Joan acknowledges that she knows how hard it is to keep their voices down: "You should have seen the teachers' meeting yesterday. If you are tired now, you can go and read." Four students depart for another section of the room, and Joan comes back to the oil issue: "I'm following what Art said: Is there more oil on the head or body?" (1.3). There is a brief discussion before they disband to read and write while a small group of selected volunteers stays to record any further observations (2.2, 8).

Of 24 students, 14 have participated in the conversation, and their ability levels vary considerably. Virtually all have participated in the whole process, including the experiment. Those students who did not actively participate in this particular set of interactions have not been idle. Throughout the discussions, Joan allows minor digressions, and the conversation remains genuine, respectful, and dialogical. Joan takes the child seriously and does not prematurely judge the child's point of view in relation to norms or standards. Although she sometimes asks questions to which she knows the answer, they are not common questions, and she does not use the standard monological format: teacher initiates, student responds, teacher evaluates—IREs (Cazden, 1988; Dillon, 1988; McDermott, 1993). These are only IRs, and they are used to move the discussion along— perhaps *IRRRR* would be more accurate, for it is the students who pose most of the questions. Joan's wait-time is extensive when breaks occur, but normally students leave little need for it. There is a constant emphasis on the process and student agency, and a complete absence of public attention to relative competence.

## SUMMARY AND IMPLICATIONS

In spite of the significant learning taking place in this classroom, Joan is not satisfied. Although she is confident about the students' progress in math, she worries that perhaps more writing should be taken to publication and that some of the students are not progressing as quickly as she would like. She worries that perhaps some of the discussions take longer than they should and that she is not striking the right balance among her various responsibilities. In part, her unease is fueled by the fact that the many extraordinary abilities she *is* fostering are not measured on the annual standardized tests. Joan is teaching her students a way of being literate with each other that reflects her deeply held values. With Freire and others (Freire & Macedo, 1987; Knoblauch & Brannon, 1993), Joan believes that a central part of learning to read print is learning to read the world and thinking about how it is represented and by whom. Her students are learning not merely about "comprehension" but about "using language to make sense of the world" (Lindfors, 1999) and, at the same time, inquiring into the language they are using to represent it. By teaching her students to take a controlling interest in the production of knowledge, she develops in them the epistemology of constructed knowers (Belenky, Clinchy et al., 1986; Johnston et al., 2001).

What makes Joan's literacy instruction unusual is her belief that becoming literate should be engaging, and that students should have a controlling interest in their learning. Central to this philosophy is her commitment to dialogue, particularly the dialogue of inquiry–response. As Lindfors (1999) observes, "I know of no more important goal in education than that the child shall discover the power of his or her own mind. And I know of no more important source of that discovery, for every child, than the inquiry that lives in the continuing exploratory dialogues of classroom life" (p. 247). Joan routinely enables her students to explore uncharted territory in which she cannot assert superior knowledge or experience. And even when she can, she usually avoids doing so. She privileges students' observations, theorizing, negotiations, crosschecking, and the group process of formulating and solving problems.

Reading and writing are an inextricable part of formulating and solving problems, sharing experience, and engaging in social and intellectual work. Perhaps because of this very ubiquitousness, they are less visible than one might expect. Instruction in all areas integrates reading and writing, and reading and writing are inseparable. At other times, however, attention is turned directly to studying language and literacy, just as any other aspect of life might be examined actively, collaboratively, and in detail. Joan's children are studying not just language and literacy but the *process* of learning to become literate—which gives them control over the why they will learn in the future as well.

Joan's students learn literacy as a social practice and in this process learn not merely to tolerate diversity but to value it. They listen closely to what each has to say and use the differences in perspective to extend their own collective and individual thinking. Joan is aware, as Lindfors (1999) points out, that "to develop ways of inquiry is to develop one's humanness—social, intellectual, personal. It matters that these three come together and receive support in classroom communities" (p. 19). It is these ways of knowing the world and knowing language that become the most important acquisitions of the students as they pass through Joan's classroom. Literacy is used in the context of inquiry and social participation marked by dignity, respect, and social commitment. These aspects of literate development are not trivial outcomes of schooling (Nicholls, 1989; Battistich, Watson, et al., 1999; Johnston, 1999; Powell, 1999). Absent from the annual standardized tests, the test for these qualities will be in the survival of our democracy.

# 4

## "Responsibility and Respect for Themselves and for Whatever It Is They're Doing"

### Learning to Be Literate in an Inclusive Classroom

GAY IVEY

When I walked into the classroom today, students were busy doing a number of different things. . . . They have been studying immigration, and they are planning an international food festival to which all of the students' families will be invited. Some students are creating personalized invitations for their family members, while others are drawing family trees or working on their autobiographies. As they work on their various tasks, students spontaneously share what they have learned about their personal histories in their research to prepare for the event:

- Jodi reports that she found her dad's family tree at home in a book. Her parents told her that there was a blizzard the day she was born, so only a few people came by to sign her baby book.

- Randy explains that he was so big as a baby that doctors and nurses made comments about his size.
- Mack shares that his paternal grandparents were born in South Carolina, and that his grandmother was born two years after the sinking of the Titanic.
- John reports that his grandmother was born in 1923 and that she is still alive.

At the end of the writing time, they listen as their teacher reads aloud *When Jesse Came Across the Sea* (Hest, 1997), a picture book about an immigrant girl's cultural heritage, which prompts even more discussion about personal and family histories. (Field notes).

Any visitor to Kim Duhamel's fourth-grade classroom in Lincoln School in Edison, New Jersey, would observe a scene similar to this one. Students typically work on a range of different projects, busy and engaged, talking as they work, usually about their task. Reading, writing, and content are connected, and activities flow seamlessly from one to the other.

Given the diversity of Kim's class, one might not expect the rich and healthy learning environment she and her students have created. Their school is located in a semiurban, densely populated, ethnically diverse area. During the year I observed this class, Kim taught 18 students representing a wide range of educational experiences and cultural backgrounds. Nine of the children were classified as special education students; 10 were of European descent, three of African descent, three of Asian descent, and two of Middle Eastern descent. Approximately 20% of the school's population qualifies for free or reduced-priced lunch.

Although Kim is an experienced teacher, having taught in special education and primary-grade classrooms for over a decade before teaching several fourth grade for the past years, her success with such an academically and culturally mixed class is due to more than just longevity. When asked to share her perspective on teaching, she compares herself to a fictitious teacher in a popular children's book series: "It's like being Mrs. Frizzle (Cole, 1995) and just kind of taking a ride through the school year. That's kind of how we set it up in the beginning, a lot of magic school bus stuff. I said, 'Let's just be that class and go wherever we're going to go and just see what happens.' " After getting to know Kim, observing her fourth-grade classroom, and talking to her students, I understand this comparison. However, I also found that although the possibilities for learning in Kim's classroom are far-reaching and open-ended, her teaching is neither haphazard nor left to chance.

My goal in observing Kim's class was to identify the characteristics of her teaching that made her classroom a productive and supportive setting for such a wide range of students. In this chapter I describe the most salient features of the classroom environment and the key features of Kim's instruction.

## THE CLASSROOM ENVIRONMENT

The instructional environment in Kim's classroom is rich and full. Virtually every minute of the day, and every inch of space in the room, are used for instruction. Children arrive at school at 9:00 A.M. and leave at 3:00 P.M., and between those times, Kim and her students are almost constantly engaged in academic activities. Likewise, the classroom overflows with instructional materials, and almost every area of the room is used by students throughout the day.

### A Typical Day in Kim's Classroom

Kim's overall philosophy on the learning and teaching of literacy is that the language arts ought to be taught in conjunction with all the other subject areas. This philosophy of integration is apparent in what happens during a typical day in her classroom, as illustrated in Table 4.1. Although there are specific times set aside for science and language arts on this particular day in January, reading and writing are clearly a part of science class, and for an outside observer, it is hard to differentiate between the two subjects.

Students are given long blocks of time to work on reading and writing tasks without interruption. Notice in Table 4.1 that students have 1½-hour blocks in both science and in language arts on this day, and overall, they are engaged in activities that involve much reading and writing (science, free reading, language arts, end-of-day journal writing) for 3½ hours of the total 5½ hours they are in Kim's classroom. They spend roughly 1½ hours out of the classroom for physical education and lunch.

During independent reading and writing times, both Kim and the special education teacher, who is assigned to Kim's room for half

**TABLE 4.1. A Typical Day in Kim's Fourth-Grade Class**

| Time | Activity |
| --- | --- |
| 9:00–9:10 | Homeroom |
| 9:10–10:00 | Students go to physical education; Kim's planning time. |
| 10:00–10:45 | *Math:* Students play cooperative card game that requires them to do mental math for addition, subtraction, multiplication, and division. |
| 10:45–12:15 | *Science:* Students work in small groups to construct paper dinosaurs from cut-outs of bones. They create names for their dinosaurs and begin to draft descriptions of the creatures they have "discovered," which may include physical descriptions, how and where they lived, and how they became extinct. They use both nonfiction and fiction books about prehistoric times they have already read (e.g., Cole's *Magic School Bus in the Time of the Dinosaurs,* 1995) to help them come up with ideas. |
| 12:15–1:00 | Lunch |
| 1:00–1:25 | *Free reading:* Students choose whatever they want from the classroom library and read silently. |
| 1:25–2:55 | *Language arts:* Class reads the next chapter of *Be a Perfect Person in Just Three Days!* (Manes, 1996). Kim gives them a writing assignment connected to the book: Students are to write a newspaper article about something the main character did. Kim shares a real newspaper article with the class, and they talk about how the author got his information, how he used interesting adjectives, etc. |
| 2:55–3:00 | Wrap-up time: Students write about their school day in their "*Carpe Diem*" notebooks. |

of the day and another teacher's room for the other half of the day, move from student to student, offering advice and on-the-spot lessons as they are needed. Both teachers also spend much time listening to students talk about their work and whatever they are reading and writing. Kim also realizes that hard work sometimes requires noise, and she is comfortable with a moderate level of talking as students go about their tasks. As she puts it, "They all know what they're doing. I know what they're doing. So if they have to talk about it, I'm fine with that."

Kim's goal for these sustained work times is that the students learn to monitor themselves—and she has certainly achieved that with this class. They know classroom routines, and they know where to find the materials they need. They also employ strategies for finding answers to questions without necessarily having to ask the teacher, such as consulting dictionaries, thesauruses, atlases, and other reference materials. Kim is confident in her students' ability to self-regulate: "I can literally walk out of the room to talk to a student, to meet with somebody individually, and [the students] don't even realize I'm gone. . . . Anybody can walk into this room, and they remain totally unaffected by it because they're busy doing what they have to do."

Kim attributes her students' ability to monitor themselves to routines established at the beginning of the school year. During the first several weeks of school, Kim sets aside time to show students where supplies and resources are kept in the room as well as to familiarize them with various systems she has developed to keep the classroom organized and instruction and transitions running smoothly. Some routines are introduced and practiced in whole-class meetings. For instance, to track activities that are part of writing workshop time, she creates a "status of the class" board (e.g., Atwell, 1998) on the side of a large filing cabinet, which holds two sets of magnetic strips: one with students' names and the other with different tasks they might be engaged in during writing time (e.g., drafting, editing, conferencing, publishing). As each student calls out what he or she needs to do that day, Kim moves the name under that task. This provides both Kim and the students with a visual reminder of what they need to do next.

Kim gives students extended periods of time at the beginning of the year to explore the room and leaf through materials while she moves around the room and points out useful resources to individuals, pairs, and small groups of students. For example, when she notices two students browsing through materials at the writing center, she goes over to show them how to use the rhyming dictionary and a book of idioms. After she moves on to talk to other students, these two continue to read and explore on their own in the writing center. Later, in the midst of writing projects, they return to these resources and others on their own. But becoming self-directed and independent also requires repeated reminders and practice. For instance, while writing a poem about himself, one student needs a correct spelling of *Pakistan*, and his first course of action is to ask Kim. Instead of telling him the answer, she reminds him about the atlas, and he promptly scurries over to the shelf and finds what he needs.

## An Abundance of Reading and Writing Materials

An emphasis on reading and writing pervade Kim's classroom from one end to the other. Her classroom library consists of roughly 800 books from several genres and spanning a wide range of difficulty levels. This variety of materials is particularly appropriate, given the fact that half of the children in this class are identified as pupils with disabilities, and a wide range of books is necessary to match individual student's needs. There are hundreds of chapter books from classic favorites (e.g., *Trumpet of the Swan*, White, 1970) to more contemporary fiction (e.g.,*The Flunking of Joshua T. Bates*, Shreve, 1984; *Maniac Magee*, Spinelli, 1990) to series books (e.g., *Maid Mary Anne: Babysitter's Club*, No. 66, Martin, 1993), and biographies. There is also an impressive picture book collection, including sophisticated texts such as *Angel Child, Dragon Child* (Surat, 1989), *The Day of Ahmed's Secret* (Heide, 1995), and *Officer Buckle and Gloria* (Rathmann, 1995), as well as easy-to-read books such as *Tales of Oliver Pig* (Van Leeuwen, 1993), *Danny and the Dinosaur* (Hoff, 1958), and *Quick as a Cricket* (Wood, 1989). Kim's library also stocks several dozen big books, including *Animals in Danger* (Amos, 1992) and *If You Give a Mouse a Cookie* (Numeroff, 1985). There are baskets containing volumes of poetry (e.g., *Where the Sidewalk Ends*, Silverstein, 1974; *Butterfly Jar*, Moss, 1989) and popular magazines for children (e.g., *Weekly Reader*; *Highlights for Children*). In addition, the listening center includes a selection of books on tape, such as *The Principal's New Clothes* (Calmenson, 1989) and *Why Do Mosquitoes Buzz in People's Ears?* (Aardema, 1975). There are multiple copies of some of the more popular books, such as the *Goosebumps* series and Prelutsky's *New Kid on the Block* (1984). Although most of the books in Kim's class are located in the corner of the room designated as the classroom library, there are scores of other books all over the room, some displayed upright and some stacked in baskets. For instance, when students were studying dinosaurs, one section of the room was devoted to books on prehistoric times. At the front of the room, displayed with all of the math manipulatives and other materials, are books such as *The Greedy Triangle* (Burns, 1995) and *Math Curse* (Scieszka, 1995), again giving the sense that reading and writing are a part of all the subject areas.

The writing center also offers abundant resources and supplies. Readily available to students are numerous pens, pencils, and markers, blank paper of all shapes, colors, and sizes, and other items such as hole punchers and staplers. There are multiple copies of dictionaries, thesauruses, and other reference books, such as *Writer's Express* (Kemper, 1995). There are folders containing instructions for creating books in unique formats: flip books, video books, pop-up books, and fold-out books, as well as a collection of books published by students, including such titles as *Spaced-Out Poetry, Mike's Fraction Book*, and *Our Antarctica Fact Book*.

Kim's extensive classroom collection was not generated overnight or without effort and creativity. Fortunately, Kim's district had begun to see the value of spending money on books, so Kim had some funds, albeit limited, to buy new books each year. Also, all teachers in her school were allotted funds to use at their discretion, and Kim spent most of hers on books. She was constantly on the lookout for special book sales by organizations such as Scholastic, as well as local used-book sales. She also invites students to bring in their own books from home, which can add well over 100 titles to the collection. Finally, Kim's school had a well-stocked media center, and although the school did not employ a full-time media specialist, Kim enlisted the help of teacher's aides and parent helpers to gather materials she needed.

## A Healthy Social Environment

A memorable incident from one of my visits came one day when students were collaborating on acrostic poems, using the names of dinosaurs. After putting the final touches on their poem, Jake and Randy proudly handed it to me to read. After I complimented them on their very impressive work, they walked back to their seats, literally patting each other on the back, as Jake commented to the Randy, "I told you people would like it—we used our imaginations." This cooperative spirit among students is a prominent feature of Kim's class. Students are supportive of, rather than competitive with, each other; the fellowship among students in this class makes it possible for them to learn from and with each other.

I do not have to ponder to understand how these students come to respect their classmates and to value what they contribute to the learning. Being respectful of others begins with students respecting and believing in themselves. Kim's students are comfortable with their own growing competence in reading and writing, which makes it possible for them to be comfortable with each other. Kim instills feelings of confidence in her students, even those with records of low achievement in previous years, by providing them with texts and tasks they can manage successfully, such as self-selected free reading and writing from open-ended writing prompts, so that no student has to struggle through assignments. She began a whole-class lesson on incorporating imagery into writing by showing students a series of photographs and asking them to imagine how the object of each scene smelled, tasted, sounded, and so on. Next, she asked each student to select a familiar person or object from their own lives and use imagery in their description. Randy, one of the lowest achieving and most timid students, was proud to read to me the poem he wrote about his mother, which I include in Figure 4.1.

Because Randy had strong feelings about the subject of his writing, his mother, he was easily able to conceptualize and apply the writing strategy Kim taught—but this might not have been the case if he had been assigned a topic or a closed writing assignment that had no relevance to his life or that he did not understand. Incidentally, Randy wrote about his mother several more times when Kim moved on to other writing strategies and poetry forms. Figure 4.2 contains Randy's favorite cinquain.

Randy was aware of his growing competence in reading and writing and the importance of reading and writing texts that were both manageable and meaningful: "Last year I didn't think it was exciting or anything, some of the books, and now I want to read to see what happens next. Last year I couldn't read a lot of the words, too, and I learned a lot more so I began to understand a lot more of it." When asked what he would like to change about his reading, he responded, "Just to be the person that's writing the book . . . that I could read my own books."

## Mom
*Smells like a flower getting sun*
*Looks like a rainbow*
*Sounds like a bird singing*
*Tastes like a sweet drink*
*Makes me feel like a candle*
*I think she is like sunlight.*

**FIGURE 4.1.** Randy's poem using imagery.

*Mom*
*Nice woman*
*Hugs, kisses, loves*
*Makes my family happy*
*Parent*

**FIGURE 4.2.** Randy's cinquain.

Kim talks to all her students as if they were experts or at least capable of being experts. For instance, it is typical for her to compare students' writing to that of published authors (e.g., "Do you know Joanna Cole has a good sense of humor? Could you do something like that in your writing?") and to imply that what students accomplish is comparable to that of professionals (e.g., "When I hang up these drawings, it will be like an art gallery in here."). Kim's students begin to realize possibilities for themselves as readers and writers, which lays the foundation for good working relationships with others throughout the school year.

Kim teaches her students how to respond to each other in the most productive ways by modeling the behavior when she gives feedback to individual students. She rarely points out whether something is good or bad or right or wrong; rather, she emphasizes the impact of their accomplishments. For example: "Jenny just came up with a great way to remember $8 \times 8 = 64$! Share it with the class, Jenny." Another example: As class members are discussing *King Midas and the Golden Touch* (Metaxas, 1992), one day, Kim notices and points out that several students used some words they had recently learned in another book, *The Whipping Boy* (Fleischman, 1986), in their talk about the book they have just read:

> "Let me just point something out to you, as I've been listening to you and what we've been talking about. I want you to understand something. These are words that you have added to your vocabulary that you amaze me with, because look how you're using them. Do you totally get it? You understand what *arrogance* and *ignorant* are. *Fathom* and *pondered*. This is so much better than I *thought about it*, isn't it? *I pondered it. I rolled it around in my mind.* You are being given the opportunity to

paint pictures and to be able to do it without saying I *thought* about it." (Field notes)

Kim's goal here is not only to congratulate students on their success but to help them see that their literate growth has implications for how they think and communicate. Jodi eagerly acknowledges that even people outside of school have noticed her growing knowledge of words: "I'm learning big words from this, and my friend—I say some of the words, and she's, like, 'Stop saying them! I don't know what they mean.' " Following Kim's lead, other students are eager to point out the reading and writing strengths in each other. When I ask, "Who are the good writers in your class?," several students are quick to cite Patty. As one student explained, "She really writes good stories, and when I listen to her I know that she's really got a handle on [the words] she uses." Another commented on Patty's creativity: "She writes big stories that are about stuff that might have happened today, and then she just makes it pretend it's happening in a magic fairy land place that's powerful." Note how the language Kim uses to describe students' learning in the first example ("You are being given the opportunity to paint pictures [with words] . . . ") is reflected in students' talk about each other in the second example ("Patty writes big stories that are about stuff that might have happened today, and then she just makes it, like, pretend it's happening in a magic fairy land place that's powerful"). In both cases, the emphasis is on what students have learned to do rather than how well they do it or whether they are right or wrong.

Kim gives students ample opportunities to experience collaboration. Starting on the first day of school, students begin working together on open-ended reading and writing projects (e.g., free reading, collaborative poem writing). These times allow students to get to know each other and to experiment with working with a variety of classmates. Kim also makes it a pivotal part of her agenda to teach students how to work together. As she explained to me:

I spend the first month of school strictly talking about, strictly getting them into working with each other, [learning] management procedures, [learning] to work independently. That first month I model everything, walk through it, do kind of mock trials with them of what should be expected in the classroom, a lot of self-esteem building activities. (Interview)

Just as important as fostering collaboration is addressing the road-block to it. Kim conducts frank, explicit discussions about dealing with individual differences in personalities and personal preferences, as illustrated in this excerpt from a class meeting:

> "I know some of you get really weird if somebody's paper is, like, one centimeter on your desk. Do you shove it across and knock everything off? It's really easy to say, 'You know, I really don't like your things on my desk.' It's just so simple. Do not do to other people what you don't want others doing to you. . . . We need to get to know each other's quirks. That way, we don't freak out when one of us does something annoying." (Field notes)

Having a class so diverse, it is important for Kim to foster positive relationships among students. The variety of instructional groupings during the day means that she is not be available to all of the students all of the time; thus students need to be able to rely on themselves and each other for help.

Kim's classroom is an environment in which all students can be active learners. Students learned to self-regulate, down-time is minimal, materials for reading and writing are plentiful, and students are both self-confident and supportive of each other. These factors not only set the stage for learning but also make it possible for Kim to implement the kinds of instruction needed for such a range of abilities. In the remainder of this chapter, I highlight the most prominent features of her instruction.

## KEY FEATURES OF INSTRUCTION

My observations revealed three defining characteristics of the instruction in Kim's classroom. First, activities and feedback are designed to meet the needs of a wide range of students, which is the reality in an inclusion classroom. Instruction is differentiated to the extent that all students are given materials and tasks that are appropriately challenging, and whole-class assignments are structured so that all students can participate.

Second, the teacher is a key participant in the learning. Kim also assumes the typical teacher roles—expert, record-keeper, classroom manager—but she balances these positions and her relationship with her students by modeling literate behaviors and by engaging in the same literate activities as her students.

Third, literacy instruction is interwoven throughout the curriculum, including the integration of reading and writing skills with rich literacy experiences, the integration of reading and writing, and the integration of literacy with content area instruction.

## Instruction that Highlights Students' Strengths

Perhaps the most compelling feature of this inclusion classroom is that the special education students could not easily be distinguished in the class as a whole. During one of my first visits to the classroom, I worked with students during a small group activity. At the lunch break, Kim asked me if I had been able to pick out any of the special needs students. When I responded that I had not, Kim replied, "Good, because that's the goal." Although all students work at their own instructional levels most of the time, struggling readers and writers in this classroom are given opportunities to engage in the same kinds of rich, open-ended literacy experiences as the strong readers and writers; they read *real* trade books (as opposed to completing skills exercises) and write *real* stories (as opposed to completing workbook exercises on grammar and spelling).

One way Kim manages to give all students access to texts they are able to read with relative ease is to include a range of different reading activities each day. Table 4.2 lists the many different kinds of reading and texts students experienced in one day near the beginning of the school year. One of the main goals of instruction during the first couple of weeks in Kim's classroom is to help students become in engaged in the process of reading and writing rather than immersing them in specific content. Thus this particular day's reading and writing are purposefully varied to help students experience the range of reading they could do and to ensure that individual students, regardless of achievement level, could participate and experiment with text.

In the morning during class meeting time, Kim read aloud from *No More Homework, No More Tests: Kids' Favorite School Poems* (Lansky, 1997) as a way to familiarize students with the collection of poetry volumes available in the classroom for self-selected reading and to inspire discussion about the topic of homework—many of the students had voiced their anxiety about the amount of homework they heard they might get in fourth grade. Next Kim introduced

**TABLE 4.2. Sample Range of Reading in One Day of Instruction**

| Reading Activity | Text(s) |
| --- | --- |
| Teacher read aloud | *No More Homework, No More Tests: Kids Favorite School Poems* (Lansky, 1997) |
| Whole-class choral repeated readings | "Homework! Oh Homework!" (from text, Prelutsky, 1984) |
| Small-group choral repeated readings and performances | Student-authored poems about the beginning of the school year |
| Teacher read-aloud | *Math Curse* (Scieszka, 1995) |
| Student independent, free-choice reading | *Scary Stories 3* (Schwartz, 1991) |
| | *Chocolate Fever* (Smith, 1972) |
| | *Magic School Bus and the Electronic Field Trip* (Cole, 1997) |
| | *There's an Owl in the Shower* (George, 1995) |
| | *Henry and Mudge under the Yellow Moon* (Rylant, 1987) |
| | *Miss Nelson Has a Field Day* (Allard, 1988) |
| Teacher read-aloud | *My Teacher Is an Alien* (Coville, 1989) |

"Homework! Oh Homework!" (*New Kid on the Block*, Prelutsky, 1984), a thematically-related poem from another book, and asked students to read it in unison several times to improve fluency and expression. This activity led to a writing assignment in which students worked in small groups to compose their own poems about homework anxiety, practice reading them until they could read accurately and fluently, and then perform them for their classmates.

Just before lunch Kim read aloud *Math Curse* (Scieszka, 1995) to raise students interest in upcoming mathematics topics as well as to introduce the author and his other popular books (e.g., *The Frog Prince Continued*, 1991; *The Stinky Cheese Man and Other Fairly Stupid Tales*, 1996). After lunch students were given a 30-minute period to read independently whatever they selected. Table 4.2 includes a sample of the range of texts students chose, from easy-to-read picture books (e.g., *Miss Nelson Has a Field Day*, Allard, 1988) to intermediate-level stories (e.g., *Scary Stories 3*, Schwartz, 1991). At the end of the day Kim read aloud from *My Teacher Is an Alien* (Coville, 1989) as a way to introduce Bruce Coville as an author and to highlight more of his books for self-selected reading.

As the year progresses, Kim integrates a similar range and volume of reading into the different topics studied by the students. For instance, one day when students were studying immigration, Kim read aloud from *When Jesse Came across the Sea* (Hest, 1997) and a nonfiction picture book about Ellis Island; she read from the chapter book *Journey to America* (Levitin, 1987) as students followed along in their own copies of the book; and students self-selected reading material from a variety of historical fiction and nonfiction books about immigration that also spanned a range of difficulty levels (e.g., *I Was Dreaming to Come to America: Memories from the Ellis Island Oral History Project*, Lawlor, 1995; *If Your Name Was Changed at Ellis Island*, Levine, 1993; *Grandfather's Journey*, Say, 1993).

Whole-class reading activities are balanced with individual reading, and when a common text is used, Kim provides the support necessary for all students to access it, either through reading it aloud to students or having them read it repeatedly to work through problems with word identification and fluency. Texts for independent reading are usually selected by the students themselves, so they can choose materials they do not need help with, and they can base their selection on reading ease or interest and familiarity with the topic.

The nature of whole-class discussions of text differ according to what students read. When all students are exposed to the same book, as with a teacher read-alouds, Kim centers the discussion on the content of that particular book. When students read different books, she focuses the discussion on a particular theme common to all of the texts available for a topic of study (e.g., such as the books on immigration). When students read a variety of texts not linked by a theme (e.g., Drop-Everything-and-Read), Kim finds inventive ways for students to talk about what they read. For instance, one day after a free reading period, Kim directed students to "sort yourselves by genre." The students congregated in small groups, according to the kind of book they were reading that day (mystery, poetry, science books), and began to discuss similarities and differences in books from the same genre.

Similarly, writing assignments in Kim's class capitalize on students' strengths and are appropriately challenging and meaningful for all students in the class. Figure 4.3 includes samples of individually written poems based on a beginning-of-the-year writing activity titled "Perfect is. . . . " Although students were given the same prompt for writing, their thinking and their products were personalized and diverse, as one would expect, and all students had interesting thoughts to share.

Once Kim ascertained what different students could accomplish in their reading and writing, she was able to design appropriate strategy instruction. Here again, Kim struck a balance between lessons that would benefit the whole class and differentiated lessons that were tailored for individual students or small groups of students. Because Kim believes in the value of teaching strategies within the context of real reading and writing, she faces the dilemma of finding a common text for whole-class instruction that all students can read. She finds that big books, typically seen in kindergarten and first-grade classrooms, are useful for teaching lessons on word identification (e.g., chunking) and writing (e.g., punctuation), but she also wants to use more sophisticated materials to draw students' attention to comprehension processes. For these lessons she mainly reads aloud to give all students, even those who are still developing fundamental decoding skills, access to a text rich in meaning. For instance, Kim gave a whole-class minilesson on irony as a literary device one day; in subsequent days, as she

| *Perfect is:* | *Perfect is:* | *Perfect is:* |
|---|---|---|
| *Florida* | *My sister* | *My excellent dad* |
| *Basketball* | *Hot wings* | *Pasta* |
| *Luke, Zack, and William* | *Soccer* | *Street hockey* |
| *My friend Tiffany* | *Football* | *Arizona* |
| *Full House* | *Giants Stadium* | *HBO movies* |
| *Backstreet Boys* | *Aqua* | *Barbie* |
| *Turkey soup* | *Number 6* | *Aqua's songs* |
| *Mashed potatoes* | *Dogs* | *The movie "Scream"* |
| *Hercules* | *The winter season* | |
| | *The letters* | |
| | | |
| *By Angela* | *By Carlos* | *By Sophie* |

**FIGURE 4.3.** Writing samples from a range of students.

read aloud to the whole class, she returned to the concept of irony and showed students how anticipating an ironic event in a story might help them to predict the story's outcome. During a read-aloud of *King Midas and the Golden Touch* (Metaxas, 1992), one lower-achieving student contributed his perception of two instances of irony: "When King Midas thought he wasn't going to touch his daughter [and consequently turn her to gold], and he did, and when [King Midas] gets to a river he has been trying to find, but when he gets there it stops flowing." Manageable and open-ended reading and writing activities such as these give all students a chance to demonstrate what they can do and what interests them.

Because Kim believes that effective instruction for word study is linked to individual assessments of development, phonics and spelling lessons are differentiated. Based on the results of the Qualitative Spelling Inventory (Bear, Invernizzi, Templeton, & Johnston, 2000) for each student, Kim divided her class into three word-study groups in which students were given opportunities to study word patterns that they had started "using but confusing," as Bear and his colleagues (2000) put it, in their writing. For instance, at one point in the year, one group of students whose spellings indicated that they had started experimenting with common long vowel patterns (e.g., attempting to spell *rake* as *raek*) began studying and contrasting words with the same long vowel sound but different spelling patterns (e.g., *fade, tape, race, slave* vs. *main, pail, faint, raid*). Another group of students, with slightly more developed word knowledge, was studying the significance of open syllables (*labor, even, ripen*) versus closed syllables (*rabbit, basket, hidden*) because they had started experimenting with these features in their spellings (e.g., attempting to spell *flavor* as *flavvor*). A third group of students, with stronger word knowledge, was studying words with common roots (con*form*, trans*form*, re*form*, de*form*ity). Although students in the three groups were studying different features in words, all of the students were engaging in activities that were appropriately challenging and using the knowledge they had already developed to learn new concepts.

## Teacher Modeling, Participation, and Engagement

Teachers need to model reading explicitly and to share what they know about the process and purposes of reading (e.g., Duffy, Rochler, & Herrmann, 1988; Gambrell, 1996). Kim certainly has gained enough expertise in her own reading to serve as an effective role model. She describes herself as "a voracious reader" who has "stacks of books at [her] house, from teachers' magazines to *Cosmopolitan* magazines to romance novels to biographies." Kim describes herself as "not as comfortable" as a writer, but that because of her own edge, she tries to help students find their "comfort level" with writing by encouraging sharing, peer editing, and constructive feedback. She also tells them that she is still developing as a writer. Moreover, she is an enthusiastic learner: "I like learning new things. I like going to different workshops and different classes that can show me how to maybe take something that I've been doing and do it in a different way. So I'm real open to learning new things and trying new things." She appreciates the value of role models in her own learning, particularly "being surrounded by excellent teachers and then asking, 'How did you do that? How can I do that?' I want to try this in my class. What can I do?' "

To say that Kim is a good model for her students, however, would be to tell only half of the story. Our observations and our discussions with Kim and her students reveal that she does far more than just serve as a good example of a reader and writer; she does so as a participant in the same literacy activities her students are experiencing. For instance, Kim demonstrates a genuine appreciation for the books her students are reading. One day before the Christmas holidays, Kim prefaced her read-aloud of the book *Olive, the Other Reindeer* (Walsh & Siebold, 1997) by sharing with the class that the book "cracked her up" and that she "laughed out loud" when she read it the first time. On another day, the class read *When Jesse Came across the Sea* (Hest, 1997), a story about an orphaned girl who journeyed alone to the United States. When they reached the part in the book that describes her wedding day years later and how her grandmother presented her with her mother's wedding ring brought from overseas, Kim spontaneously shared her own reaction to the book: "Doesn't that give you goosebumps?"

Kim also demonstrates to her students that she is a participant in the learning going on in the classroom. In introducing a book on Kwanzaa to the class, for instance, she prefaced the reading by saying, "I want to share with you, for those of you who don't know, myself included, a little about Kwanzaa." Likewise, as several students spontaneously shared with her what they learned from a book on dinosaurs, she reacted with "I find that fascinating, don't you?" She makes an effort to point out specifically what she finds interesting, as when the class studied a newspaper article they were using as a model for their own work: "Let me read the Spice Girls article to you. 'The Spice Girls are the only spices on the planet with no taste.' " Both Kim and the students laughed at that line, but Kim also drew their attention to why she finds this article useful: "I like the adjectives [the author] used. Frumpy frocks. Dumpy duds."

Kim's modeling of literate behavior goes beyond inspiring students to emulate her; her actions serve as an invitation for them to join her. Kim becomes a part of the group effort in math, in particular. For instance, one time she announced to the class "I need to study this myself," when they all got stumped by a challenging math puzzle. When asked what she does in science and social studies discussions when there is ambiguity about some issue or a particularly difficult question, she replies, "I tell [the students] that I don't know the answer to it, and we can go look it up, go on the Internet." Numerous times during our observations, Kim prompted students during class discussions with "Let's think about this for a minute." She also demonstrates the value of hypothesizing as part of learning to her students. While reading *When Jesse Came across the Sea* (Hest, 1997) to the class, she stopped spontaneously to think aloud about the implications of the two main characters, who were from different cultural backgrounds, marrying each other: "She's Jewish, and he's Italian, or maybe. We don't know Lou's last name, do we?"

Students in Kim's class are also encouraged to use their imaginations. Kim's inspiration to her students is evident in this excerpt from a class discussion of alternative fairy tales after reading *Yeh Shen* (Louie, 1982):

KIM: Do you know what would be a funny story? . . . What's the story I read to you? *The Jolly Postman* [Ahlberg & Ahlberg, 1995]? Where he goes and he hands the mail out to everybody. Wouldn't it be kind of cool if they met each other, like Snow White and Cinderella? Like they go out for a cup of coffee.

STUDENT: A tea party!

(*Lots of other students yell out their ideas.*)

STUDENT: I know a good version. Yeh Shen's evil stepmother is chasing her through the woods, and Cinderella's evil stepmother is chasing her through the woods, so they meet. So they run, and then the evil stepmothers plot together, and they say, "Let's get them!"

KIM: So the evil stepmothers come together and plot together?

STUDENTS: Yeah!

STUDENT: Then they find another Cinderella.

(*Students yell out a string of other ideas.*) (Field notes)

Notice how Kim points out connections between *Yeh Shen* and other literature as a way to model strategic thinking and to fuel students' imaginations. Although she does not respond to each and every idea, she continues to urge students to envision multiple possibilities.

One of the goals of modeling good literacy and learning behaviors, according to Kim, is for students to learn from each other as well as from her. Sometimes this means that Kim and her students reverse roles. For instance, one day as Kim went to write the word *shiny* on the board, she hesitated and consulted the class:

KIM: Anybody know how to spell *shiny*?

STUDENTS: S-h-i-n-y.

KIM: Anybody want to challenge that? You know I'm the worst speller in the world. Look it up.

(*Students tear into their dictionaries to confirm that their spelling is correct.*)

RANDY: Told ya! If you add a *y* to a word, sometimes you drop a vowel.

KIM: That might help me remember that. (Field notes)

She often asks students to explain how they reached a particular answer so that they can benefit from each others' thinking. On numerous occasions I observed students supporting each other's work. For example, during writing time, students make suggestions to each other on standard conventions ("We didn't indent—you have to indent on a new paragraph") and on style ("We need a better adjective"). Some students even share tips on maintaining fluency in writing. For instance, one day when writing a mock encyclopedia entry on a dinosaur he had researched, one student asked, "How do you spell *theory*?" and another responded, "It doesn't matter. It's just a rough draft. The computer will catch an error." In this classroom, students consistently look to each other for advice and inspiration.

## Multiple Levels of Integration

In Kim's classroom, most subjects are interconnected and integration exists on a number of levels. At the most fundamental level, reading and writing skills and strategies are incorporated into real reading and writing experiences. As Kim explains, "What I try to do is incorporate all the language arts through the literature and the writing. I try to make the connection that way as opposed to the language book with the worksheets." Sometimes this means examining books as models for their own writing. For instance, one day Kim engaged students in a mini-lesson on quotation marks using a repetitive big book that contains a lot of dialogue and is easy enough to allow all students to participate. After they spent some time examining how and when the author used quotation marks, one student noted that the author's repeated use of the word *said* was monotonous. So, in response to this student's observation, Kim shifted the lesson to a discussion of ways to make substitutions for bland, overused words such as *said*. Students suggested that instead of *said the bird*, the author could have written *chirped the bird*, and in place of *said the owl*, the author could have written *shrieked the owl*.

The integration of reading and writing is also a prevalent theme in Kim's classroom. Specifically, what students read often serves as models or inspiration for their writing. As Kim explained,

> "[The students] do every type of writing, from news articles to persuasive to explanatory, depending on what we're reading or the theme we're working on. . . . Now we're doing historical fiction, so they're doing several different diary entries of famous people in history from the perspective of that person or someone from that era." (Interview)

Reading–writing connections were emphasized not only for fiction texts but also for informational reading and writing. For instance, at one point in the year each student chose a state to research and present to the class in some creative way. One student, Jenny, explained what she did after reading about North Carolina, a state she had never visited: "First, I made a travel brochure that was blank. Then I wrote down some information on North Carolina. Then I made up some stuff, like you could go to North Carolina, and you could visit some stuff like the memorial of the Wright Brothers." She added that, "[Next] we all have to study the [country] our ancestors are from, and we're going to do almost the same thing as the states reports."

Students used reading and writing to learn in all of their subject areas. Kim's philosophy on content literacy approximates what McKenna and Robinson (1990) refer to as the ability to use reading and writing to acquire knowledge in a particular discipline. One unit of study that integrated science, social studies, reading, and writing in Kim's class exemplifies this notion. For several weeks the class studied prehistoric times, and Kim made available scores of books and information on the topic. The entire class read *Magic School Bus in the Time of the Dinosaurs* (Cole, 1995), another easy text for fourth grade that was accessible to all of the students, even those with learning disabilities, and students were also free to read any number of the other books on their own. The culmination of this study was for students to "discover" their own dinosaur and describe it through a written biographical sketch based on what they had learned from the reading. The following is an excerpt of what happened in class one day when I visited.

KIM: You've discovered this thing. You've created it. So name it, and write a description of it. You can play around with it. What period they lived in. Were they a plant-eater or a meat-eater? It's your discovery.

STUDENT: When we do this, we can give it our own name? Should we go by the book and tell what each part of the name means?

KIM: It's totally in your hands. (*Students scatter into their small groups to work.*) You are working as a team of paleontologists. You can't argue with each other, or your work will fall apart.

(*Each group is at a different point. Some groups begin to discuss their dinosaur biographies. Kim conferences with one group at a time. A couple of boys grab dictionaries from the shelf. I ask them what they are looking up.*)

STUDENT: We're looking up *rex* to see what it means.

(*They cannot find it in the dictionary, so they go to the section of the room where there are many books on dinosaurs and begin to skim. They find that rex means king, and that T-rex is king of the tyrant lizards.*)

KIM: (*to the whole class*) Just like you would look up *dinosaur* in a book, that's what you're writing up.

STUDENT: We could describe it our own selves?

KIM: Right, because you're the paleontologist. (Field notes)

The final product from Malcolm, Chelsea, Sean, and Janelle is shown in Figure 4.4. Although their writing contains misunderstandings about some of the things they read and grammatical errors, they have used reading and writing to think and learn—which is the goal of content literacy.

This active, inquiry-based model of content area instruction is a sharp contrast to what Vacca and Vacca (1999) refer to as "assign-and-tell" (p. 6), a practice that predominates in many upper-grade elementary and secondary classrooms. The all-too-familiar assign-and-tell routine involves the teacher assigning a text to read, followed by the teacher telling students what they should have learned from the text through a lecture or a question-and-answer session governed by the teacher. In Kim's classroom, however, the students are much more responsible for their learning, and what they conceptualize about the content is based on reading a wide range of texts rather than reciting and memorizing from a single text.

The integration of skill and strategy instruction within real reading and writing experiences, the integration of reading with writing, and the integration of reading and writing across the content areas give Kim's students numerous opportunities to engage in reading and writing across the school day. More important, perhaps, it helps students understand that the purposes of reading and writing are to think, communicate, and learn. Students learn that not only that they can become expert readers and writers but that they will use reading and writing to aspire towards a range of identities, be it poet, historian, or paleontologist.

## LOOKING AHEAD

My time with Kim and her students opened my eyes to the complexity of teaching reading and writing in an inclusion classroom, and it reinforced my belief that all students can become good readers and writers if they receive high-quality instruction. I do not believe every fourth-grade classroom should look just like Kim's. Children differ,

### Jurekasaurus

This amazing discovery of a new dinosaur was found in the forest of the Everglades in the year 1998.

We paleontologists think that this dinosaur might have eaten cycads, conifers, and fresh grass. This dinosaur, claimed to be called "Jurekasauras," liked to wade around in low-lying swamps.

Jurekasaurus had many relatives of his kind such as Brontosaurus. All long-necked dinosaurs were relatives of the long, thick necked Jurekasaurus.

Jurekasaurus was named after living in the very-violence Jurassic Period. This very strange necked dinosaur was also named for the enormous neck it had.

Jurekasaurus had yellowish-brown scaly skin all over its outside. Its tummy was a peachish color almost light pink. The paleontologists discovered dull and crushed yellowish teeth that looked as if it had chewed fresh grass which proved it was a herbivore. It had lived over one hundred forty-two and a half million years ago and had weighed fifty tons in all.

It is not yet known how Jurekasaurus got extinct. Our theory about its extinction is that there was a terrible and horrible drought for a very long time limit. Dinosaurs such as Jurekasaurus couldn't survive living without water and died. Proof has shown by some old, rusty bones.

By Malcolm, Chelsea, Sean, and Janelle

**FIGURE 4.4.** Collaborative student writing from research project.

and so do teachers. But some lessons I learned may be universal, and I have been passing them along to other teachers who are trying to sort out meaningful and effective ways to meet individual needs in their own diverse classrooms.

When I hear teachers lament that finding a way to teach struggling readers and writers seems impossible in a regular classroom that contains a whole spectrum of students, I think back to Kim's classroom and the following questions come to mind:

- Are all students in your class provided with many books that they are able to can read and that they *want* to read?

- When students write, do they get to write about what they know and care about?
- Are students given plenty of time to experiment with and practice reading and writing?
- If you want students to do something (e.g., work independently, work in small groups), do you first teach them how to do it?
- Do all students get opportunities to demonstrate and use their strengths in reading and writing, or do the reading and writing activities accentuate their weaknesses?
- Is literacy integrated across subjects, so that students see reading and writing as a way to learn and communicate?
- Do your students get to learn by watching you as a learner?

As may be the case in many places around the country, state curriculum standards and testing present new demands for instructional time and focus in Kim's district. Nevertheless, she maintains an unshakeable belief that having students read and write meaningful things, matching students with texts they can read and want to read, and designing instruction that is responsive to students' literate development rather than to a set of criteria will ultimately lead to higher achievement. Consequently, high-stakes tests have not affected Kim's instruction significantly. Kim shared with us that she feels lucky to work with administrators who trust her to do what is best for children, for, as she explained, "I'd hate for somebody else to make up the formula." While many fourth graders are now spending their time throughout the school year studying content and strategies for test-taking, Kim's students continue to read and write. Perhaps Kim's hopes for her students cannot be measured by any test:

> I want them to leave here with a sense of responsibility about their job as a student, with a love of good books, with a richer vocabulary, with a different way of looking at things without just taking everything at surface value, to question and wonder what's going on and why, and to ask why . . . but mostly about responsibility and respect for themselves and for whatever it is they're doing and trying to do their best. (Interview)

---

**Gay Ivey, PhD,** is an associate professor of Reading Education at James Madison University. Her research and teaching interests include the learning and teaching of struggling readers in the upper elementary and middle grades. She is coauthor of *Pathways to Literacy* (Guilford, 2001)

# 5

## "Focus on the Real and Make Sure It Connects to Kids' Lives"

RUTH WHARTON-MCDONALD
JUNE WILLIAMSON[1]

This chapter describes the teaching and learning that unfolded in June Williamson's classroom over two school years. June teaches fourth grade in a rural district in southern New Hampshire. The school serves primarily lower-middle-class families; historically it has been a blue-collar community but has had a number of professional families move in during the last decade or so. During the years described, June had 23 and 19 students, respectively. Approximately 15% of her students carried special education labels; 10% belonged to minority groups.

"Let's come down to group." These words are uttered several times a day in June Williamson's classroom. They signal to her students that it is time to assemble on the rug for group instruction. The

---

[1] This chapter was written from the perspective of the first author but represents the collaboration of Ruth Wharton-McDonald, a researcher/observer, and June Williamson, the teacher in focus.

78

topics of these "lessons" range from new information about electricity to the use of literary devices in a current novel to the ethics of lying. Regardless of the topic, group discussions—and any time students are in group, there is discussion—are characterized by mutual respect, widespread participation, and a focus on learning. The environment in June's classroom supports learning in a host of overt and subtle ways.

June starts out the year with a plan, interweaving academic, interpersonal, and individualized student goals to create a community of students who are, at once, independent and interdependent learners. Beginning on the first day of school, the students work together to create class expectations whose primary objective is making the classroom a better place to learn. June introduces this task on the first day of school by reading the picture book *Miss Rumphius* (Cooney, 1982), in which the main character, is charged with making the world a more beautiful place. For homework, students are asked to compose lists of suggestions for how they could make the classroom a more beautiful place—for learning. Miss Rumphius, she explains, was concerned with aesthetic beauty. *They* are to focus on suggestions that would promote beauty in learning. Students take this task to heart; a summary of one class's suggestions appears in Table 5.1.

From this initial list of suggestions (many of which are presented multiple times, by different students), the class creates a list of about ten "expectations"[2] for classroom learning and interaction that they all agree to honor. The involvement of students in creating this list is typical of June's classroom: Student voices are valued and heard throughout the day and the year.

## STUDENT VOICES AND DIALOGUE

Consistent with the emphasis on student involvement, much of the learning that takes place in this classroom is done cooperatively with partners, small groups, or the whole class. In each instance, all students have opportunities to share in the learning and the decision

---

[2]June notes the important distinction between *rules* and *expectations* here: Rules demand compliance with an outside authority, whereas expectations imply a commitment to a group effort.

**TABLE 5.1. Student-Suggested Ways to Make the Classroom a More Beautiful Place for Learning**

| | |
|---|---|
| Make at least one person smile a day. | Have a big skylight. |
| Do lots of projects. | Walk, don't run. |
| Everyone play together. | Don't yell. |
| Everyone be nice to each other. | Don't bother people when they're working. |
| Have lots of math and science games. | Treat other kids like you want to be treated. |
| Have a pet in the classroom. | |
| No yelling. | |
| Everyone be everyone's friend. | Meet other classmates. |
| Put flowers in the windows. | No making fun of people. |
| Have plants around the room. | Keep the inside of your desk clean. |
| Keep the classroom clean. | Be organized. |
| Keep it fun but serious. | Have desks in rows. |
| Have a really nice teacher. | Share things. |
| Say something nice to people each day. | Acknowledge someone when they do something nice. |
| Sit next to new people at lunch every day. | Don't draw on your desk. |
| Help each other out. | Hang things from the walls. |
| Listen to each other. | Don't litter. |
| Have lots of colors. | Don't poison the water. |
| Have lots of activities and fun games. | Decorate the walls. |
| Everyone should have a smile on their face. | Respect people's property. |
| | Display projects. |

making that takes place. June ensures widespread participation by creating a community of students who know one another well, respect one another's strengths and weaknesses, and are responsible for themselves and their learning.

She begins the school year with units on biography (including autobiography) and Impressionism. Students read biographies of famous artists and begin to think about their own impressions of their classmates and themselves. As she explains to students during the second week of school, "We're doing biographies at the beginning of the year partially because it goes with what we're doing—getting to know each other and getting to know ourselves a little better." As part of this unit, students complete surveys of their likes and dislikes and learning preferences and create Venn diagrams with partners to identify the commonalties and unique characteristics. The completed Venn diagrams are displayed on a central bulletin board, so they are available for students to peruse at their leisure—learning about their classmates as they do.

The students in June's classroom talk to one another throughout the day. They ask questions, offer advice, share insights, laugh, and work together to solve problems. This talk is not incidental. June's instruction is designed to facilitate student talk. In fact, she once said, "I hate when I have to have a lesson where kids can't be talking to each other."

In some classrooms where student voices are valued, the voices of a handful dominate. These tend to be the students who are confident and knowledgeable (you have to know *something* just to pose a question). Discussions in June's classroom are characterized by widespread participation and questioning. It is clear from observing the classroom that all kinds of students believe that they are valid contributors to these exchanges. June facilitates this attitude by encouraging students to question, consider, and connect with the ideas. Moreover, she deliberately accepts a wide range of responses to the questions she poses. When a student offers an interpretation that is clearly incorrect, she probes to understand how the student is thinking; often, she is able to identify the exact point of confusion and clarify the student's understanding on the spot. The way she does this validates the learning process as being more important than finding a "right" answer to a question.

Indeed, the questions are at least as important as the responses in June's classroom. Questions provide opportunities for learning through shared experiences and understandings. For example, as the class was beginning a mini-unit on newspapers, Ethan asked, "Why do they *have* newspapers instead of just listening to a TV?"

"Wonderful question, Ethan" June responded. "Does someone want to answer that besides me?" This led to a lengthy discussion of the media, and the advantages and disadvantages of its various incarnations. As the example illustrates, June approaches the fourth grade with a curriculum and a set of goals and objectives that provide the framework for her instruction. However, it is the questions, suggestions, and other input from students that frequently determine the depth of the lessons.

In many classrooms where students are encouraged to participate in discussions, the teacher–student hierarchy remains, such that the teacher (authority) poses questions and the students are then encouraged to hash out responses among themselves. Thus, the teacher remains separate from the community of students. One of the most interesting characteristics of discussions in June's classroom is her participation as "one of the group": not as the discussion director, but as another interested participant. I frequently observed her puzzling alongside her students. For example, during a read-aloud discussion one day, students were trying to figure out who in the story knew what (and when). There were references to literary devices and strategies for reading mysteries. At one point, June chimed in, "Yes. I was wondering about that, too. How did he [the character in a book] know that already?"

Throughout the day, June shares personal experiences, questions, preferences, and anecdotes in a manner that models interest and enthusiasm for learning without implying that she necessarily has the answers. In fact, she teaches students explicitly to question any response before accepting it as truth. In a discussion/review of prime numbers one day, she admonished students, "*Never* believe everything I say. Never believe everything any adult says. I might *say* five is prime, but can you prove it?"

At the time of these observations, June had requested that the individual student desks in her classroom be replaced with tables, based on her belief that students working at tables are better able to share ideas and collaborate on projects. For years, her request was denied because, she was told, if she were ever to leave, her replacement would surely prefer desks and the exchange would be too costly. June resubmitted her request for several years and was eventually successful in convincing the administration that tables were a critical support for the kind of learning she valued and fostered in her classroom. At the time of this publication, she reports that the tables are an effective support for dialogue and collaborative problem solving.

## LEARNING ORIENTATION

A sampling of the comments and admonishments that June uses daily in her classroom conveys some of the ways in which she reminds children of the reasons for being in school:

> "I'm here to learn and I hope you all are, too!"
> "Yes, it's a game, but you're also learning some very important electrical knowledge."

"I shouldn't have to remind you to focus on learning and not
   your neighbors."
"Remember that wonderful word *effort*? If you try it here, you
   won't have to try during recess."
"I want to be your teacher—not a police officer."
"You're interrupting people's learning." (Field notes)

In June's classroom, students are in school to *learn*. During the
first week of school, June tells her class, "I want you to leave here
learning something every day. Your effort is what counts the most."
The focus on learning is not an unspoken assumption in this classroom but a central and explicit one whose primacy permeates all of
the activities in which students engage.

The classroom atmosphere is perhaps best captured by one student's suggestion to make the classroom a beautiful place by "keeping it serious but fun." During one conversation with me about the
elaborate holiday celebrations and art projects taking place in other
classrooms, June explained, "I think I am totally anti-cutesy. . . . To
me, it's got to have some scholastic relevancy or it shouldn't be included in the school day." This aversion to curricular "extras," however, does not mean that her students do not observe holidays or engage in art projects. What it does mean is that students learn about
the history behind the holidays, and the art they create contributes in
deliberate ways to their understanding of curricular concepts and
ideas.

The movies they watch are also carefully selected to contribute
to the curriculum. After reading *Tuck Everlasting* (Babbitt, 1986),
for example, the class watches the movie version of the story and
then lists the differences between the book and the movie. They also
write essays explaining which version they prefer and why (all but
one student prefers the book).

In an impressive example of meaningfully integrated artwork,
June teaches a writing unit based on Beth Olshansky's image-writing
techniques.[3] Over the course of several weeks, students created a
series of collage papers using paint and other mediums. They then
used cut and torn shapes from the papers to create collages that

---

[3] Image writing is an approach developed and is taught by Beth Olshansky at the University of New Hampshire; it encourages students to use collage art to generate language for
writing.

served as the impetus for generating poetic story writing. The poems and stories created through this process are impressive in their vocabulary, their originality, and the way in which they combine images and writing to evoke settings and feelings. The artwork in this project was integrally related to students' writing; in fact, in many cases, it enabled students to develop their writing (and their perceptions of themselves as writers) to higher levels of understanding and success.

In addition to the learning emphasis that permeates the classroom environment, June uses a number of specific strategies and techniques to support students in keeping learning in the foreground as they go through their days in school.

## CLARIFYING THE PURPOSE

One of the ways June keeps students focused on learning is by being very clear with them about the goals and purposes of their activities. At the end of a lesson on revision and editing, for example, as students prepare to return to their writing, June reminds them, "What am I looking for? Usually when I give you an assignment, I have a purpose. What's the purpose here? How well you can revise and edit. I know you can all be neat. I *expect* that. But I'm looking to see how well you can revise and edit your work." By making both the purpose and her expectations explicit for students, she increases the efficiency of student learning and reduces frustration in students who do not have such context for their assignments.

## THIS WEEK'S NEWS

Each Friday, students review what they've learned during the week through a letter entitled, "This Week's News" (see Figure 5.1), which they take home to their parents. This letter is written by each student via a series of discussions held on Friday morning. As a group, students summarize their learning for the week and make connections within and across the curriculum. Then, individually, each student composes a letter describing his or her personal learning, with examples.

During one Friday morning discussion in January, for example, students describe the multiplication problems they can now solve, re-

Parent initial _____

Date _____

Dear _____,

In math, we are learning about _____.

Here is an example of the kind of problems I can solve now:

```
┌──────────────────────────────────────────────────┐
│                                                  │
│                                                  │
│                                                  │
│                                                  │
│                                                  │
│                                                  │
└──────────────────────────────────────────────────┘
```

Our literature lesson was about _____.

I am reading a book titled _____.

The class read-aloud is _____.

Here is a new word I can web for you:

```
_____        ┌──────────┐        _____
                       │          │
_____        └──────────┘        _____
```

In writing, I _____

_____.

| Here is a new grammar, spelling or punctuation rule I learned about this week: | Here is a wacky way to remember how to spell the word: |
|---|---|
| ```┌──────────────┐│              ││              │└──────────────┘``` | ```┌──────────────┐│              ││              │└──────────────┘``` |

**FIGURE 5.1.** This Week's News.

view the elements of a quality newspaper article, create a semantic map for the word *news*, discuss what they know about the Midwest (social studies), and remember to encourage parents to sign up for parent conferences. Moreover, during the 40 minutes or so devoted to this activity, June also provides mini-lessons on spelling strategies, the role of the editor at a newspaper, the role of economics in advertising, the distinction between a lake and an ocean, the purpose of the social studies read-aloud book, and strategies for succeeding in a spelling bee. Thus, students use this time not only to summarize what they've learned already but to build on it and make connections in new ways.

## WORKING BULLETIN BOARDS

Another source of learning in June's classroom is the wall space. In contrast to some classrooms, where the bulletin boards are primarily decorative, the wall space in June's classroom serves as a perpetual source of information (see Figure 5.2 for examples). Students can refer to the boards and walls for information related to science, social studies, math, and writing topics. In addition, some bulletin boards contain questions and information about topics not in the curriculum, per se, but of interest to students. One section of a large board is called the "Why" board; its space is reserved for students' questions about how the world works. Topics of interest have ranged from the preparation of mummies, to the dangers of electrical shock, to how it is that fingernails can grow when they are made up of dead cells. Another section of board is devoted to "Wacky Words." Here, students learn and review mnemonic tricks for spelling and understanding words. Some of the strategies are in written form, others are graphic. Students *use* the bulletin boards throughout the day to find information, confirm hypotheses, support their arguments with other students (one such discussion I observed concerned the evidence for plate tectonics).

## STRATEGIES AND STRATEGY INSTRUCTION

Consistent with June's overwhelming focus on learning, her curriculum is infused with strategies instruction. She not only teaches strategies explicitly, she teaches students when to use them, why they are useful, and how they will contribute to their ability to solve a problem. During one lesson, which ultimately culminates in a class-written book, June has students brainstorm a title for the story they are composing. As students begin to suggest titles, June intervenes long enough to instigate a discussion about the definition and pur-

**FIGURE 5.2.** Top photo: On the left, a bulletin board early in the year provides background information related to the book, *Miss Rumphius* (Cooney, 1982), which students use as a model for creating classroom expectations. On the right, students analyze similarities and differences between classmates using Venn diagrams. Bottom photo: In the back of the classroom, a bulletin board encourages mathematical curiosity, models fascination with numbers, connects a newspaper unit to local news, and provides news media related to a unit on World War II (including a consideration of the effects of war on domestic animals.)

poses of using brainstorming as a strategy. Though most of these students have been asked to *use* the brainstorming strategy for several years, it is clear that many have not clearly understood the process nor have they considered its purpose prior to this conversation.

One of the broad strategies June emphasizes is using a variety of resources to solve problems and answer questions. For June, the definition of a good resource is one that can be used efficiently and that accomplishes the goal the student seeks to meet. Sometimes that means using traditional strategies to solve problems; other times it means that you use whatever works. On the second day of school, June breaks ranks with a long line of teachers who have taught students to use the dictionary to ensure accurate spelling. "The dictionary can be a great tool. But do you know what? After teaching fourth grade for many years, I have found that the dictionary is not such a great tool for learning how to spell. You know what's better? The Spelling Ace, or the Franklin Spellers." As the discussion continues, elaborating other alternate strategies for learning correct spellings, June reminds students that "it's also okay to ask your neighbor. Or you can ask me. I don't want you to always be asking me, but I'll tell you: As an adult, if I don't know how to spell a word, if I'm in a group, I ask someone. And that's an okay strategy." Later in the semester, she praises a student who uses the lunch-count list to spell *Wednesday*. "What a great resource! It's so much faster to take ten steps over here than to look it up in the Spellex."

Consistent with her emphasis on using strategies that work in the real world, there are no spelling tests in June's classroom—but many, many spelling *strategies*. Students learn at least one per week, in fact. As she explains to her students, adults do not take spelling tests. "I don't wake up on Monday with a list of spelling words I need to learn. But what I do encounter in adult life is this: I come across a word, *calendar*, let's say, and is it *e-r*, is it *a-r*—how do I spell that word? And I need to have in my brain some resources that I can then use . . . to find out how to spell that word correctly." Thus her spelling goal for her students is to know which resources are available for a particular task and how to use them. One of those resources is mnemonic devices. In the case of *calendar*, she tells her students that a calendar is full of days and the word *days* has an *a* in it. So, *calendar* is spelled with an *a-r*.

When it comes to comprehension and studying, June teaches a number of strategies explicitly, and others through modeling. Many are presented, modeled, and practiced during read-aloud, making them accessible to readers at all levels. She often thinks aloud as she reads, modeling her approach to understanding text and to resolving confusing interpretations. On one morning during the newspaper unit, students read an article about a decapitated statue chosen specifically for the comprehension difficulties it might pose. As students review the article, June describes her own process of understanding what it is about: "When I read this the first time, I just looked at the picture [of a headless mermaid] and I thought it was a real person. Then I read the first line and it said, 'Diver searches for missing head,' so I thought, 'Okay. It's a real head.' I kept reading and it said, 'Little Mermaid.' So I thought, 'Well, there's no such thing as real mermaids, so this must not be about someone real.' " Since several other students have had similar experiences trying to sort out the meaning of the text, a discussion ensues about the metacognitive processes involved in understanding text (though not in those words).

Some of the strategies June teaches are planned in advance, while others are in response to student need. Following a comment about the title of a read-aloud book, for example, June advises her students, "When you read, don't just read literally. Think about what the real meaning is. Some people [students] have said they don't understand *The Big Lie* [Leitner, 1992]—the title of the book. Pay attention to the ideas when you read, and see if you can figure out why it's called *The Big Lie*."

Among the strategies June teaches are those for setting goals, monitoring time, and regulating one's own learning. Early in the year, as students work on a writing assignment with less than ideal focus, June interrupts. "Let's look at the clock now. You've got about 15 minutes until recess. You've been here for an hour now. Think about what you've done here—what you've accomplished. By recess time, you should be pretty much done with your rough drafts . . . so if you're nowhere near done, then you should be doing less chit-chatting and focus more on your work."

Later in the fall semester, I overhear her checking in with a particular student who struggles with writing. She is working on an alliterative A-B-C book and appears to be overwhelmed by the task (26 letters!). June pulls up a chair beside her and compliments her on some of the pages she has already completed. "Okay, Jana," she says. "Let's make a goal. How many are you going to get done before recess? What's realistic?" They agree that three more letters before recess is reasonable, and as June moves on to another student, Jana looks much relieved; she starts in on the letter *N*. By providing frequent opportunities for students to think strategically about their learning and check in on their own work processes throughout the year, June helps students develop the habits and strategies of effective, self-regulated learners.

## CONNECTIONS TO THE REAL WORLD

According to June, students' abilities to hear something on television or read it in a magazine and make the connections to something they have learned in school is one of the most important indicators of a teacher's success. Many of her students' parents report that their sons and daughters bring home topics and discuss them at the dinner table or in the car on the way to soccer practice. This ability (and desire!) to pursue "school" topics outside of school is a measure of June's success. And it is one of her explicit goals.

June models the making of such connections for students daily. For example, when they are studying Impressionism, June brings in an article from *The Boston Globe* featuring a Monet exhibit at Boston's Museum of Fine Arts. She introduces it by telling students, "There's something interesting going on in the *real world* that you know about." She encourages students to share what they observe about the painting on the cover and enthusiastically describes the difference between seeing a reproduced print of a Monet and seeing "the real thing." Moreover, she suggests that students' own recent attempts at painting and preserving their artwork might help them understand why art museums are so careful with the paintings of artists such as Monet. Later in the year, when the East Coast is recovering form power outages caused by ice storms, June connects the local headlines to what students have learned about electricity and circuitry.

My favorite example of June's connections with current events takes place on the day when she explains to students that it was, in fact, hotter than Hell. On one hot day in May, June describes a radio announcer she had heard on her way to school who had called the town of Hell, Michigan (a real place), to check on the temperature. June reports that the temperature in Boston that morning is, in fact, hotter than the temperature in Hell! This story involves references to the radio as a source of news, the location of Michigan (which is linked to an earlier social studies unit), and the use of linguistic expressions such as "hotter than hell."

June's emphasis on making school learning relevant for students translates directly into her curriculum and assignments. Her students, for example, do not write book reports. They do not write book reports because June believes that the process of writing one turns the whole purpose of reading on its head. "We [adults] read a book because we want to read the book and discuss and talk about the book, and that's what I want them to be able to do—to take from the book and really to share something about that book, like an adult does." What students do write, however, are letters to politicians in which they express their feelings about war. They do this during a unit on World War II and, in the process, learn to use the elements of a formal letter—for a real purpose. In the aftermath of the World Trade Center attacks, June's students wrote letters to President Bush relating what they had learned about the effects of war and considering alternative ways of responding. In contrast, other fourth-grade teachers frequently have their students write hypothetical letters which do not get sent—often, to fictional characters.

At the end of the unit on World War II, June and her students engage in a lengthy discussion triggered by her question, "What have you learned in this unit that you could apply to your own lives?" Students describe recent local and national incidents of hate-related crimes and discuss the realization that, as one student puts it, "there is still hatred in the world." For many students, this is a new experience; they had not connected what they perceived as historical events and cultures to their own current situations. It is June's demand that they connect "school ideas" with their lives that enables them to see such connections.

During this same lesson, students begin a conversation about the world's supply of weapons for mass destruction, trying to understand the purpose for having enough bombs to "blow up the world 20 times." June mediates the conversation, encouraging students to think aloud about their relevance of the big ideas in the unit to students' lives, without imposing her own values or interpretations. The importance of integrating the subjects of history, science, math, art, and writing into the daily lives of students is emphasized explicitly throughout the year. June does not assume that children will necessarily make these connections on their own. She creates scaffolds and creates contexts for students to use as they learn to relate school to life on a daily basis.

Deliberate connections between the real world and the curriculum are built into the units June plans and the materials she uses. At least as powerful, though, are the daily examples she uses to help students develop conceptual understandings. For example, in science, June describes a series circuit by relating it to the World Series: "There is one game after another, and if you lose a game, you're out." Similarly, she explains that in a parallel circuit, "electricity finds another way to go, kind of like when you're caught in traffic: Sometimes you can find another path around the jam."

Some of the topics and issues addressed in June's classroom are controversial; some are even disturbing. Many would not be seen or heard in a typical fourth-grade curriculum. Rather than avoid issues such as violence and abuse, June draws them into the curriculum in ways that students can make sense of them and begin to understand them in the context of the larger world. Students in her class study World War II, including the effects of Hiroshima and the experiences of children in concentration camps. They do this largely through planned read-aloud books and the discussions and writing these books provoke. But in addition to planned lessons on these topics, students benefit from June's willingness to answer questions and facilitate discussions about difficult issues.

Many of the students who attend her rural elementary school have never been to a large city, despite the fact that Boston is an hour's drive away. Compared with many schools, there is limited racial or ethnic diversity in their community, and students rarely confront overt racism in their walks down the school hallways. It would be easy in such a setting to argue that children should be protected; that their "sheltered" status is a privilege to be preserved. June's perspective, however, is that despite their apparently sheltered lives, the children who are her students—like most students in the United States—are exposed to stories of murder, destruction, and injustice in the media every day. It is not accurate to contend that they have no exposure to adversity, injustice, violence, or fear. The problem, in June's opinion, is that, "they are just not asked to *think* about it." In June's class, students are not only *invited* to think about topics such as the Holocaust (e.g., by reading *The Big Lie*; Leitner, 1992), children's survival (*Maniac Magee*; Spinelli, 1990), and potential justifications for lying (*Shiloh*; Naylor, 2000)—they are required to do so.

In this process, they learn more about the world and about themselves.

## CONNECTIONS ACROSS THE CURRICULUM

Learning in this classroom is not compartmentalized. One of the ways students come to understand the connections between academic learning and the real world is by integrating subject areas across the curriculum. Thus a unit on newspapers extends across several curricular areas and naturally pops up throughout the day in a variety of contexts. In language arts, students learn to use the wh-questions (who, what, where, why, when) to understand newspaper articles as well as to write their own. In math, they are studying large numbers, so for homework June asks them to search the newspaper for examples of large numbers and then bring them to class. This leads to discussions about the use of numbers to make a point in advertising. On another day, June invites a local editor to visit and talk about everything from the elements of a "good" article to the cost of advertising. Still later in the unit, a question about opinions versus facts is related to earlier discussions about war propaganda. Thus, with June's scaffolding, students easily connect topics in language arts, math, and social studies through a short unit on newspapers.

Throughout the day, students are expected to make such connections across curricular areas. Consistent with June's style, these connections range from the explicit to the implied. Her instruction appears to be grounded in the assumptions that math is relevant to social studies and language arts; that reading is a tool that crosses all boundaries; that science is used in understanding history; that writing serves multiple purposes.

In fact, writing in this classroom is rarely done in isolation. Rather, students write in response to books they have read or ideas they have discussed; they compose stories and poems to accompany elaborate collage books; they develop their knowledge of electricity and geology into a series of metaphors. In one activity modeled after the book *Quick as a Cricket* (Wood, 1989), a student writes, "I'm as slow as a rock that sat on a glacier for a million years and only moved one inch. I'm as fast as electricity. Before you know it, I can reach out and stun you."

## READ-ALOUD AS THE CENTERPIECE OF INSTRUCTION

One of the primary ways in which June teaches strategies, integrates learning, and strengthens student dialogue is through her daily read-aloud. In contrast to many upper-grade elementary classrooms, read-aloud in June's room is not an instructional segment to be fit on days when the schedule allows—it is the centerpiece of her curriculum. In her word, "The most important thing is read-aloud. If I had to keep one thing in the whole schedule . . . that would be the thing that I would fight for the most." June deliberately schedules read-aloud at one of the rare times in the day when all of the children—including those receiving intensive remedial services—are present. In her view, those students who are most likely to be pulled out of the classroom (the struggling readers) are precisely the students who stand to gain the most from the intensive instruction of read-aloud. "You need to be read to, to learn to read," she says. Resource room teachers rarely consider reading to students to be a valid use of their instructional time. Moreover, read-aloud in June's classroom involves a great deal more than listening.

"In the beginning of the year," she explains, "I think [students] just thought I was going to read and they were just going to listen. . . . It wasn't going to be a two-way interactive street. . . . I think they thought it was almost going to be, like, 'I can just relax and almost zone out,' versus, 'this is work time.' If you say, 'okay, you can color while I'm reading,' then the message you're sending is that you don't need to be listening 100%." Instead, read-aloud in June's room is a time when students are fully engaged and actively participating in the learning. Read-aloud is the arena for perhaps the richest instruction of the day—in vocabulary, strategies, literary devices, a huge range of content, and the process of reflection.

Many teachers take advantage of the opportunities read-aloud provides for teaching vocabulary. Not surprisingly, June can be counted in this group. What makes her vocabulary instruction so effective, however, is that rather than tell students the meanings of unfamiliar words, she teaches vocabulary by teaching and scaffolding active comprehension strategies. For example, when they encounter the word *parsonage* in the book *The Upstairs Room* (Reiss, 1987), June knows that some children will not know what the word means. Rather than tell them what it means, she poses a question: "If you didn't know what a parsonage was, how could you tell from the context of what I just read?" With this lead, students proceed to model for one another their problem-solving strategies. In the end, they not only acquire a common understanding of the word, they become more strategic readers.

In addition to the extensive strategy instruction that goes on during read-aloud, June models her love of good literature and ideas. It would be hard to leave her classroom at the end of the year without understanding the power of language in reading and writing. Her appreciation for good literature is transparent in her discussions with students. Over the course of the year, even the most reluctant readers become avid participants in the exploration of literature.

In part, students become part of this book-loving culture because June helps them to see the relevance of specific books to their own lives. When they connect what they read to other things they know, suddenly reading becomes purposeful and they feel some ownership for the language and the content. When June introduces *Shiloh* (Naylor, 2000) in January, she situates the story in the genre of realistic fiction and offers some background information about the author and the experiences that lead her to write the book. There is a brief discussion of Gary Paulson, another popular author who writes realistic fiction based on his own experiences. Then she shares the reason why *she* likes this book so much: "I think this is one of my favorite books because it has so many literary devices in it. Do you remember when we read *The Ice Cream Heroes* (Corbalis, 1988) at the beginning of the year? It had a lot of literary devices—a lot of cliff hangers. [There are] a lot of good writing devices that I'll be pointing out to you as we go." Not 5 minutes later, she asks students to name the device that describes phrases like "tail sticking up like a flagpole" and "tail going like a propeller" (from the book). Having written their own books of similes students are quick to respond.

During the unit on World War II, students have many conversations about Nazi goals and atrocities and make at least an initial attempt to understand the concept of "the final solution." Throughout the unit, which includes several novels, June helps students grasp the power of words to communicate ideas. She encourages them to choose words carefully in their own writing and to think about the words other authors use in theirs. One day, as she reads about Jews being transported to Auschwitz in *The Big Lie* (Leitner, 1992), she stops mid-sentence and goes back: "Herded. What gets herded? People?"

A student responds, "Animals."

"Animals. They weren't even treated like people. They were treated like animals. That was a great word for the author to use there because it makes us think about how the people were treated like animals." By thinking aloud and modeling thoughtful reading, June teaches children not only to love literature but to read it strategically and thoughtfully. Moreover, the discussions and reflections that punctuate her read-aloud are carried over to students' writing—when it is *they* who are using the power of words to create the meaningful and moving pieces of writing.

## ENCOURAGING INDEPENDENCE

June's most important goals for her students are: "They can think for themselves; they can be advocates for themselves with their own learning; they have a good broad base of knowledge in all subject areas; they can speak intelligently about the topics [they] have studied." In the fall, when she is explaining fourth grade to her new students, she promises them, "If I teach you nothing else, I want to teach you how to be responsible."

At the end of the year, when June is asked to talk about students who have made significant progress over the course of their fourth-grade year, she inevitably mentions their gains in risk-taking and independence. For example, in the fall she described Megan as a competent reader, but one who would not turn in any work or participate in discussion unless she was certain that she had the correct responses; she needed to check with June about every decision. In discussing her progress at the end of the year, June happily reports that "she makes a lot of decisions on her own now and then tells me about them. She has kind of come into her own this year and she is . . . thinking for herself. She is not just giving answers and what she thinks I want to hear anymore. She has been a person who has transformed, I would say, from a more average student to an above-average student because she feels more confident. . . . [She is] asserting herself more, speaking up. She is more like a leader to her peers, too." When I ask June what she thinks she has done to contribute to this transformation, she replies, "Just let her be herself. I don't ask for particular answers. I accept anything reasonable—with justification."

Independence and risk-taking mean different things to different students, however. For Elizabeth, a shy and struggling reader, June explains that her goal was to convince Elizabeth to ask questions when she didn't understand something. In June's words, "at some point, [the learning process] is not solely my responsibility. It becomes a joint responsibility. Yes, I need to teach Elizabeth, but she needs to ask for help when she needs it, too. . . . With Elizabeth, it came down to telling her, "When you don't understand something, you get up here and you just stand beside me until I notice you." And in the spring of fourth grade, Elizabeth is doing just that.

By the spring semester, it is clear that June's students have developed into self-regulated learners who are more confident than they were in the fall. They ask questions, take responsibility for their own learning, and have strategies for solving problems on their own or with their peers. This kind of development does not just happen as children get another year older. It is carefully scaffolded and deliberately supported.


## CONCLUSION

Exemplary teachers do more than teach—or perhaps it would be more accurate to say that they redefine common understandings of what teaching is. Teaching in a classroom like June's is both individualized and community-oriented; it is focused on learning in ways that value both process and product; it is explicit as well as opportunistic; it enables students to become agents of their own learning.

From the first day of school, students in June's classroom work together as a community. They do not merely have *opportunities* to talk with one another, they are expected—*required*—to work together to think through and solve problems. They push each other (and I include June in this mix of thinkers) to reach new understandings and challenge misconceptions. In a perfectly logical irony, June teaches students to become more independent learners by teaching them to rely on and utilize effective resources—and the most important resource they tap throughout the year is each other. Experts solve problems by talking through the possibilities with colleagues. Students in June's class learn to be just such experts. June teaches them to do this through planned and opportunistic modeling, and by deliberately creating projects and assignments that require students to challenge their understandings.

Students are willing to accept June's approach and instruction because they are able to connect what they are doing in school with what they know about and experience in the world outside of school. One of the most powerful outcomes of a year spent in June's classroom is the understanding that school learning is directly related to what students perceive to be "real life." School is not just that stuff that happens between 8:30 and 3:00 when the rest of life is on hold. It is *part* of that life. And as students come to understand that fundamental interconnectedness, they become visibly empowered to participate in that part of life that happens between 8:30 and 3:00. In June's classroom, she makes certain that those hours are spent engaged in thinking, questioning, dialogue, and learning.

**Ruth Wharton-McDonald, PhD,** is an assistant professor in the Department of Education at the University of New Hampshire. Dr. Wharton-McDonald's research interests are in the experiences of teachers and students in classrooms where children are learning to read and write. In particular, she has studied the characteristics of exemplary literacy teachers and the perspectives of students in their classrooms. She is coauthor of *Learning to Read: Lessons from Exemplary First-Grade Classrooms* (Guilford, 2001).

# 6

"We Learn from Each Other"

*Collaboration and Community*
*in a Bilingual Classroom*

Jeni Pollack Day

It's science class in Sandy Kniseley's classroom, and the students are presenting experiments related to the class unit on water. Each student has chosen an experiment from several books available, practiced it at home, and written up his or her procedure, results, and conclusion. Students are now demonstrating their experiments and sharing papers with the class. As the students sit wide-eyed and engrossed in what their classmates are saying, Sandy asks, "Are we learning things from each other?" "YES!!" exclaims the class. (Field notes)

This vignette exemplifies how Sandy Kniseley uses formal and informal collaboration to help her students become both learners and teachers in a community bound by a common love of learning. By allowing students to work together, expecting them to teach and learn from each other, and by permitting and encouraging student talk, Sandy has created an environment in which students own their learning and are responsible for themselves and their classmates. How

99

does she run her classroom? How did she get in running that way? These are two questions we strove to answer as we observed Sandy and her students over the school year.

## SCHOOL CONTEXT AND DEMOGRAPHICS

Sandy teaches on the edge of a large West Coast city. She has a class of 31 students who are primarily second-language learners. She has more second-language learners in her class than do other teachers because she speaks Spanish and wanted to work with Spanish speakers. The school is poor, with 72% of the student body receiving free or reduced-price lunch, and the student population is fairly transient: In the last 2 months of school, Sandy was assigned four new students.

Sandy's class is considered a bilingual classroom, and she has students in her class at all levels of proficiency in English. The goal for the program is to provide assistance and some instruction in Spanish, but to transition children to using English as quickly as possible. Sandy's program uses reading materials and textbooks in Spanish, but her schedule includes specific time for instruction in reading and speaking English. Sandy teaches primarily in English during whole-class activities but uses Spanish to shelter students' language levels. Her class this year is mostly working on grade level, with few students receiving special education services, although she says this is unusual.

## TEACHER BACKGROUND

Sandy is finishing her fifth year of teaching and although not a new teacher, she remains extremely energetic and informed. She earned her master's degree in special education while teaching and works as a mentor teacher for her district. She is very conscientious and spends considerable time reflecting on how her students understand her instruction, how she can meet their needs better, and what new areas of need have been revealed to her through her activities. In an interview she remarked, "I really enjoy it when I can just sit and watch. That really helps me improve my own teaching and I know my kids a lot better." She often paused while observers were in the room to wonder aloud, "Next time, I think this would be better if I tried having them work in small groups first," or "They don't seem to be getting this as well as I'd hoped. I think I need to go back and do another lesson on proofreading."

## DAILY SCHEDULE

Students arrive in Sandy's classroom around 8 A.M., unpack their backpacks, turn in their homework, and begin writing in their journals. Several students approach her with questions, news, and problems to share. She also uses this time to greet students, find out about their lives, and to look for and respond to notes and requests from parents. After students are settled and have had time to write, Sandy provides time for several to share with the class what they have written, motivating them to write by giving them an audience. The rest of the morning is spent in PE or art, math, recess, and integrated language arts, which includes read-aloud, guided reading groups, work on class novels, and 30 minutes of small-group instruction in English. After lunch the schedule includes writing workshop and science or social studies.

Sandy has a wall chart that helps students keep track of the weekly schedule, and she writes daily activities on the board each morning. Although she needs to keep to her schedule as much as possible due to school scheduling constraints, she often allows an activity to flow into another section of the day if students are engaged or need more time. A typical day's schedule might look like this:

| | |
|---|---|
| 8:00–8:30 | Collect homework, write in journals |
| 8:30–9:00 | PE or art |
| 9:00–10:00 | Math |
| 10:00–10:15 | Recess |
| 10:15–11:40 | Integrated language arts/ESL |
| 11:40–12:25 | Lunch |
| 12:25–12:35 | Homework and goals |
| 12:35–1:25 | Writing workshop |
| 1:25–2:25 | Science or social studies |
| 2:25 | Dismissal |

Integrated language arts begins with reading right after recess and continues until the writing workshop. Sandy uses a combination of elements to create her language arts program. During small group time she uses the district required basal, although she uses it in unconventional ways. Rather than proceeding sequentially, Sandy pulls stories that fit the interests of her students and that relate to the science, social studies, or health theme they are studying. For instance, while studying California's history, the students read two related historical fiction stories about life in California missions from the basal; when they were studying water, she skipped to a piece on scientists who use knowledge of water in their fields, such as meteorology and oceanography. Sandy supplements the basal program with novel units she does with the whole class. She also uses a Spanish basal program, "Bridges," with her Spanish speakers in much the same way as the English basal, picking and choosing what she considers most important and useful for her students. She notes that she looks at the teacher's guide for suggestions, especially when using a new textbook series, but often modifies the ideas or develops other possibilities based on observations of her children.

Sandy begins the integrated language arts time with read-aloud, one of the favorite parts of the day for the whole class. Children gather around Sandy, seated on chairs or the floor or desks in the carpeted reading area near her desk as she shares another chapter of an exciting children's novel.

After read-aloud, she meets with her reading groups: two English groups for students who are fluent, and two transition groups for Spanish-speaking students. In the beginning of the school year the two transition groups use the Spanish basal, but by spring they are working in the English basal, using easier text than her fluent English speakers. Group composition remains flexible, and she often moves students into different groups to reflect their developing English ability. She notes that the students do not think of them as high and low groups but as English and Spanish groups. She shared that her Spanish readers are sometimes more fluent in Spanish than the English readers are in English.

Each group meets four times each week, two times with Sandy and two times with the assistant or student teacher. Groups meet for about 20 minutes and then the students return to independent work. While Sandy and her assistant work with approximately half of the class in groups, the other half of the students spend 20–30 minutes on silent self-selected reading, work on projects involving the class novel (such as *Charlotte's Web* [White, 1952], which the students are reading independently), or complete assignments they began in group time. Students are given the choice during this time of working independently or in groups of two or three.

One day a week, usually Friday, students do not meet in groups but instead participate in whole-class activities involving the novel, such as acting out scenes, discussing the book, or sharing pertinent projects. Independent novel projects involve reading a section in the text and completing activities based on it, such as writing letters to characters or the author, illustrating favorite scenes, or working with its vocabulary. Because everyone in the class is reading the same novel, Sandy has copies in English and Spanish. This year, all of her students are able to read the novel, although she often allows slower readers to partner-read, taking turns to read aloud in pairs, in order to help students who are less fluent.

The next part of language arts is Bridges, the English as a Second Language (ESL) program. During this time, several teachers and assistants throughout the school work with students they have grouped across classes by English competence to work on reading and speaking English. Several of Sandy's students remain in her group, while others work with other teachers or assistants, and students from other classes join Sandy's group. The Bridges program involves reading cohesive texts and practicing English through speaking exercises, such as drama activities. Fluent English speakers read self-selected novels or work on self-initiated writing projects during this time, allowing the teacher extra time to work in small groups with students who generally need it most—second-language learners.

After lunch, students spend 10 minutes working on "homework and goals," in which they use a notebook to keep track of homework (due on a daily basis) as well as create their own nighttime goals for long-term projects. This provides instruction and practice in self-regulation on assignments.

In the writing workshop, right after lunch, students work independently on various pieces of writing that are at various stages. They work at their own pace, within the teacher's deadlines, through drafting, conferencing with other students and the teacher, revisions, and finally presentation and publication. Assignments alternate between teacher-chosen and student-chosen topics. At any given time during writing workshop, students might be drafting, reading aloud their piece to another student or group of students, conferencing with Sandy, or setting up time to share with the class what they have written.

The last hour of the day is dedicated to science or social studies.

Sandy usually focuses on science in depth for two weeks and then social studies for two weeks. She employs experiments, art, drama, and group activities to give students opportunities to explore topics they are studying and to practice English-speaking skills. Science and social studies are integrated with language arts as students use the library, trade books, and textbooks to answer research questions and creative writing to explore what they are learning. As noted, although Sandy uses the basal textbooks for science and social studies, she does not use them sequentially but picks and chooses readings and other activities that meet the particular needs of her program. For instance, wanting to give her students a sense of the different groups of people who settled California, she assigned one section of the chapter to each of five groups rather than have each student read about all five groups. Each group was assigned to read its section and plan a way to teach that section to the rest of the class, so that students became experts in one part of the chapter and shared that expertise with the others.

## CLASSROOM ORGANIZATION

The foundation of Sandy's classroom organization is mutual respect. She is respectful with her students and listens and responds to what they have to say. She takes a genuine interest in their lives and their ideas and spends much of the free time before and after school, or during lunch and recess, conversing with them. She often asks them about ongoing situations in their homes or communities and shares information she thinks will interest them, such as news of a new library book on a topic a student has become interested in or a community event she thinks they will enjoy.

When problems or disruptions arise, Sandy strives to understand the source of the difficulty, often asking, "What don't you understand?" or "What is the problem?" instead of chastising them for not working. When unable to talk to a student immediately, Sandy will make a point to find that student later and listen to him or her. She reprimands students gently—without negative tones or emotion—by simply reminding them, "You know better." She is also quick to seek help when dealing with serious problems, often calling home or consulting with the school nurse, counselor, or principal before the situation becomes debilitating for the student. She is also quick to build up the students' pride in their class by comparing it positively with other classes and, more importantly, comparing the students with themselves earlier in the year. She takes the time to prepare them for potentially difficult behavioral situations. For example, prior to a school performance she comments, "These students are very brave to perform in front of the whole school and all the parents. How do you think they will feel if they make a mistake and someone laughs?" She routinely reinforces specific examples of appropriate behavior: "I appreciate your respectful listening in the assembly." And, "Remember the first week when we had to really work at walking quietly? Now you guys do it automatically."

Sandy also spends a great deal of time teaching students personal and academic responsibility and long-term planning by allowing them choice in the projects they select and the time schedule they work out for themselves. She spends 10 minutes after lunch each day on "homework and goals," in order to transfer responsibility for planning and completing projects to students. During this time, students copy short- and long-term assignments from the chalkboard and determine their daily goals for completing various projects. Sandy has modeled how to break up long-term assignments into their own personal daily goals and encourages them to consider whether goals they set in the past have been too easy or difficult to attain, asking them, "How did you do last week? Were your goals too easy or difficult? What would be a reasonable goal for today if you need to turn in your final draft on Friday?" These sheets also contain questions that teach students to reflect on their behavior by answering quick yes/no questions on a daily basis: Did I try my best? Did I complete all my homework? Did I clean my desk? Was I respectful? She does not expect them to act completely independently, yet she teaches them independent decision making by modeling how to plan and make short-term and long-term goals.

## INSTRUCTIONAL DECISION MAKING

Sandy uses several sources to guide her daily decisions about instruction. First she considers students' scores on annual district and statewide tests to determine the areas in which her students had difficulty the preceding year. These tests measure knowledge of math problem solving and computation, reading comprehension, and factual knowledge. She also considers district requirements and topics that are part of the fourth-grade curriculum, such as California history and geography in social studies and animals and water in science. The district uses holistic reading and writing evaluations, in the form of rubrics and checklists, which help to inform her instruction. Finally, she considers students' needs and strives to make the external requirements fit these needs. She frequently evaluates whether an activity met a particular student's needs and what new needs became apparent through an activity. For example, on one day she commented, "They seem to get brainstorming webs when we went over it, but I don't see them using it in their writing. I need to figure out why not."

Sandy's school district recently purchased a new basal series. Because of her role as mentor teacher, Sandy feels it important for her to become familiar with the contents of the program. She does not believe in proceeding straight through the program, however, instead taking the time to find activities that match her students' needs and interests and find ways to integrate the basal into her science and social studies curriculum. She says it creates far more work for her, but that she couldn't imagine simply doing activities for the sake of doing them.

## EXEMPLARY READING INSTRUCTION

The students have finished reading the first six chapters of *Charlotte's Web*, their current class novel, and have discussed characterization. "Quick," says Sandy, "in the next 2 minutes review the last chapter and think of a question you would like to ask one of the characters. Think about what you know about the character and what might be an interesting question. When you have a really good question, come and whisper it into my ear." After each student skims the book and finds a question, Sandy assigns 10 students to act as the characters in the book and answer questions from their classmates. Students laugh and listen as they try to think like the character and answer questions such as, "Why didn't you want to help Wilbur, Templeton?", and "How did you feel about going to the fair, Wilbur,' or, 'Would you have done the same thing again, Fern?" (Field notes)

"Okay, let's go," Sandy says, as she hands out copies of a recipe photocopied from a popular cookbook. "We've got some read-

ing to do before we start." She's working with a beginning
Spanish-speaking ESL group during Bridges time. The group is
making gingerbread, an activity the students chose after several
readings of *The Gingerbread Man* in English. "Let me know
what you need to do first. You're making this, not me. How are
you going to be sure you have everything you need? Are we going to have time to finish this before lunch?" Sandy prompts students who haven't read the entire recipe. (Field notes)

The key to Sandy's reading program is the balance she achieves
between modeling and presenting strategies and providing purposeful opportunities to practice and use those strategies. Activities in
reading are divided into several major areas. Students meet in small
groups for 20 minutes every day. This time is divided to include
guided reading and strategy instruction, although Sandy uses them to
cover any other topics relevant to her students' reading and writing,
such as explaining rules for using apostrophes with possessives, or
making spelling patterns explicit. While small groups work with her,
the rest of the class works alone or in groups on Drop Everything
and Read (D.E.A.R.) time, independent long-term activities centered
around class novel units, and assignments from small-group time. After small-group time, the teacher organizes whole-class or group activities around the novel the students are reading.

Students spend time each day reading books of their own choice.
Because her schedule leaves little room for whole-class free reading
(D.E.A.R.) time, Sandy has students schedule their free reading during independent work time. She assigns 30 minutes of reading at
home each evening. Students keep track of their reading through log
sheets that the parents sign. This allows Sandy to keep track of what
books students are reading and which students are ready to transition from Spanish to English books or from easier to more challenging books.

Small-group lessons are pulled from the basal program and
adapted to her students' needs, as determined by her observations of
as well as checklists from the district (see Figure 6.1). Lessons for
more proficient readers including learning spelling and grammar
conventions, practicing reading strategies, and doing oral reading or
comprehension activities. Groups that are working to transition from
Spanish are taught similar comprehension strategies and skills as well
as awareness of English phonetic and syntax rules and their relation-

DEVELOPMENTAL READING STAGES

| PRE-EMERGENT | STAGE 5 |
|---|---|
| • Not yet interested in stories/books<br>• Not yet aware of print and its function | • Reads fluently with expression most of the time<br>• Uses a variety of strategies when reading<br>• Makes a wider application of the literal facts of text<br>• Demonstrates understanding of material read in a variety of ways: retellings, dramatizations, Visual Maps of Thinking, art, discussions, writing, cooperative activities<br>• Independently connects text to own ideas, experiences, and knowledge<br>• Reads silently with sustained concentration |
| **STAGE 1** | |
| • Listens to/enjoys a wide range of literature<br>• Has favorite books<br>• Curious about print (e.g., asks to be read to)<br>• Attempts to reread their own words or stories<br>• Makes comments about pictures/story<br>• Pretends to read by making-up story; exhibits read-like behavior<br>• Notices/"reads" Environmental Print (e.g., stop sign, cereal boxes, McDonald's)<br>• Memorizes/chants rhymes, songs or poems<br>• Beginning of directionality<br>  • Front to back | |
| | **STAGE 6** |
| | • May explore multiple possiblities of meaning by interpreting and analyzing text<br>• Cites text to generate, validate, expand, and reflect on their own ideas<br>• Recognizes and differentiates between literal and figurative meanings<br>• May challenge the text by posing questions, taking exception, agreeing, disagreeing, and/or speculating |
| **STAGE 2** | |
| • Recognizes story comes from print<br>• Development of directionality<br>  • Understands story begins where print begins<br>  • Recognizes left to right page sequence<br>  • Knows that text goes left to right<br>  • Recognizes words that begin with the same letter<br>  • Can find repeated words in text<br>• "Reads" familiar, repetitive text and/or <u>own</u> language experience stories<br>• Begins to use letter/sound association | |
| | **STAGE 7** |
| | • Recognizes that different kinds of text require different styles of reading<br>• Chooses to read for a variety of purposes<br>• Welcomes challenges as a reader<br>• Makes connections to other texts or works of art<br>• Challenges the text<br>• Takes risks<br>• Locates and draws on a variety of sources in order to research a topic |
| **STAGE 3** | |
| • Begins to use meaning and language to predict words<br>• Matches word-by-word when tracking<br>• Immediately recognizes some words<br>• Distinguishes between fact and fiction<br>• Indicates comprehension by retelling the story | |
| **STAGE 4** | |
| • Begins to integrate language structure, meaning, and letter/sound relationships when reading orally<br>• Uses punctuation to support understanding of text<br>• Demonstrates a grasp of the whole work, but at a literal or simplistic level<br>• Demonstrates a basic understanding of key literary elements: plot, character, setting<br>• Connects the text with personal experience<br>• May need encouragement to take risks<br>• Begins to develop fluency with familiar text | |

**FIGURE 6.1.** Checklist from report card.

## WRITING STAGES

### PRE-EMERGENT WRITING
- Scribble writing with no format
- Scribble writing with some directionality
- Dictates:
  - words for objects
  - words for pictures
  - captions for pictures
  - sentence(s) for pictures
  - individual & group experience stories

### EARLY WRITING
- Writes his/her name
- Writes some letters (reversals), no spacing

### STAGE 1—WORD WRITING
- Writes some high frequency words like mom, dad, cycle words
- Sense of word length
- Spaces between words, reversals
- Absence of conventional spelling and punctuation
- No apparent sense of audience
- Very literal

### STAGE 2—NEW WORD AND PHRASE WRITING
- Writes new words
- Recombines phonemes
- Writes pattern sentence ending using a word and/or phrases:
  "I see a _____." "It is a _____."
- Consistent Initial consonant, reversals
- Writes captions for pictures
- Writes single or unrelated phrases

### STAGE 3—SIMPLE SENTENCE WRITING
- Uses literature as a model to compose several pattern sentences
- Writes simple, non-pattern, non-related sentences which require phoneme recognition

### STAGE 4—SIMPLE SUBJECT/EXPOSITORY
- Writes a brief paragraph consisting of a few simple related sentences
- Sticks to the topic
- Consistency of invented spelling
- Some organization
- Composes thank-you notes, invitations

### STAGE 5—EARLY STORY WRITING
- Writes story of simple sentences using narrative style with plot development/happening
- Lots of "ands"
- Random capitalization and punctuation
- Some assisted self-editing
- Beginning standard spelling

### STAGE 6—STORY WRITING
- Descriptions include colors and other simple words
- Writes a story that has a beginning, middle, and end
- Writes simple poems using rhyme
- Writes riddles
- Uses some compound and/or complex sentences
- Guided self-editing for phonemic consistency and content
- Initial capitalization
- End punctuation (periods, ? marks)
- More correct use of capitals
- Reversals almost disappeared
- Fewer "ands"

### STAGE 7—ADVANCED WRITING
- Uses patterns other than noun-verb or noun-verb-noun such as:
  - sentences using adjectives and adverbs to expand meaning
  - sentences using connectives
  - sentences using prepositional, adverbial, and adjectival phrases
- Uses initial capitalization and ending punctuation
- Uses correct spelling of basic word
- Uses punctuation of written dialogue
- Uses commas in a series
- Uses a literary device such as:
  - alliteration
  - metaphor, simile
  - onomatopoeia
- Uses a topic sentence with supporting details to write:
  - a descriptive paragraph
  - an explanatory paragraph
  - a persuasive paragraph
- Edits written work for:
  - structure of paragraph
  - content of a paragraph
  - run-on setences
  - complete sentences

### STAGE 8—CAPABLE WRITER
- Writes two or more paragraphs using appropriate transition given each of the following styles:
  - narration
  - explanation
  - description
  - persuasion
- Writes an introduction and a conclusion
- Writes a story of two or more paragraphs using the following story elements:
  - development of setting
  - development of character
  - conflict in plot
- Edits written work for:
  - development of setting
  - development of character
  - conflict in plot
- Edits written work for:
  - punctuation
  - grammar
  - audience
  - spelling
  - thought
- Writes to inform:
  - thank you notes
  - business letters
  - news articles
  - book reports
  - friendly letters
  - responses to forms
  - editorials
  - autobiography
- Writes to entertain and express:
  - short story
  - diaries
  - poetry
  - journals
  - essays
  - drama
- Uses writing patterns
  - summary
  - sequential
  - classification
  - problem/solution
  - generalization
  - enumeration
  - cause and effect
  - comparison/contrast
  - directional
- Writes a report based on research of two or more sources and demonstrates the ability to:
  - take notes
  - outline
  - compile a bibliography

**FIGURE 6.1.** *(continued)*

ship to Spanish. For instance, in English, adjectives generally precede nouns (white house), while in Spanish, the noun generally precedes the adjective (*casa blanca*). Rather than telling students this rule, Sandy shows them several examples they have encountered in their reading and asks them to predict the pattern. In this way, students become more aware of Spanish as well as English and begin to see that, by carefully observing patterns, they can learn how language works.

During group time, Sandy does not do all, or even most, of the talking. Instead she begins by having students brainstorm what they already know about a particular topic or making predictions about the story. Rather than tell students what they need to know, she uses a series of questions to involve them in finding patterns and predicting and confirming theories about a particular topic. Sandy provides hints to students who do not yet understand, but she allows them to find answers for themselves as much as possible. Groups often provide experiences of collaboration as well, as students interact with each other in trying to figure out the problems Sandy has posed to them or in sharing and solving questions of their own.

While Sandy or the assistant works with the groups, other students focus on their independent projects related to *Charlotte's Web* (White, 1952), including answering questions, finding meanings to vocabulary words, or creating art, computer, or writing projects related to the novel. Often these independent activities prepare students for whole-class activities or discussion around the novel. The classroom buzzes with activity during this time, as students typically work in groups of three or four. Students would often stop to ask questions of each other regarding what the teacher said about turning in rough drafts, how a sentence sounds, or what a word or phrase means. This kind of student collaboration frees the teacher to work with groups uninterrupted, since she does not need to stop and answer students' questions. The students use each other as resources when studying the text, working on the assignments, and in clarifying the teacher's expectations, as well as for immediate feedback and evaluation on work in progress.

Making sure her bilingual students practice speaking and reading in English without falling behind in other subject areas is one of the most important challenges of Sandy's program. To make sure *all* her students engage in reading, Sandy obtained copies of several books, including *Charlotte's Web,* in both English and Spanish; every child reads this novel in English, if possible, and in Spanish, if his or her English is not sufficiently advanced. While the ESL students read and write about the book in Spanish, both formal and informal class discussions are conducted in English, which allows them to practice their English in a context with which they are comfortable. Although this method is effective, Sandy acknowledges that it works only because she has no below-grade-level readers in the class, as long as children are allowed to read in their language of choice. Many of her ESL students are reading on grade level in Spanish, and Sandy encourages this until they are able to transition to reading in English.

Sandy also uses read aloud-time to help her students become familiar with English. Before beginning to read aloud a story in English, she summarizes in Spanish what the passage is going to be about, casually translating key vocabulary words from English to Spanish, and making a point to note cognates—words that are similar in Spanish and English, such as *animals* and *animales*. This allows her Spanish speakers to follow along more easily and pick up more English as she reads. She also often stops to paraphrase in Spanish to help her students comprehend.

Sandy spends a great deal of time working to build a love of literature and books in her children. Indeed, this is the central goal of her read-aloud time, although she fosters it in many other ways. Read-aloud is a special time. Sandy gathers her students in one area of the room. She reads with expression, flinging her arms out in frustration when the character is stymied, changing her voice to a low, angry tone when the mean antihero comes on the scene, and smiling and laughing with the students when a character does something funny. She also interjects comments and questions and often stops to help students think more deeply about the story by asking them to review, predict, or relate the book to their own personal experiences. She might ask: "How do you think he felt?" "Why is he curious?" "Do you think Old Dan will fight?" " 'Walking like a tomcat' . . . hmm . . . how does a tomcat walk?" "Do your pets know when you are leaving? What do they do?" Most questions are intended to involve students in the characters' lives in order to draw them into the book. When reading *Where the Red Fern Grows* (Rawls, 1989) Sandy allowed one student a day the privilege of holding her stuffed raccoon during reading time, a connection to a character in the book.

Sandy also encourages students to make connections to other books they have read, based on content or author's style. When one student pointed out how Wilbur in *Charlotte's Web* and Little Ann in *Where the Red Fern Grows* are both described as *runts*, Sandy and the students compared the two texts. Sandy also encourages a love of books by making reading exciting; she often stops reading for the day at an exciting section and allows her students to predict what might happen next in the story. Rounding out her comprehensive approach to cultivating literacy, Sandy also shares with students the exciting books she is reading for her own pleasure and tells them how important reading is to her.

### EXEMPLARY WRITING INSTRUCTION

As I observe the class working independently while the teacher works with small groups, I hear a constant buzz of activity. Moving closer, I can make out individual conversations.

Two students are trying to determine if Mr. Zuckerman and Homer in *Charlotte's Web* are the same character. They debate for several minutes, then reach to the book for evidence. They determine it is the same person.

A student, frustrated that he can't figure out what to say next in his writing, asks the students at his table to listen to what he has written so far.

Three students buddy-read through an especially difficult chapter. Now and then, one stops to ask the other two a question about the book

"¿Como se dice 'anaranja' en Ingles? [How do you say 'spider' in English?]" one student asks another. "Spider. S-p-i-d-e-r. Do you want me to write it for you?"

A student listens to a classmate read a summary he has written, then comments, "You need to add a period here and a comma over here. Plus, right here, I don't understand what you mean. And this paragraph doesn't make sense. Wilbur didn't know that right here, see, in chapter six . . . " (Field notes)

In talking with students, both in formal interviews and informal conversations, I found that they all love to write and the most began to love writing in Sandy's classroom. Her classroom is itself a testament to the love of writing. Student writing is displayed on every wall, hanging from the ceiling, standing on tables, and published in class books. It is part of computer projects and science experiments and social studies projects. It is presented informally to the class on a daily basis and formally to the class several times a month. Sandy also encourages her students to enter writing contests and to take advantage of other opportunities inside and outside school, which many do. One student told me that having his work entered in one of these contests was the beginning of his love for writing, an interest he now pursued both in and outside school.

Sandy alternates between teacher-selected and student-selected writing genres, and although she allows free writing, she has a schedule of when final drafts should be completed. To provide models for them, Sandy reads from a variety of genres during read-aloud, including memoir, mystery, fairy tale, and even recipes, and often finds that they copy the style of the genre in their writing. She then gives them 45 minutes to an hour each day to work on drafting, proofreading, and conferencing with her or another student.

She begins a typical conference by pointing out to students what they have done well before helping them with areas that need attention. She describes her role as that of facilitating students' abilities to self-monitor. First she asks the student: "What do you think you need to work on next?" Sometimes the student and Sandy agree, and sometimes they do not. Once Sandy reported; "I was hoping she would say, 'I need to put in more periods,' because all her sentences run together." When this student did not see a need for periods, Sandy read it without periods, and asked, "How does that sound?" The student then realized a need to signify pauses, and Sandy showed her how periods could solve that problem. Another time a student asked her, "How do you spell *distant*?" Sandy responded, "How do you think it's spelled?" When the student spelled it correctly, the teacher said, "Good, go write it down." At the same time, if a student doesn't see an error, she is quick to give them feedback, helping them see when they need to correct something and why. She and the student then jot notes of the conference on a chart, so they can refer to it throughout the year and maintain the conventions the student has learned as well as celebrate progress.

Sandy has high expectations for her students, expecting them to write a lot—"You can do five paragraphs"—but also expecting it to be good—"Read it over and see if it sounds right." She has students keep a chart that tracks the one area they need to work on for each new piece. They keep this chart in their writing folders, where they can refer to check the current week's goals, the start and complete dates for each piece, as well as what they have worked on in the past (see Figure 6.2). She expects them to be responsible for the items that make it onto that list, which are negotiated by teacher and student,

| Date begun | Date Completed | Title of piece | Goals | Comments |
|---|---|---|---|---|
|  |  |  |  |  |
|  |  |  |  |  |
|  |  |  |  |  |
|  |  |  |  |  |
|  |  |  |  |  |

**FIGURE 6.2.** Sheet in writing folder.

and include areas such as the use of capital letters at the beginning of sentences, the use of periods at the end, more interesting adjectives, and finding words other than *said*.

Sandy created a rubric for grading writing that is based on the district's report cards (see Figure 6.3). At the beginning of the year, Sandy spends time familiarizing students with what each item on the chart looks like by sharing examples of her own and past students' work. As the year progresses, she also connects the students' work and the items on the rubric to the context in which they wrote: whole-class, small-group, or one-on-one settings. This helps students own what they have accomplished and identify what they need to work on in their writing, producing literacy independence.

During the writing workshop, Sandy allows students to talk and move around the room to be near friends as they work. Because her expectations are very clear, talk stays centered on the writing projects. Furthermore, the students' own goals for the day, based on the teacher's parameters, will be turned into Sandy and their parents at the end of each week—which provides another level of incentive to remain focused on assignment expectations and requirements, factual information, composing ideas, and grammar conventions. I hear comments such as: "Do I need a capital letter here?" "Listen to this, something is missing—what do you think I still need?" "I can't think of what to say next—listen to this and see how it sounds so far." Sandy's students are *very* serious about their writing.

## INTEGRATION OF SUBJECT MATTER

It's social studies time and the students are grouped around the classroom; markers, huge pieces of butcher paper, and their textbooks are their tools. They spill over with ideas, and the talk is serious, even urgent. Sandy has assigned each group to take a small section of the textbook and teach it to the rest of the class. Students interrupt each other in their enthusiasm to share their ideas. Quickly the markers come out and thoughts are jotted down on paper. (Field notes)

Sandy has the students read a small historical fiction story set in the period of their state's history they are studying. After the students read, she reviews the major conflicts and issues with them. She then asks them to compose a list of all the main charac-

**Scoring Rubric for Language Arts**
Fiction

| READING COMPREHENSION | SEQUENCING AND ORGANIZATION | SPEELING AND PUNCTUATION |
|---|---|---|
| *How much information did you include from the story? Are you right?* | *Do you focus on the right things? Is it in a logical order?* | *Are your sentences written well?* |
| **4** | **4** | **4** |
| Great job! You told a lot of good things from the story. You only told things that make sense for the prompt. | Your response is well organized and makes sense. The ideas flow logically. The main idea is explained with details from the plot. | Your sentences are correctly written and show variety. Your words are expressive and are spelled right! |
| **3** | **3** | **3** |
| Good job! You told some details from the story. You might have made a couple of mistakes or you might have told some things that don't matter for the prompt. | You might have gotten off the subject or you might have repeated something but most of your response answers the prompt and makes sense. The ideas are in pretty good order. | Your sentences are correctly written but they're mostly the same and kind of boring. The words you chose are okay but they're not very expressive or vivid. |
| **2** | **2** | **2** |
| You tried to answer but your answer doesn't have very much information in it from the story. It might even have some pretty big mistakes. You may have said things that have nothing to do with the prompt. | You tried to organize the information in your response but it came out unclear and illogical. You didn't explain the things you said and the ideas don't flow in a reasonable manner. | Your sentence may have serious mistakes of grammar and spelling. Your sentences are not at all expressive. Words are okay but not interesting. |
| **1** | **1** | **1** |
| You gave no correct information | There's no logical plan. | Many, many errors. |

**FIGURE 6.3.** Rubric in English/Spanish.

### "Rubric" para evaluar el uso del lenguaje
Ficción

| COMPRENSION DE LECTURA | ORDEN Y ORGANIZACION | ORTOGRAFIA Y PUNTUACION |
|---|---|---|
| *¿Cuántos hechos incluíste del cuento? ¿Tienes razón?* | *¿Pusiste el énfasis en las ideas centrales? ¿Hay un orden lógico?* | *¿Escribiste bien tus oraciones? ¿Las deletreaste bien?* |
| **4** | **4** | **4** |
| ¡Sobresaliente! Incluíste muchas buenas ideas que leíste en el cuento. Lo que escribiste tiene sentido y está relacionado a la tarea inmediata. | Tu respuesta está bien ordenanda y tiene sentido. Tus ideas corren lógicamente y están explicadas con hechos que están de acuerdo con el cuento. | Tus oraciones están muy buenas y demuestran variedad. Las palabras que escogiste son muy expresivas. |
| **3** | **3** | **3** |
| ¡Buen trababjo! Dijiste algunas cosas del cuento. Te equivocaste dos o tres veces o contaste cosas que no importan y que no tienen nada que ver con la tarea inmediata. | Dejaste el asunto o te repetiste pero la mayoría de lo que dijiste tiene sentido y relación con la tarea inmediata. Las ideas de tu respuesta están bien ordenadas. | Tus oraciones están bien escritas pero están todas parecidas y más o menos aburridas. Las palabras que escogiste son buenas pero no son muy espresivas. |
| **2** | **2** | **2** |
| Intentaste responder pero tu repuesta no tiene mucha información del cuento. Es posible que te equivocaste mucho y que dijiste cosas que no tienen nada que ver con la tarea inmediata. | Intentaste ordenar los hechos en tu repuesta pero el resultado no es muy claro ni lógico. No explicaste las ideas que presentaste y tus ideas no corren con soltura. Tu respuesta no es muy razonable. | Tus oraciones tienen errores graves de ortografía y de gramática. Los oraciones no son expresivas. Las palabras que escogiste son razonables pero no son interesantes. |
| **1** | **1** | **1** |
| No diste hechos correctos. | No hay plan lógico. | Muchos errores. |

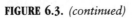

**FIGURE 6.3.** *(continued)*

ters, and assigns students to be those characters and retell the story together. As they reenact the story, she asks each student/ character, "How do you feel?" and "What do you think?" After they have finished, Sandy asks all the students to write a letter to one of the main characters and offer advice on "his" or "her" current problem. She reminds them what they know about how to set up a letter. (Field notes)

Sandy has been learning how to use the multimedia presentation software, Hyperstudio, and has her class working on summaries of *Charlotte's Web* using the program to present to the rest of the class. (Field notes)

These are only a few examples of extensive opportunities Sandy provides for students to use reading, writing, and conversation to support their learning in the content areas. Students engage in reading activities that utilize textbooks and trade books from the school and classroom library towards the goal of locating information on a topic. They use historical fiction short stories to discuss and act out how historical characters might have thought and acted, and what their lives were like. For instance, a story from the social studies textbook that explored the Mexican tradition in which it is the youngest daughter's duty to stay unmarried and take care of her parents as they age, led to a long discussion about the problems and benefits cultural expectations. Students wrote letters to characters in the story, suggesting ways to solve "her" problem. Sandy then connected this story to her students' histories by telling them to "ask your parents if they remember family members that upheld this tradition and be prepared to report back."

They read science books to find experiments they can present to the class and to learn more about ideas in which they have become interested. When studying water, Sandy began by having students find, practice, and present to the class an experiment with water. This experiment led to the development of research papers, as students explored further the topic of their experiment, such as water density and freezing and boiling points. Sandy also uses readers' theater— having students act out events from history, reading their parts directly from the book—as a means of practicing oral reading (especially powerful for Spanish speakers).

Writing is used to explore what students have learned as well as what they are learning and thinking at the time. Students write summaries of information they read and share opinions about topics they are studying, such as whether they would prefer to live in a rancho versus a mission during California's early history, and why. They explore characters' motives and feelings through questions and letters written to the characters. They explain how they are making sense of science experiments and use their writing to derive applications and generalizations from what they are learning.

Sandy pulls technology into her program in many ways. She uses writing programs such as Story Book Weaver to draw in reluctant writers and create published work through word processing, kid pix, and the presentation program, Hyperstudio. She connects literature to video and music, and has created a listening center in the room where students can read along with stories on tape (especially useful for Spanish-speaking students who need to connect spoken English to text).

Sandy uses drama, art, and debate extensively as avenues for students to explore what they are learning in content areas. Debates allow them to formulate and support opinions regarding what it was like to live during a particular period of their state's history, such as the debate on living in a mission or a rancho. Participating in group presentations of experiments helps children make sense of what they are learning in science and provides another venue through which they can share their tentative understandings with classmates. Making posters and murals helps students make sense of content areas such as the water cycle, and the art is often used by one group to teach the rest of the class about the topic. These activities engage students in their immediate tasks but also start them thinking about serious issues in history and science. Discussions around these activities helped students to empathize with cultural figures, grasp the complexity of historical dilemmas such as arranged marriage, and relate issues of the Spanish conquest of California to their present lives. Because they are expected to teach others what they are learning, students have to gain a deeper understanding of the information themselves; the prospect of a real audience and a real purpose encourages them to take the task seriously.

## VERBAL ENVIRONMENT

The students have finished learning about the difference between ranchos and missions in California's settlements. "Where would you rather live?" the teacher asks them. "If you would rather live in a rancho, stand at the front of the room. If you would rather live in a mission, stand at the back. Let's see if any of you can convince people from the other side to join your side." The students move to different areas of the room, and the debate is on. When they have exhausted their reasons, and many students have changed sides more than once, the teacher has them return to their desks to write about what they have learned from this experience. (Interview)

One characteristic that stands out in Sandy's classroom is how much the student talk that occurs throughout the day is directly related to learning. The nature of talk in her classroom is worth exploring in depth because of its unusual nature and the role it plays in shaping student motivation and advancing student collaboration.

Talk in Sandy's room can be divided into two categories: formal talk or presentations and informal or incidental talk. Formal talk, usually prepared beforehand or orchestrated by the teacher, includes presentations of science experiments, computer projects, writing pieces or teaching sections of the textbooks. It also includes "character chair," in which students answer questions as if they were the characters from books; and debates, drama, or reader's theater involving stories they have read or topics they have studied. Sandy encourages her students to participate actively by asking questions and offering comments and evaluations. Each of these activities supports student learning explicitly, by creating an authentic audience for the student presenting, and providing the esteem of a public performance and implicitly, through the valuing of students' work by according it worthy of classroom time.

Informal talk includes teacher and student conversations about reading, writing, schoolwork, and student concerns; teacher and class conversations; and students' conversations among themselves. In Sandy's class such talk is common because it is encouraged by rather than stifled by her. Students frequently talk with Sandy, sharing their news and asking for her opinion. They also meet with her at least weekly to conference about their writing progress.

During whole-class activities, Sandy does not dominate the talk but allows the discussion to be shaped by student conversation. Although she has a plan for her class discussions, she often allows the discussion to go in directions the students spontaneously pursue and builds on their ideas, rather than requiring them to stick to her agenda. She often uses questions to elicit what students already know about a topic and to encourage them to reflect on their own expertise—as they did when discussing family traditions held by Mexicans and Californians. During read-aloud one time, a student interrupted to mention a parallel between the current book and another read-aloud from earlier in the year. Sandy acknowledged the student and sent her to the class library to find the book so they could compare them. When the student returned with the book and found the page, Sandy stopped reading and held up the book, encouraging students to compare the two sections.

The most impressive aspect of classroom talk, however, was the amount of productive student-to-student conversation that occurred during work time and that led to productive collaboration—thereby reducing Sandy's workload, who did not have to spend time answering questions and evaluating work. Because Sandy required students to use their peers as a resource before coming to her, the students saw themselves as competent to act as teachers and sources of information. When a student had a question or needed advice during work time, another student would invariably offer specific answers or advice. Past success and clear understanding of what the teacher expected made them comfortable taking on the role of expert.

The students' ability to stay on-task during independent work time is due to several factors. The work was related to the class novel, which the students were enthusiastic about, as well as interesting and meaningful to them personally. Second, each student was responsible for his or her own work. Because Sandy works with them to develop their daily goals and models planning and accountability for them, they are clear on *what* they expect to finish *when*. Because the goals are ultimately created by them, students have more investment in completing them. Lastly, they are very aware of the teacher's involvement in their learning as she constantly points out their success: "You improved? GREAT!" "Look how well you did this time compared to September." "See, you almost never forget periods and capitals anymore!" "These summaries look really good—you guys make me so proud!" Her genuine enthusiasm makes them proud of their accomplishments, and the pleasure of success makes them want to continue to improve.

Several educational researchers have noted the lack of student talk that often characterizes classrooms (Nystrand, 1997; Goodlad, 1984). Sandy works to overcome this engrained behavior by allowing her students to participate actively in discussions and even influence the direction of instruction, and by allowing for collaboration via spontaneous conversation. During a science experiment, for example, when an egg failed to float in salty water, the students are quick to suggest reasons: "Maybe the egg is too big." Or: "Did you get a hard-boiled egg by mistake?" Sandy turns back questions to students, encouraging them to answer their own or her questions. This approach keeps them involved and interested and reinforcing their growing belief that they are competent and knowledgeable partners in learning.

Sandy Kniseley's room is a busy place full of students who consider their work important and take seriously their roles in the classroom as both learners and teachers. Sandy believes that by verbalizing their ideas, students make sense of what they are learning and, at the same time, learn how to learn—by recognizing what they know and what they do not know. In our conversations, Sandy frequently mentioned the adaptations she makes for individual students, which reflects her desire to work with each student, at whatever level, rather than try and fit each student into one unbending program: "With an ESL classroom, especially, students are at very different places in reading or speaking Spanish or English. You just have to be flexible."

In all the time I worked with her, I never heard Sandy complain about educational policies or systems as beyond her control, nor did she blame parents, colleagues, administrators, or community for what they did or did not do to support her classroom. She considers her students her responsibility. "I've taught with nothing, with bad books or materials," she commented one day. "The secret is the teacher, being creative, making things games, such as through working in teams, and sharing tasks." Although she makes her classroom an enjoyable place, she is very businesslike and serious; she expects her students to work hard and exert their best effort at all times. The result is that Sandy's classroom is a comfortable, challenging, *and* exciting place to learn.

**Jeni Pollack Day** is a doctoral candidate at the University at Albany, State University of New York, and a research assistant at the Center for English Learning and Achievement. She has conducted research on classroom talk, the needs of struggling readers, and the effect of policy on teachers and teaching. She is coauthor of *Moving forward with Literature Circles* (Scholastic, 2002).

# 7

## A Caring, Responsible
## Learning Community

PETER H. JOHNSTON
MARY ELLEN QUINLAN

Mary Ellen Quinlan teaches in a small rural community hit hard by
the loss of manufacturing jobs in the northeast region of the United
States. Empty factories and warehouses provide evidence of a once
thriving industrial base, now departed. Many children (40%) at this
K–5 elementary are eligible for free or reduced-price meals. Many
children have been classified as pupils with disabilities. In September,
Mary Ellen's new class included, along with the 26 other students, a
student who came bearing the label "emotionally and behaviorally
disordered." Four other students also bore labels of one sort or another, but Brian distinguished himself with verbal outbursts and a re-
sistance to working with others. His problem was considered serious
enough that his Individualized Education Plan specified a one-on-one
aide. By the beginning of November, displaying virtually no outbursts, he was generally indistinguishable from the other students. By
January he was almost gregarious, participating in partner reading
and sharing ideas in book discussions, and with no outbursts. He
was, in Mary Ellen's classroom, emotionally and behaviorally nor-

mal, a contributing member of a strong and caring literate community.

Mary Ellen is aware that she cannot work this magic alone, that it takes a caring classroom community to make possible such miracles. Another incident featuring Brian makes this clear. One day, as his reading group is silently rereading a section of their novel, Brian becomes agitated by a tear in his copy of the book. After a short period of this barely noticeable, but intense, agitation, his neighbor reaches over and quietly trades books.

Because Brian is a student who is considered both at risk, and a risk, he is a useful indicator of the condition of the classroom. Consider a third vignette featuring Brian. One day in November, the class is working on different projects, one of which is a worksheet follow-up to their reading of the illustrated book the story of *Ruby Bridges* (Coles, 1995). The worksheet contains the following prompts:

- "What does *discrimination* mean?"
- "Can you think of ways that you can help fight discrimination?"
- "Why was it important for Ruby Bridges to continue to attend the school?"
- "How do you think you would feel if you were Ruby Bridges? Explain."
- "Describe Ruby using character traits. Back up your character traits from the article."

Each student is supposed to complete this sheet, but as she passes by, Mary Ellen notices that the two are collaborating and that one of the boys' sheets is empty and the other's is complete. Mary Ellen's response is instructive. She comments, "I see you guys finished. Wow! But your sheet's got nothing on it, Brian."

His neighbor says, "He was thinking. He has good ideas."

Mary Ellen replies, "Oh, I know he has good ideas. He's a good thinker." She leaves it at that and moves on. This vignette is typical in several ways. First, Mary Ellen responds first to what is going well. Second, the other student is supportive. Third, Mary Ellen has analyzed what she wants to accomplish with the worksheet. She wants these issues to be thought through before class discussion and realizes that this has occurred. Fourth, she knows the students well and knows when to push and when to leave as is. The attributes embedded in these responses contribute to the development of strong and caring communities in and out of school.

Brian is not a unique case in Mary Ellen's class. In fact, because of her ability to normalize such students, she is routinely assigned them. She requests the same aide, Barbara, who is free to work with other students and small groups—at which, through Mary Ellen's training, she has become very effective.

But Mary Ellen has her holdouts, too. Diamond, another classified student, has refused to do her homework all year; she is not taking her Ritalin and is very stubborn. She has had lunch detention every day. One day, Mary Ellen had her do the next day's homework in advance, leaving a tiny bit for home, which Diamond still didn't do. The next day, Mary Ellen finally explains that at her house, kids know there are consequences to their actions. There must be consequences in class, too. For the first time ever, she tells Diamond, she will have to exclude a student from a field trip. Miserable, she comments honestly that, "It makes me feel like a failure, a rotten teacher."

DIAMOND: Why?

MARY ELLEN: Because I just can't reach you.

The next day Diamond reports to Mary Ellen that she has come up with a plan for doing her homework that involves six other girls in the class who have included her in their lunchtime basketball game. At night she is to call these girls to tell them what she has done or what problems she is encountering. Mary Ellen is ecstatic. "You're a genius!" She exclaims to Diamond. "Did you come up with this? I've got to have all these kids again next year. They're team players. Great attitude, Diamond. You're so smart. How come I didn't think of that?"

The alchemy of Mary Ellen's classroom is grounded in several core values, or principles, which she consistently implements:

- Build, and insist upon, a caring and respectful literate community.
- Interact with students in ways that help them build productive narratives about their literate lives.

- Build an epistemology that includes a respect for, and interest in, learning.
- Arrange for interesting, challenging, and *accessible* literate activities.
- Model everything.

## CARING, RESPECTFUL COMMUNITY

There are numerous, often subtle, ways in which Mary Ellen goes about building her learning community. She makes it clear that in life, in general, and in this class, in particular, they should expect to struggle, but that struggle is easier with company, and that they should expect to have fun. Her open question at the end of one day is, "Is anything bothering anyone? Life just gets harder so you should have fun here. I'm here to be your helper." She actively fosters collaboration and caring, and her ground rules for the class are shaped by respect, responsibility, fairness, and justice.

### Collaboration

Working collaboratively is a fundamental characteristic of Mary Ellen's classroom. She observes, "I think it's very important that children learn to work in groups and talk to one another and to give and take, and to share ideas—and know that, if you're right, other people can be right also." In rehearsing a song they have written to perform for the other fourth graders, Mary Ellen exhorts, "Come on John, we need your help. Excellent. You have a great voice. . . . Most people were right on target, and your voice helps your neighbors. We're going before all the fourth graders . . . and we want them to get our message and also see that we work together and have a good time learning . . . " She pauses, and the kids know to fill in the word *together*. She regularly structures group work around reading and research.

### Caring

Lining up for lunch break, Mary Ellen asks her students, "Does anyone have any compliments?" Used to being asked this question, nine students' hands shoot up. Jean points out that Beth has been working hard. Mary Ellen agrees and there is applause—then three more compliments. "See how kind you can be," she says. "Remember, we're a team." The compliments are often little things, but they make the students stand taller. They have learned which students, in particular, need compliments, and they know who is working on improving which aspect of his or her behavior—because that, too, is a normal part of classroom conversation. When a student returning from the library comments that he did not find what he needed but that he did get a good book for another student whose project he is familiar with, it comes as no surprise. The students have been socialized to attend to the collective needs of their intellectual community. They have a beginning idea that, to the extent that they can improve the intellectual community in which they live, they also stand to improve their own intellectual possibilities.

Her students have also developed an expanded social imagination and are aware of other's feelings. In helping children think through their disagreements and misbehaviors with one another, she draws their attention to the other student's feelings. But she also consistently fosters this social imagination and empathy as part of her literacy instruction, pointing out audience and character in their writing and reading. For example, when reading about Ruby Bridges' first day at school, she stops and asks, "What is she feeling? I want everyone's hand up." Then she goes around the room, exploring the range of contributions offered. "What do we know about what kind of person Ruby is?" she asks, drawing their attention to character traits.

These kinds of discussion are a common part of her literate conversations that, at once, develop comprehension and community by eliciting answers to questions such as, "What would you feel if you were in this position?" "What's another feeling?" "Keep your mind on the character's feelings." Her consistent modeling and fostering of social awareness and empathy create an environment in which students learn to care about each other and about others in the world— and, in the process, she fosters an important social value. When they take a few moments to rehearse a new song, she comments, "For me, the key word in this [song] is *tolerance*." Although there is only one minority student in the class, an African American boy, these children read a great deal of multicultural literature as part of Mary Ellen's efforts to inspire not just tolerance but an appreciation for others' cultures and experiences.

## Fairness, Trust, and Justice

Fairness and trust are a constant theme in Mary Ellen's interactions. Comments such as "What would be fair?" and "That was a fair decision" and explicit commitments to live up to her promises are common. Mary Ellen expects her students to be honest, responsible, and fair and to become concerned when things are not fair. The students often mark their own papers, and she simply admonishes them to "be honest." Her students do not want to disappoint her. She engages them in discussions of what would be fair in terms of how they treat each other and in her own interactions with them. For example, she asks, "What would be fair for math homework? There are 28 problems." She does not wish to lose their trust by appearing unfair. After straightening out a problem between two students, leaving one somewhat disgruntled, she concedes to him that "I could be wrong, but I had to make a judgment."

Mary Ellen's concern for fairness and justice also imbues book discussions and research projects (reading *The Story of Ruby Bridges* led to extensive discussions of fairness and justice) and includes learning that what people write and say, in the media and in official documents, is not always accurate or just, and that it must be questioned and sometimes contested. A research project on fair housing raised similar issues and strong feelings.

When a student complains about another cheating in a game, Mary Ellen shows her disappointment and stresses the importance of earning trust. In response to another complaint, she admonishes firmly, "honesty and trust," and sets them going again. One student admits that his mother helped him with his sentences, but they weren't the ones he wanted because they were not his. "Thank you for your honesty," she says.

## Respect

Respect is basic and demands listening. Early in the year Mary Ellen reminds the class, "Now when somebody shares [their writing], it's time to stop everything and respect the person who is sharing." Students give comments on the shared work, and then applaud. The comments include affirmations of what went well and questions about interesting parts and future directions. When one student is about to share and the others are not ready, Mary Ellen tells him to "Wait, wait—and give them that teacher look."

Mary Ellen constantly listens to what the students have to say; from the moment they arrive in her classroom, she wants to hear about their experiences and their opinions. She genuinely finds them interesting. And when she is engrossed in listening to a student, particularly if they are having a conference about reading or writing, she does not brook interruptions. To one student attempting to interrupt, she says, "I don't want to be interrupted in a book talk like that. It would have to be an emergency." To another, she says, "I'm with Beth just now and you can't interrupt. It's not fair." She also "walks her talk." For example, when she asks a student to come for a conference, and he responds, "Can I finish this [writing piece] first?" Mary Ellen simply says, "Fine," and goes to the next person.

She makes it clear that she learns from them and values their interests and what they have to say. For example, giving feedback to students, she says, "Poems come in all sorts—thin, fat, crazy, factual, rhyming. You guys have a lot of excellent poems and I've learned a lot from them." Her students' interests and concerns matter. She asks to be able to read the books they are reading that she has not yet read herself. In doing so, she is able to facilitate productive discussions with them as well as show them that she values their judgment.

Although the bulk of Mary Ellen's comments are positive, she will also offer, in a friendly but persuasive tone, occasional feedback such as, "You forgot something there. I don't want to see carelessness like that today." Or, "It's got to be your best cursive writing. Look at me, Lucy. Your *best* cursive writing." On another occasion, she reminds students to pay particular attention while editing, "If you have an abbreviation . . . [or] capitals . . . no excuses." From Mary Ellen's perspective, respect also entails respecting yourself and doing your best.

This is the sort of approach referred to by Compton-Lilly (2000) as "staying on" students, as she does with Diamond. On one occasion, she reprimands a student for being late to school a second time. Taking aside the student, she talks to her quietly about the problem and then adds, good-naturedly, "I'm late for everything—except school." Such interactions make it clear to her students that they have both the right and responsibility to be in control of their learning narrative. At the same time, she takes a very active hand in shaping the story they tell.

## PERSONAL LEARNING NARRATIVES
## OF AGENCY, RESPONSIBILITY, AND SUCCESS

When Mary Ellen introduces the university researcher to her class, she asks, "And what do you think I told him about you?" The students chorus, "We're the best."

Much of Mary Ellen's classroom talk is directed towards helping students see themselves as personally and academically good—independent and intelligent people who work together as a team and care about and respect one another. When behavior becomes disruptive, she treats it as a brief aberration rather than a reflection of any deeper problem of character or intellect. Mary Ellen's concern for respect extends to self-respect: She expects her students to respect themselves and to take their learning seriously. When asked, "What did you do better today?," a student answers, with little hesitation, "I wrote better and longer sentences." There is little hesitation because this is a normal conversation. Students are expected to pursue goals in their learning; there is no room for slacking off. She gives her students free choice of books but admonishes them to "Choose books that are challenging and interesting, not too easy." Through personal conferences with all her students, she checks to make sure they are doing just that. When they are not, she helps them to think through their next selection and offers more productive options. She does not allow them to "rest on their laurels" or produce less than their best work. On one occasion, after students have shared their current affairs homework, she observed, "Some [are] excellent—some a little shaky. I expect your best work when you do things."

### Success

Part of the trick is getting students to give their all is arranging for success through managing task difficulty. A second part is turning children's attention towards their successes by giving praise about a specific accomplishment and ensuring that responsibility for the achievement is owned. For example, Mary Ellen might say, "I love the way you chose those words—they sound so good together." A third part is finding ways to reinforce the effort it takes to do one's best on a daily basis. For example, when Mary Ellen sees one of her weaker students return from the library with a book for his project and another for a peer, she observes, "You had a good day today."

He responds, "I'm getting better," and Mary Ellen adds "How does it feel to be doing so well?" Drawing his attention to the feelings associated with success helps solidify the external praise into internal feelings.

These features avoid the problem of hollow praise that plagues some classrooms (Brophy, 1997). Indeed, there are many ways in which Mary Ellen conveys praise without giving it directly. For example, when reading a child's writing, she spontaneously asks her to read it out loud to the class and calls for students' attention. The focused feedback the child receives makes the praise specific.

Mary Ellen emphasizes engagement and accomplishment not comparative ability. Her focus is on *agency*—the belief that one possesses the ability to solve problems and get things done. She values all attempts and draws attention to what went well, and why it went well, particularly which parts of unsuccessful attempts were productive— "noticing the partially correct" (Clay, 1993). In this way, students become aware of their successful (or almost successful) efforts. They are invited to think of themselves as strategists, and the specific strategic behaviors are brought under their conscious control.

## Agency

In Mary Ellen's classroom certain kinds of learning narratives are fostered. She insists that children take an active protagonist role. They expect to encounter, even seek out, problems and challenges, and they expect to solve them, even though it might take some time.

MARY ELLEN: What's the hard part of research, Brian?

BRIAN: Well, I don't have much facts yet.

MARY ELLEN: Well, the facts come slow. Rachel, could you tell everyone how long it took you to write this poem?

RACHEL: About 2 hours.

MARY ELLEN: And then she reworked it again and again.

Several aspects of classroom talk foster productive narratives. To begin with, everyone is expected to be working on problems—including social ones such as behavioral self-management, in which case Mary Ellen helps the student set productive short-term goals, and others, made aware of these goals, are expected to assist.

One of the most important features of Mary Ellen's classroom is the process-oriented talk that becomes part and parcel of the students' way of thinking and behaving. For example, Mary Ellen frequently asks, "How did you do that? How could you figure that out? How else? Has anyone else had that sort of problem? How did you solve it?" This kind of wording normalizes the expectation of encountering problems *and* of solving them, possibly using multiple strategies, and reveals the strategies available. Other related comments include: "Good decision," "What's the next step?," and "Do what works for you."

When students face a temporarily unsolvable problem, they are encouraged to seek support. For example, when a student is asked a question in a whole-class session and cannot answer it, even with sufficient wait-time, Mary Ellen throws it open by asking, "Can anyone help?" This does not take the problem away, but it does place it in a collaborative context.

Mary Ellen deliberately offers possible identities for students to try on, so to speak. These identities are ones that are likely to sustain longer-term action. For example, she offers comments such as the following:

> "I came in this morning and saw [your painting] and thought, 'Wow! What an artist.' "
> "Oh, boy. You're getting a lot of information. You're a great researcher."
> "You are such a wonderful little writer."
> "Oh, wow, that was wonderful. Ben, I think you are a very gifted young man to write such poems."

Mary Ellen routinely takes aside individual students to give compliments as well as remonstrations. For example, after one student gives compliments to two peers, Mary Ellen quietly says what a great job he did and observes, "That's the kind of character traits I look for." *Good* behaviors are attributed to character traits—stable features of personality; *poor* behaviors are attributed to momentary lapses in judgment—errors and aberrations. Another student asks to share a piece of writing. It is a letter to a classmate that includes an apology for calling names. The other student responds with "apology accepted." Mary Ellen casts this interaction as a matter of correcting an error and highlights the importance of correcting such errors. An *error* means that the problem is temporary and does not represent normal behavior or feelings.

Several additional features make these productive narratives possible. One is the engagingness and relative difficulty of the activity. A second is that in this classroom, children are not focused on the issue of who is better, but on how they can solve a problem or improve some idea or product. So strong is this orientation, in fact, that, when asked who were the good writers in the class, the student simply declined to make such a judgment, pointing out that it was not a productive line of conversation.

A third important feature is the range of literate pursuits available; students are always in the process of developing a variety of interesting areas of expertise through their reading and writing. They have choices regarding research topics, and Mary Ellen often invites them to take on additional projects in areas of interest. For example, picking up on a loose end in a discussion of Ben Franklin's biography, Mary Ellen asks, "Anyone want to investigate lightning rods and inform us? . . . Okay, Rachel."

Mary Ellen extends the students' development of productive narratives that maintain a sense of agency to include the children's views of themselves as knowers—their epistemologies.

## PRODUCTIVE EPISTEMOLOGIES

For Mary Ellen, complex and controversial issues are the most interesting, and she views her role as helping to expand children's independent and interdependent thinking:

> "If it's an answer that isn't black and white . . . first of all, I ask them if they can research it. . . . Many times I'll say 'I really don't know. I have no idea. Let's find out.' Because I really *don't* know, and you know what? I'm interested to find out myself . . . and I think it's good for them to see that."

In keeping with this stance, she encourages—indeed requires—children to use multiple and potentially conflicting sources of information and to collaborate in the process. She makes comments such as, "Okay, let's list the places where your sources disagree, and we'll look for confirmation." In her teaching she emphasizes the process as much as the knowledge that is the product. She asks, "Okay, how did everyone do with their research?" There are lots of affirmations and some qualifying comments. She inserts, "You know what? Ryan had an interesting thought here. This is a middle-of-his-life book [no information about childhood or later years]. Rebecca, tell us about yours. What was difficult? Okay, you read and forget and have to re-read." She would often pursue the *how* questions further.

Mary Ellen feels that multiple perspectives on an issue are particularly important. Consequently, authority is distributed across the classroom. Each person's experience and expertise is valued as an important, and potentially enlightening, piece of the puzzle. But authority brings with it responsibility—the need to provide warrants for one's position. Consequently, Mary Ellen would ask questions like, "Do you know for sure J is faster than K? How can you be sure?" In response to the student's assertion she inquires, "Why do you think that?" When other students start to offer suggestions, she interjects, "Give him time," insisting on a thoughtful response rather than an immediate answer. Her questions extend to book preferences. "Who's your favorite character? Why?" Or, "You said you love the book, but *why?*"

KAITLYN: It's really good.

MARY ELLEN: Why? You have to have some reason.

KAITLYN: It's interesting.. (*Mary Ellen presses further.*) It's historical and has lots of details. . . .

## ENGAGING AND ACCESSIBLE ACTIVITIES

Mary Ellen has a passion for children's literature. She started the teachers' book club when she couldn't get into her local one because she couldn't guarantee her presence at every meeting because of her teaching and family life. "I'm really an avid reader. I mean, I have to read every day. I have to have a book going or I feel like . . . I'm missing something. I love books. I love literature." Recommending a book to a student, she comments, "You've got a good sense of humor. You'll enjoy [this book]." Or, "I know you're interested in mysteries, and I've got that Barbara Park book."

Through her read-alouds, personal recommendations, and discussions, she infects her students with the same avidity. Her view of literature and its value in the classroom is also important:

> "I think that's what's great about literature. . . . Everybody reads the same thing and gets something different. Tara . . . got so much out of *Miss Rumphius* because she was studying Rachel Carson. Now she never would have related to that book unless she had had that experience. . . . she just loved it . . . and she reread it over and over again. . . . You know, she's a very poor reader. So I think if you just keep trying new things with the children, fiction and nonfiction. . . . I mean, it really makes it all a lot more fun for me, and I feel like I've accomplished more myself."

Although she argues that everyone can read the same thing and get something different, it is uncommon for her to have everyone read the same thing. She does not ask comprehension questions to ensure that everyone got the same meaning; rather, she engages students, individually and collectively, in discussions about books. For example, in listening to a student recount a new book, Mary Ellen puzzles, "Now I'm a little confused. He seems to have changed his mind. Why do you think he would change his mind? . . . "

The students read a wide range of books appropriate to their current competence. Studying character traits, for example, can be done across a wide range of books. On the wall is a list of character traits students have generated from their books and discussions. Mary Ellen stresses *character traits* as a way to help them connect their reading with their own experience of, for example, feelings of pride, and she connects it to their writing by asking them to write about themselves, who they are and what they take pride in doing. Furthermore, she argues that, to understand plot, you need to understand character traits.

Her philosophy on literature also informs her grouping practices, which are flexible:

> "I go from groups to independent books. You know, right now I probably have half of the kids in two groups and the rest of them are . . . independently reading books of their own

choice. . . . Now, these kids that are in the groups, the groups are made for particular reasons [including common interests, curricular projects, and student needs]."

There are six or seven core books (sets) she can choose from, some connected to social studies. But, she points out, "I don't like to do the same books every year because then I find I get stale."

Although children's literature, both illustrated and nonillustrated, holds a prominent place in the classroom and is carefully displayed to attract passing eyes, children's individual research projects are also emphasized, which involve them in reading nonfiction and doing library research. Over the course of the year the children write in a wide range of genres, from research reports, to poetry of various kinds, to letters, book reports, and a variety of narratives.

In addition to her own enthusiasm, recommendations, and read-alouds, Mary Ellen uses students' work to make reading contagious. She routinely has students sign up for oral book reports, shows them how to give them, and afterwards asks of the class, "Who else would like that book?" In response to this question, students give astute recommendations, taking into account the other students' levels of reading ability. Although students are well aware of each others' relative competence, this is the only time at which such evaluations are relevant.

## STRUCTURE

Part of what makes the class run smoothly is the organizational and interpersonal structure of the classroom. Mary Ellen's desk is in the corner, piled with incidentals. She spends no time at it. She spends most of the day working with small groups at the conference table, organizing class discussions, teaching the class, or roaming the room offering encouraging remarks, and holding individual conferences with the students. When in brief conferences with students about their reading or writing, she gets down to their height, eye-to-eye. She also constantly makes connections among students. For example, "Sonny, Alice has two sentences I'm going to have her read to you because they're kind of funny." Alice does so, quietly, and Sonny laughs.

The day's schedule is clearly written on the board, and the class normally sticks to the schedule fairly closely. Each day has its routines and rituals—the morning warm-ups (10 minutes of fast-paced math practice problems), the compliments, snack time, and so forth. But given the caring and personal nature of the classroom, the pace of the work and the speed of transition from one task to the next are surprising. For example, bringing their research project time to an end, Mary Ellen announces, "Ladies and gentlemen, you only have 4 minutes left. Use your time wisely." After the 4 minutes, she asks, "What did you learn about today?" Kate tells about the spine, nails, traction, and speed of cheetahs. Angela explains, with prompting, about leopards. Brad describes, with occasional prompting, how bats use echo location to catch food. Jake comments about movie sound effects. Mary Ellen leans on Justine for "one more fact."

There are, of course, exceptions to the careful scheduling. For example, Mary Ellen might notice that their energy is flagging on a hot afternoon and shift gears to a different activity, or realize that an interesting, teachable moment can be captured; or another teacher may need the class to serve as an audience. And she has priorities that can change the schedule. For example, when the reading teacher came to get some students during their discussion of *The Story of Ruby Bridges*, Mary Ellen would not let them go until the discussion had ended.

## MODELING

Mary Ellen offers herself as a role model for the students' developing narratives through all of her literate interactions and in her presentation of herself as a learner. She expects students to interact and behave in particular ways, and she herself lives those expectations. She makes it clear that she loves books and has specific favorite authors. For example, she comments to Ben, "Oh, this is a great one. Ken Follett wrote that. He also wrote *Eye of the Needle*, which is one of my favorites." She makes it clear that she is involved in book discussions outside of class: "I went to a book discussion group yesterday with other teachers. Some of them really liked the book and others didn't especially." And there is no mistaking her love of learning: "I hate to close the research [time] because I really like it." It is an example that is easy for them to follow because of her constant invitations and enthusiasm. For example, part of their homework one night was "to look at the moon, observe it, describe it." Mary Ellen also did the assignment, and the next day there was an interesting discussion about what was seen about the process of observing.

She commonly models (1) what she is thinking when reading or doing shared writing, (2) her decision making while teaching, and (3) her theorizing about science or social studies matters. She also uses the students as models. For example, when the students are in the process of writing biographies, Mary Ellen asks one of them to describe how she has proceeded so far. The others then offered feedback on her current product.

Mary Ellen's modeling is consistent in the way she treats others. Just as she expects students to be responsible, she takes her own responsibilities very seriously, as her interaction with Diamond indicates. At no point does Mary Ellen blame parents for a student's poor performance. In one interview she described how the mother of her lowest-achieving student had cried during a conference, saying, "I don't know what to do. I'm a terrible mother." Mary Ellen's responded much like she would respond to a student: "No, you're not a terrible mother. You just don't know what to do. I know what it is to have kids, and have somebody sick and have a commitment." She believes that "helping parents, not trying to criticize but to *help* them" is important—important enough to give up another lunch break because the mother's work hours prevent her from coming at another time.

Mary Ellen's classroom normally runs very smoothly and that all of the children appear to be naturally responsible, caring learners— which she often asserts they are. These children are from a working-class neighborhood, and over a third of them receive free or reduced-price lunches. Management, however, is not a problem in Mary Ellen's class, for several reasons: She sets engaging and manageable classroom activities, in the context of which she arranges for students to manage themselves. This situation allows her to highlight their success frequently, which also means that they are rarely in the position of having to do something to save face. She personalizes her instruction through brief academic and nonacademic interactions with individual students several times each day. She knows them well enough to recommend books, to know when to push and to back off, when to answer a question and when they can figure it out themselves, and to recognize problems that need to be solved. This personal knowledge, together with her fairness, gives her credibility with her students. They trust her. Importantly, they also care for, and trust each other, which makes it possible for children who, in other places, appear abnormal, to appear, and become, normal.

This complexity, made to appear so simple, is extremely difficult to address in research on teaching and teacher education. And it never stops evolving. Each year Mary Ellen changes the ways she does things—different students, new challenges, more planning, new ideas. She is, like her students, constantly a work in progress.

# 8

## "I Want Students Who Are Thinkers"

PETER H. JOHNSTON
TRACEY BENNETT
JOHN CRONIN

Tracey Bennett is an African American teacher who teaches in a sub-urban K–grade 5, with 498 students, very few of whom are poor (2.3% free and reduced-price lunch) or minority (14%). She teaches in a multiage classroom in which she is responsible for 24 children (11 fourth graders and 13 third graders), 16 boys and 8 girls. Three students are minorities, two African American and one Asian American. The adjoining multiage grades 3–4 class is taught by her friend and colleague, Kathy. Tracey places a very high value on their collaborative teaching, scheduling, lesson planning, and conferencing on portfolio-style assessments. They share a great deal philosophically, and their frequent, reflective discussions at the end of the day lead to mutual growth and improvement, even though on some points they "agree to disagree." Their relationship is such that neither would want to team with anyone else, if given a choice.

Tracey has been teaching for 8 years and is always trying to improve her practice. She points out that the district provides many opportunities for in-services, and there are various teacher get-togethers; "I love going to workshops. . . . The district supports us on that. We work in a very, very supportive district where colleagues share information with you. . . . I read *Language Arts* and I read *Reading Teacher.*" These educational experiences lead to regular changes in her teaching methods. She explains:

"What's different this year is that we've used the writer's notebook more to play with words. . . . And Anne [one of the students] has taken topics that she wrote about last year, and she's doing what I do in my writer's notebook. I write about the same topic all the time—different genre, different craft, different way of presenting the structure—but the topic's often the same. She is doing that now, and you can just see her growth as a writer, pulling in different crafts that she's willing to try."

Tracey regularly uses reflective writing for her own benefit. She keeps a journal in which she writes down lines she reads and likes, things she hears her daughter say, and so forth. She also reads a range of books and shares her reading with her students. Her favorite part of the curriculum is "reading and writing, but I like teaching the other areas because you get to see the whole kid."

Tracey and her co-teacher encourage extensive communication with parents. In addition to what parents learn at the well-attended parent conferences and initial parent–teacher night, they send out a substantial amount of information at the beginning of the year explaining the nature of their program and their expectations. The materials include a conference planning guide to make sure parents communicate important information. For example, one entry prompts: "What you should know about my child: as a learner, as a participant in and out of school activities, and as a family member"; in addition, parents are asked to identify particular goals for their child that educational year, and what they are intending to do to help. Other sections contain responses to frequently asked questions about their multiage class, their rubric for grading homework, and unique curriculum features of their district. They also hold monthly morning teas with parents in one of their specials periods. Though the attendance rate at these meetings varies, their availability makes it possible for a number of the parents to remain up to date on what is happening with their children, as individuals, and in the classroom as a whole. In these sessions they also explain some of the logic of their teaching and the basics of children's academic development. The school's mission statement, which they also give to parents, is also their mission statement. Supporting spokes of the "learning never ends" and "everyone can learn" wheel include the following:

> . . . when diversity is expected and valued, when curiosity and reflective thinking flourish, when trust and respect support the community, when play and humor weave through the learning environment, when problems are solved together, when self-confidence and self-esteem are nurtured, and when high expectations lead learning.

In her classroom, Tracey fosters children's participation in the construction of knowledge by encouraging them to grapple with complex issues that include conflicting perspectives and sources of information. She views her role as one of helping them to become independent and interdependent thinkers:

> "I want kids who are thinkers. I don't want kids who are going to wait to be told every step to make. I want you to know what to do when you don't know what to do. . . . These are all the possibilities; Which one makes more sense to do at what particular time?"

She wants students who will "question every single thing" they read and hear and see going on in the world. The classroom is not quiet. She believes that learning is fundamentally social, so she values the conversations that take place in her classroom. Tracey feels that "as long as they're talking about what we're talking about, that's fine."

Students' personal experiences are important to Tracey and she wants them to recognize the relevance of their learning to their daily lives. For example, in studying Martin Luther King, Jr., Tracey notes that they have all this information about how he changed America and then challenges them, "How will you change today? What effect did this man's life have on yours?" Her question prompts one boy's observation that his doorbell wouldn't ring each morning—which is when his African American neighbor comes over to play. Another observes that Tracey probably would not be their teacher. These comments spark a discussion of *The Story of Ruby Bridges* (Coles, 1995) which includes imagining themselves in different roles in the book—as the parents, the National Guard, and the students walking the alley between them. Tracey notes, "I try to make it relevant to real-life experiences, so that you understand that there's a purpose for learning." Authority for knowledge construction is thus distributed throughout the classroom because children's experience is valued. The classroom is distinctly dialogical. She encourages students to expect and to value multiple perspectives, and she arranges for them to be encountered.

Tracey also values inquiry and often begins project work using a wide range of materials that generate numerous questions from the students—a list of which provides a place for students to make decisions about which threads to follow as individuals and as a class. Children then begin their research; throughout the process Tracey helps them to examine, evaluate, and rethink their research strategies. For example, having begun their research on Martin Luther King, Jr., they went to the library to gather material but found themselves overwhelmed by the volume of questions they had raised as a class. They took a step back to gain perspective and realized that sometimes the information they located, though not relevant to their own questions, was important for another student's work.

Although Tracey's view of teaching is clearly constructivist, there is a touch of Baptist preacher in her classroom presence—a legacy from her grandfather—which she occasionally announces with "All right, I have to start preachin' here." The children, aware of this part of her, eagerly chant, "preach, preach, preach." Tracey is firm and holds high expectations but is, at the same time, playful.

## A STUDENT VIEW

One way to get a feel for Tracey's classroom is to interview the students. Let us introduce Megan, an average reader and writer in her class and, from our interviews, a fairly typical respondent. Asked to describe herself as a reader, she says:

> "You get to go somewhere else and it's like, if I was reading in my bed, I wouldn't feel like I was in my bed anymore because I felt like I was in the story. I'm not that fast at reading, but I'm good at it, though. And I like to read, too."

Asked whether there are different kinds of readers in the class, she makes no mention of relative ability. Instead, she notes:

"Some kids in my class only read a certain kind of genre or a certain kind of book. [She gives examples.] There's a kid in my class, she likes to read picture books, 'cause I sat next to her and she always had a picture book that she was reading. . . . She also read chapter books, but not as much. . . . Other kids in my class, they like to read science fiction books . . . [and] other kids like to read books that are funny and make you laugh."

If she wanted to find out about another person as a reader, she would ask what kinds of books they like and whether they have any favorite books "because then maybe we would have something in common." Indeed, Megan regularly recommends books to her friends. Aside from books like *Charlotte's Web* (White, 1974), she and her friends

" . . . like mysteries. . . . We also read a lot of sequels from other books that we read. Like, we read the book *Shiloh* [Naylor, 2000] in a literature group and then we found out there was a sequel called *Shiloh's Season* [Naylor, 1999]. And then another sequel called *Saving Shiloh* [Naylor, 1999]. So Anna, she read *Shiloh's Season* and she recommended it to me, so now I'm reading it. And she's reading . . . for her personal choice book, she's reading *Saving Shiloh*. And I'm probably going to read that one next."

She has favorite authors. For example, "I like Roald Dahl, who wrote . . . *Charlie and the Chocolate Factory* and *James and the Giant Peach*." Megan likes to participate in the literature discussions, though she prefers not to actually start off the discussion, and she is not afraid to disagree with classmates' views.

Asked if there are any good authors in her class, she answers, "I think that all the kids in my class are good writers." Does she enjoy any one in particular?

"I like reading most of Martha's work, 'cause she was a new student in the class, but she writes mostly, like in her books, she uses people's names that she knows already. And she makes them act really funny and weird and stuff. . . . I like Priscilla's also because, like, she writes, like, mostly about gymnastics. And she writes . . . and she wrote about her mother once. And she writes mostly about things that happen to her, like her life and stuff. I also like that 'cause . . . I get to know more about her. And I get to know her also, better."

She herself likes "to write almost any kind of writing . . . because you get to express yourself and you get to write down what you're feeling." And she writes a lot. Declining to choose her "best" piece of writing, she states that all of her writing is good because she revises it until it is good. For example, she didn't like her first version of a biography: "It wasn't that good. So I changed it, and now it's, like, it's the same information, but it's a lot different and it's better." In particular, it has "a better beginning that would really want somebody to keep on reading." She will concede, however, a current favorite piece, a poem that she began in her writer's notebook: "I had some of it already in my mind and I was writing it down. But I added more to it as I was writing it because my ideas just went through my head." Then she took some lines out and added new ones. Then she wrote it two different ways. She likes it because "it makes me think that anything's possible." She got the idea from a book of poetry that a classmate shared with her. She thinks it is different from her other poetry because "my [other] poetry that I've published are, like, funnier. They are not really serious." Indeed, as a writer, her most recent new learning is "how to write different kinds of poems. Like, at first I only wrote poems . . . like poems, but they weren't like a certain type of genre, poem, like a limerick or something." She demonstrates, pulling three different genres of poetry from her folder. In other writing, as in her reading, she has crafted sequels, one in collaboration with two of her classmates. She also has done research, particularly as part of social studies, where it is often collaborative research. If in the course of her research she comes across conflicting sources of information, she resolves the problem by writing down both: "I would say in my report, like, some people think that this does that and other people think this."

Megan's views of literacy and of herself as a reader and writer are important achievements in themselves (see Chapter 10) but also because they reflect a classroom environment in which there is more than one teacher. Children's peers are teachers, too. This is a classroom in which students expect to work collaboratively and to manage their own learning, where they respond directly to each other rather than through the teacher. So let us look at this classroom in which Megan is becoming literate.

## THE VISUAL ENVIRONMENT

Books representing a range of genres, cultures, and levels of difficulty are prominently and accessibly displayed throughout the classroom, and there is comfortable space available to read them. The wall is also used to display the students' published work, such as their Martin Luther King, Jr., projects. The message: Students' work is clearly valued. In addition, posters provide guidance, rubrics, and inspiration. For example, one poster proclaims: "You are not finished when you lose. You are finished when you quit." Another proposes: "Recipe for success! Responsibility, diversity, compassion, cooperation, respect, honesty." Photographs and names of African American leaders occupy a substantial area. The "Reading expectations" list (Figure 8.1., which was included in the material sent home to parents) is a year-round staple.

Tracey shows considerable interest in words and people's choices among them, particularly those of authors. She encourages students to play scrabble, and some do so at lunchtime. On the wall, the "Word soup" list contains *scarcity, discrimination, empathy, philosophy, aerobic, racism, stomach,* and *Caucasian.* Tracey makes sure that words of interest come up by liberally using more advanced words phrases such as "strictly optional, not mandatory." A "Scientifically speaking" list provides the words *powder, crystal, mixture, suspension, solution, variable, translucent, acid, base, pH, interac-*

---

- We are always prepared with a book to read, log, folder, pencil, book.
- When we read independently we record our responses on the reading log.
- Each book that we read is recorded on the (yellow) record sheet.
- During reading time our room is *quiet.*
- We may not leave the room during reading time (bathroom, drink, etc., except in emergencies).
- When we are done with a book we will refer to our fishbowl list for questions to respond to. Our response will go in our reading journal.
- We will be prepared with our reading assignments when they are given.
- Before we abandon a book we will discuss it with Mrs. Bennett.

Another chart provides "Punctuation rules everybody needs," and "Birthday wishes" is decked with cupcakes inscribed with students' names by month.

**FIGURE 8.1.** Reading expectations.

*tion, reaction,* and *physical change.* She uses word sorts and word finds as part of her spelling program.

## CORNERSTONES OF CLASSROOM COMMUNITY

There are four cornerstones to Tracey's creation of a classroom community. The first of these is respect. She notes that "I've got to create a community where it works for all of us, where we all compromise but, at the same time, we all feel like we are respected. We all feel that we are valued. That's *my* job." Her use of *I, my,* and *I chose* shows her strong sense of responsibility:

> "It is my job to create a safe atmosphere for my classroom, and that means not getting into a confrontation. I can say I have respected every kid in my class. I'm a parent, and I know I want to make sure my daughter's teachers . . . have ultimate respect for my daughter, so . . . keeping that in mind, I would never disrespect the kids. And the bottom line is: I respect you; you respect me. I have to earn that respect . . . showing you that I respect you first."

At the beginning of the year she selects Mildred Taylor books for the class which, she points out,

> "are very controversial. . . . They talk a lot about injustices and how people are treated, they provide one way to establish community in a classroom. That's why I chose those books at that particular time. . . . Then we started talking about what's fair and what's equal, and the respect that they have for one another, and understanding that there are going to be differences of opinion but we respect them, as long as we can justify them with specific examples from the literature."

A second cornerstone of her classroom community is teaching students to take responsibility for their own management. Her students are constantly involved in the decision making—the governance—of the classroom. They make plans and later "reflect . . . [on] what's working and what's not [and] what we can do to change those things that are not working." (Note the use of the pronoun *we*.) For example, when planning a party, Tracey asks, "How would you like to go about doing this?" and writes down their responses. She asks them to be aware of what they are trying to accomplish and offers, "How can I help you? Let's come up with a plan." She helps them plan their time management, both in the classroom and with regard to their homework. She says, "I keep telling parents that, as a parent, it is so easy for us to do things for kids, because it gets done quicker, but what message are we sending them? I'm really trying to create independent thinkers." She helps her students obtain the information they need to plan. For example, she makes sure they know the time frame in which they are supposed to accomplish each task: "Friends, you have 15 minutes to get this done." They are also encouraged to internalize useful criteria. For example, she asks, "Friends, what will it look like and sound like when you're ready?"

Children in Tracey's class are constantly being encouraged to take control of their own learning, to manage their learning lives. Students participate in generating the rules by which they live in the classroom and even the rubrics by which their work will be judged. Tracey is persistent in her efforts to impart a sense of agency and identity in her students by repeatedly reminding them that they are in control of their learning and their behavior, not just as students but as *scientists* and as *authors*. She often asks them to consider the books they read and their own writing in terms of the authors' and their own intentions. They are urged to act and to think about the implications of their actions, both for themselves and for others. Consequently, along with the agency that she espouses comes responsibility for behavior and choices. Her approach to helping children plan and think through the consequences of their actions extends to individual problem solving with children who are experiencing social problems.

A third cornerstone of her classroom community building is her knowledge of individual children. Tracey goes out of her way to give an individualized personal greeting to each student entering the classroom in the morning. She takes a few moments to listen to each child's personal news, to convey her caring, and to mark his or her entry to the classroom community.

When conflicts arise, she takes the time to work through the problem rather than solving it by edict. After one such occurrence, she explains:

"It took us 15 minutes to have that discussion but we needed to . . . because the other person wasn't aware of what our intentions were. Feelings are hurt and if you don't deal with them, the child walks away being angry, and I don't want that to happen. [Instead I say something like] 'It wasn't your intention to hurt his feelings, but you were angry. I'm just trying to get you to understand why he would respond the way he did and why you would respond the way you did. . . . I don't want to invalidate how you are feeling . . . just understand why you are feeling the way you do. . . . then we'll all have a better understanding of one another.' "

The understanding among students that Tracey fosters is distinctly related to her teaching of reading and writing, where she wants children to imagine authors' and characters' intentions and audiences' reactions. It is also associated with her interest in building problem-solving independence. For example, three girls were struggling with a disagreement, and Tracey's response was:

"I need three things from you girls . . . you need to talk about what's going on. That is the first thing. Two, I need to know, do I need to change any seats because you are sitting next to each other? And the third thing I want to know, I want to know what are your future plans so we don't have to deal with this again? I'm going to check my mailbox and I'll come back after five minutes."

When she returned, they said that they needed more time, and got it, after which it was down to two students with whom Tracey took up the discussion to help them solve the problem.

A fourth cornerstone of Tracey's classroom community building is arranging for students to have choices in, and ownership of, many of the things they do in class: in particular, project topics, writing topics, and reading books. However, she is well aware that the ability to choose productively is a learned skill, so she takes steps to expand the options from which they will choose. For example, she points out:

"The kids just have an incredibly broad spectrum of reading. But that's also because I try to do that too. In my literature groups, I

expose them to books that I don't think they would normally
pick up on their own; for example, books that have dialect in
them—that Southern dialect, which is my favorite—it reminds
me of my grandmother. And to be able to read that is challenging, because the makeup of my classroom—a lot of them have
not had that experience. But because they get [the message] from
me that 'I'm going to help you do this,' and knowing that they
can make it through, they're now picking up books that contain
dialect, they're now looking at their writing . . . and saying, 'You
know what, I want to write a book like that.' "

She also teaches productive choosing in a direct way. For example,
she tells the class, "Before you put a book back because you didn't
like it, let me know so I can give you some direction to help you find
a book that you'll get something from."


## GROUPING


In general, the students are seated in groups in the classroom, organized so that positive role models for learning will be accessible to
all. Tracey groups the students for reading and writing in several different ways. In book club groups the children choose their own
books and decide on a common way to share them. Students in literature groups read the same book. Both are commonly heterogeneous.
Students take turns leading the group and selecting the assignment
for the day. Tracey also has the class participate in a program of
reading buddies with one of the kindergarten classes, which provides
an opportunity for the least capable readers in her classroom to be
particularly successful. Writer's notebook groups are selected in several different ways to ensure diversity. Sometimes the assignment is
random, sometimes students select the groups, sometimes two third
graders and two fourth graders are put together. Sometimes, when
the students pair up to learn, Tracey asks how they expect to be
learning from this particular person, for example, as a writer. After
group work Tracey sometimes asks, "I want you to tell me how
[group discussion] went." Each group reviews the process with
prompts from Tracey, such as, "What went well?" and "What kinds
of questions [were raised]?"

Tracey's purpose for literature groups is different from her purpose for personal choice books.

"My purpose in a literature group is to take part in discussion. And so I need to make all kinds of arrangements for that kid, so that at least he has gotten the reading done, [even if] that means I have to get the book on tape, I have to tape it myself, or somebody has to read it to him. Then they form their own interpretations because I want them to know that I value their opinions. But their personal choice book shouldn't be something that they're struggling [with]. It should be for their own enjoyment, but they should be able to talk to me about what you're reading."

Students use Post-its to mark their comments in their personal reading books; these comments are the foundation for later group discussions.

Tracey facilitates small-group discussions around a common trade book the group is reading mostly silently. Sometimes students will read aloud favorite parts of the book, or read with a partner before the group discussion. Tracey is aware of those students in her room who struggle with reading. At one point in the year, she "invites" these students to join a group whose text is less difficult, and they appear to feel privileged by the invitation. The remaining third and fourth graders elect to participate in one of two literature groups, one of which is facilitated by a reading specialist who comes into the classroom at these times. On other occasions Tracey and the reading teacher switch roles. Some children elect to be in neither literature group, and it is acceptable for those with invitations to a certain group to refuse. A third option students have is to participate in book clubs (McMahon, Raphael, Goatley, & Pardo, 1997). The students in the book club read books they have personally selected on any topic, with the stipulation that they choose particular genres when the whole class is working on them. These groups are entirely student-facilitated once they become comfortable with conducting conversations around reading and writing—something Tracey demonstrates and shapes all year and gives examples of past students' practices. She also provides cards containing conversation starters in case the students are unable to initiate their own conversations.

Tracey monitors the groups to make sure that they are successful, and they regularly discuss the ways in which groups are functioning successfully, or not, and how to manage group processes.

Whether students are reading poems, mysteries, biographies, or another genre, they are doing so with books that they can actually manage. Through group participation and individual conferences, Tracey keeps track of their progress and helps them to stretch themselves. She links their reading experiences together in group and whole-class discussions about genre and process: "Why do we write this way? How can you captivate your readers' interest? How do you create an atmosphere of suspense? How can you express that differently so we can understand that chapter more clearly?" Students of all competencies in Tracey's class have opportunities to engage in reading at their independent level while also being "on the same page" as their peers in terms of content. Tracey achieves this commonality by focusing on the learning process regardless of content covered. As a result, students of all competencies see themselves as learners and do not focus on their deficiencies. How they learn and what they can do to learn more remain the focus. Students do not define their achievements as relatively inferior or superior to their peers.

## CONVERSATIONAL ENVIRONMENT

Tracey treats her students as authors and insists that authors have intentions and make choices in line with those intentions. Readers have to be aware of those intentions and choices, both so they won't be unwittingly controlled by authors, and so they can exercise control as writers over their own readers. "What I expect from kids as readers and writers is to look at reading as an opportunity to take themselves to another place, as an opportunity to think. I want critical thinkers . . . a commitment to themselves as thinkers. . . . Question every single thing." She fosters this commitment by asking, as a matter of course throughout the day, "So what do you think? So you have this problem. What's your plan? How can I help you?" Or, "I noticed that this is what you did, so what do you think could improve it?" She avoids, "Let me tell you what to do."

Tracey encourages students to make comparisons among books and stories. For example:

TRACEY: How are the *Bailey School* books different from the *Boxcar* books?

STUDENT: *Bailey School* is more predictable.

TRACEY: So *Boxcar Children* is a lot longer to read . . . the author leaves you to work through more of the story.

STUDENTS: Yes.

She also compares movies and books. In her teaching unit on mysteries, for example, Tracey draws from television as well as the books they are reading. She asks whether anyone watched *Shelby Wu* on Nickelodeon, and many have. "Anyone have a story that started with the crime?" She moves to the wall chart on mysteries and uses an example from the TV program to elaborate each of the elements (Figure 8.2). "What are your comments about your author's use of a particular element? [There are several interchanges.] Now, [in] my book the author was real slow getting into it." The students readily agree and elaborate. One student notes that there was no suspense in his because there was only one suspect; two others describe their books; then one describes a TV mystery that showed the crime and all the detail at the beginning and then how the detective solved the case. Tracey adds, "So, friends, as a writer those are the decisions you have to make."

One student notes, "So you need to decide whether you want to start your story from the detective's point of view."

Another points out, "That's what happens on *Shelby Wu*."

Tracey comments, while writing these on a chart, "That's right. Or you could take yours starting with witnessing the crime."

Literature discussions are dialogic. Tracey wants students to un-

### Mysteries' six elements

1. Case or crime (criminal, victim).
2. Setting (unusual details).
3. Witnesses (saw or know something about the victim or crime).
4. The clues (red herrings writer puts in to throw the reader off the track).
5. Suspect (motive—reason).
6. Plot.

**FIGURE 8.2.** Wall chart on mysteries.

derstand that in discussions they must have "respect for one another
. . . [and] understand that there are going to be differences of opinion, but we respect them, as long as we can justify them with specific
examples from the literature." She also wants her students to talk
about what they read in analytic terms, emphasizing both text structure and authors' intentions and strategies. Consider the following
sections, edited from a longer discussion, to emphasize Tracey's role.

TRACEY: Let's talk about the story in terms of what the author did.

(*A student explains the character introduction in her book and then
proceeds into a retelling.*)

TRACEY: Okay. Talk to us in terms of the elements. In the beginning,
the author introduces the character and then the setting is presented. Then certain events take place where clues are provided.
That's what I mean by talking in those terms.

(*The students discuss their books in these terms.*)

TRACEY: (*in response to a student*) So the person who everybody
thought was a criminal was really a victim?

STUDENT: Yeah. And they don't know [another character] is the
criminal. She's all nice. But at the end she confesses.

TRACEY: So what we hear is some irony. We didn't expect things to
happen the opposite of what everyone first believed. Okay.

STUDENT: (*Tells about her book.*) In most of her books she tells
about the character and then goes on to tell a story.

TRACEY: Okay. So how does she tell about the character? You have
to have an author that's a mentor for you.

STUDENT: My author hides the clues so you have to figure them out.

TRACEY: Like how?

STUDENT: You want an example?

TRACEY: Of course.

(*The student searches through the book to find examples of the clues;
there are other exchanges about clues before the group ends.*)

TRACEY: I think we can do writing like other authors do and think
about choices the authors made. I can think, "I want to do what
Robert Kimbal did when he put many mysteries in one."

TRACEY: Jess, what does your author choose to do in the first couple of chapters? (*Jess responds.*) So she sets up the purpose of the story through the two brothers talking to one another? That's like Kevin's story. He started off telling us his character is a lonely boy to get us caring about the main character. You (*looking at Kevin*) made a conscious choice.

The outcome of this kind of instruction is that students voice new desires and questions: "I want to try something like that in my writing." Or "I notice that he's written short chapters. I want to do something like that." Or "Why would an author do something like that?"

Aside from whole-class and group meetings, Tracey also holds regular conferences with individual students about their writing. In one such conference, she demonstrates cutting and pasting while helping a student expand what she has written. She says, "Tell me more about Violet." The student extends the piece. Tracey prompts again, "What was it about the flower that intrigued her?" The student explains. Tracey prompts again, "So this flower was alive all that time. Tell me about that." The student explains and Tracey adds, "How did Lily get her hands on it? You can play around with the words later, cut and move the words around so you don't have to rewrite everything."

Tracey focuses much of her classroom talk on the processes used to read, write, research, and solve problems. She encourages children to share their ideas as well as the processes they used along the way. For example, she says, "You come up with a great line, you like that line, you share it. There are lots of opportunities to share—mini-lessons." She also encourages experimentation: "How many people did something different in their writer's notebook? What did you do?" Students are eager to share a process or strategy. Tracey uses the children's writing as the springboard for mini-lessons by pointing out, for example, what she observed one of the other students doing in his or her writing and connecting it to another author. She says, "I've got a bunch of resources right at my fingertips—my students. I don't have to come up with everything."

Tracey encourages students to *try*, with the expectation that they will make errors and that they will learn from those errors. She models owning up to errors by announcing, for example, that she was responsible for confusing them and explains why she didn't get it straight. It was not clear to the students whether they should analyze their own mystery story or the book they are reading. She asks which they would prefer and meets divided opinion. "What about both?" she asks and gets a collective "No." "How come?" she asks, "Is that asking too much?" On receiving agreement that it is, she suggests that they choose whichever one they want.

Tracey does not expect to be the only teacher in the classroom. She observes, "There are times when I am trying to teach something, and I have just run out of ways of getting it across effectively. I am very comfortable with saying, 'Do me a favor. Go over to Elsa and talk it over with her. Come back and let me know what you guys talked about.'"

## INTEGRATION

In Tracey's classroom, reading and writing are thoroughly integrated with other subjects, particularly social studies. Students are frequently assigned to research and write biographies on historical figures, as when they researched Martin Luther King, Jr., and issues of segregation and the civil rights movement for an inquiry project presented to the whole school. Relevant biographies, research projects, and poetry have led to fertile ground for critical reading and conversations about multiple perspectives and issues of fairness, power, and democracy.

The genre study of biographies entails not only researching historical figures of interest through trade-book biographies, note-taking, and question-asking, but also writing biographies on the historical figures to share with classmates and writing biographies about classmates based on interviews. Initially a 10-minute exercise, biographies of classmates are produced from partnerships between a third and a fourth grader, in which each lists five things the other does not already know, then they trade lists and write short biographies. Students often choose to spend 20 minutes before gym class revising their pieces, rather than getting together for the read-alouds they love so much. Upon returning from gym, Tracey leads the students in examining their biographies by dialoguing with them:

TRACEY: Why do we write biographies anyway?

STUDENT: Because you're interested in a person's life.

TRACEY: So what might you include?

STUDENT: How you were inspired by a person.

STUDENT: You write for the reader's sake.

TRACEY: What do you mean?

STUDENT: A reader doesn't know about them, so you need to include a lot of detail.

TRACEY: Yeah. Ask yourself what your author's doing to make you keep wanting to read.

STUDENT: Famous persons' biographies start out really boring.

TRACEY: You think so

STUDENT: Well, like really regular—the interesting part is usually later, when they do whatever makes them famous.

TRACEY: (*writing students' comments on biographies on the easel chart*) How does your author start the biography? When do you get to the meaty part of the person's life? How does the author keep the reader's attention? What I want to know is, why did the author write that book. What does the author want to learn about that person? What does the author need to include?

STUDENT: What they did.

TRACEY: (*writing*) What are their accomplishments? What are their struggles? Like Martin Luther King, Jr., and his struggles. Remember when he was young? What was a big struggle for him?

STUDENT: He lost his best friends.

TRACEY: Yeah. He was told his two best friends couldn't play with him anymore. Do you think that affected his life? Did that struggle lead to his accomplishments in civil rights?

The consistent thread, whether reading aloud, conducting individual conferences, or moderating literature groups, is getting students to ask questions about what they read and what evokes interested in them. Another example: In studying the Iroquois, students first skim through the books, generate questions, collect the questions together, then choose books to address the questions. They go to the library but quickly feel overwhelmed by the number of questions they have generated, They return to their classroom and consider what has worked and what has not. They then group the questions into categories, and each chooses the questions for which he or she is responsible. Returning to the library, they know what each other is researching and when they come to that information, they make a note and help each other. For example, there are four groups studying New York: community group, location group, landscape group, housing group. Each is multiage, and Tracey uses students to act as leaders. Commenting to one group, she said, "Matt and Sam, you are the experts here from last year. I expect you to head the group in the right direction."

The study of science is also integrated with the study of reading and writing. For example, students make daily records on the metamorphosis of the caterpillars for which they have been caring. Tracey reads aloud the book *Monarch Butterflies* (Gibbons, 1991), and they compare the monarchs with the pink ladies they are raising. As she reads the book, she pauses regularly to check their understanding of the terminology:

TRACEY: What does *transparent* mean?

STUDENT: See-through.

TRACEY: Yeah, see-through, like the glass over there. You can see through to the other side. Metamorphosis. Some of you are reading those *Animorphs* books. What does *metamorphosis* mean?

STUDENT: You completely changed.

(*Students begin to respond, without prompting, to the terms describing various parts of the butterfly: "Proboscis!" a student exclaims, recognizing bees in a pollination project earlier in the year. "It sucks up the sweet stuff." Tracey then encourages the students to generate questions they would like to learn about while they study butterflies, just as she has done in other projects in social studies and language arts.*)

TRACEY: Why do they fly south?

STUDENT: They'll freeze.

TRACEY: Is that why?

STUDENT: There's no food.

TRACEY: So when it gets cold, the plants die and there's no food.

STUDENT: Why don't they just stay in the south?

TRACEY: Good question.

Tracey adds this to the list of questions taking shape on the easel chart and then continues to read aloud: " 'They follow where the milkweed plants are'—good job—it's like you're predicting." She writes down terms the students want to know from the book. "Now what you guys are referring to is the life cycle. What's the first stage?" The students readily volunteer the various terms (*egg*, *larva*, *caterpillar*, *pupa*, and *butterfly*) and how long each stage lasts. Many of the students are familiar with some of the terms from the pollination study, but there is confusion about the larva and pupa stages, which Tracey then clarifies by asking students to classify the current stage of their butterfly.

TRACEY: Pay attention to the illustrations, too. Do you notice any changes taking place with your caterpillars?

STUDENT: Mine is starting to hang.

STUDENT: Mine has stripes now.

STUDENT: Will a bird that eats a monarch butterfly caterpillar die because a monarch butterfly caterpillar is poisonous?

STUDENT: Well, why don't we do some research on that?

TRACEY: Yeah. That's what I say. (*She adds it to the list.*)

Tracey is concerned that her students gain disciplinary knowledge and terminology while still maintaining some sense of control over the inquiry taking place throughout the conversations inserted into the read-aloud. Tracey's conversation, interwoven throughout the read-aloud, models the reading process and makes the material accessible to the full range of students. The students who otherwise would not have access to this material are invited into the conversation through talking about what they already know about butterflies and what they still wish to learn. In the language arts block she introduces *The War with Grandpa* (Smith, 1984), which they read together as a literature group, tying the conversations into the life-cycle theme. This book is one of the set books in the curriculum and is chosen because its text is manageable for virtually all of the students; at the same time, it leads to rich discussions that fit well with other curricular areas.

## EXPECTATIONS AND ASSESSMENTS

Tracey also holds students to high expectations, and she does not readily accept failure. For example, when Ed fails to finish his reading at the desired rate, she tells him to "use your class reading time to finish this book. It must be done by Friday. I know you can handle it." On one occasion three students have not finished writing their comments when lunchtime arrives. Tracey instructs, "Finish your comments. I'm walking these guys down to lunch, and I want to hear what you have to say when I return." Two of the students finish quickly and leave for lunch. One is left. When she returns, Tracey says, "Jim, take it with you to lunch. I want to read what you have to say when we get back." Later it turns out he has not done it. She says, "Jim, I'm trying to work with you. You will not leave school today until that is done." In this way, she "keeps on" the students to make sure they do not fall behind.

Tracey also encourages her students to hold themselves to high standards: "The examples have been shown to you. What do you expect of yourself? What message do you want to give the audience?" Responding to a student who does a particularly good job, she says, "Joshua, that is the difference between mediocre and going the extra mile." One group's presentation contains a discrepancy. They argue that Martin Luther King, Jr., did not meet President Kennedy but that he worked with him. Tracey points out the problem and explains that they need to fix it.

Although she insists on high standards, she also recognizes the tension inherent in expectations:

> "I'm trying to keep everything individualized, but I'm also trying to keep the grade level in perspective in terms of what I'm expecting. . . . I can't expect [she names a low-achieving student] to produce in the same amount of time that everybody else is, although I have the same . . . high expectations for her. . . . I make homework modifications, spelling modifications, depending on the kid. The biggest obstacle is making sure that every child's needs are met. For example, when you have someone who is in the higher end of the spectrum, you have to make sure that that child is challenged. Sometimes people think that things come easily to them, that they don't have to stretch themselves. . . . How do you get them to see that they need to stretch them-

selves? The other [challenge] is when you have that other kid, who is at the other end, the lower end of the spectrum, making sure that I've got enough materials so that that kid is comfortable and . . . just tapping into all the resources that I need to so that I can get the kid prepared. Sometimes that takes a little networking, which takes a little bit more time."

Keeping track of her students' development is an important feature of Tracey's teaching. First and foremost, she is an astute observer of her students' progress, or lack thereof. For example, when asked to describe particular students' growth in literacy throughout the year, she notes:

"Steven reads more analytically now. He reads a lot for enjoyment. . . . His vocabulary is incredible. But now when he is reading, he is questioning more what he reads. He is thinking more about the author's intentions, I think, so he is more aware of the craftiness of the author and how that impacts the story—which I think is different from what he did at the beginning of the year. . . . He is a really good writer, but I think Steven has changed now in that he does things intentionally. I mean, now he can tell you what he is doing, he can explain a process that he is going through. In the past it was like, 'Wow, this is good,' but I don't think he really understood why it was good. Now he's got a better awareness of decisions that he makes as a writer.

"Elsa likes to extend herself. For example, during the mystery unit, I didn't know that there was another book, a sequel to that one, and she found it and read it. She has read the book we are reading now, and she has read the third book. So she is challenging herself by looking for sequels, and that's how she has changed as a reader. I think she is more conscious about being as creative as she possibly can—for example, taking that piece and revising it constantly so that it is different and better. Or when she reads now, she takes what she reads and puts it into her writing. For example, she and some other fourth-grade girls, even from the other team, were reading some poetry books. They started composing their own poems, following the patterns that were in that poem they had read. I am seeing that [initiative] more in her writing—using things that she has read and incorporating that in her writing. She did that for the mysteries."

Although Tracey uses a checklist to evaluate progress in reading and writing, she also takes notes of what the children have to say, what they choose to focus on, and so forth. The checklist helps her to remember all the "things that I need to be aware of." Her record-keeping involves whatever "works for me." When writing children's report cards, she doesn't rely on her records a great deal because, she observes, "I know my kids." When necessary, she can refer to the data, including students' journals and reading logs. "It's my job to have that information. . . . When I write report cards, I write them as if I were having a conversation with that parent. And I have to adjust how I write my comments depending on who's going to be reading them." She points out that report cards often take quite a while. However, she has help. Her students are involved in self-evaluation, with the help of her prompting:

> "Take a look at your reading record sheet. What kinds of books have you read? How do you feel about the number of books you've read during this time period? What types of books have you been reading more of? What kind of goals have you set for yourself? Where do you want to go from here? What plan do you have? What are some areas you feel good about?"

Self-evaluation in other areas is also fostered through rubrics, some of which have been generated with the students.

Students are invited to the conferences. Tracey describes one of these.

> "I had a conference with Henry. His mother requested that we meet to discuss Henry's feeling overwhelmed. And this is Henry. He feels that school is hard. He says his time is limited, and he is afraid he can't finish activities in the amount of time he has in class. Henry ran this conference. Everything that you see here is what Henry said. He is having trouble with cursive, reading cursive, so then we talked about strategies, ways that we could solve that. And I also wanted him to know, 'Henry, you know you are putting too much pressure on yourself. You are doing much better than you think you are.' Here I wrote, 'Mrs. Bennett will print when sharing with the class.'
>
> "Henry will exchange spelling words prior to the spelling test with his partner because of his concern that he couldn't read

the cursive. We shared Henry's success in school, in math, his understanding of, and ability to complete, the assignments. He works cooperatively with others; in science he follows his safety procedures, understands all the vocabulary words and scientific terms, and is able to interpret the data. In reading, he has insightful responses to the text, is able to make inferences, responds to comments made by peers, and has completed all of the projects. 'So what if it takes you longer to do it?'

"We also had to make some seat changes, and we will make time modifications when necessary. I will check in with Henry to see how things are going, and Henry will check in with his teachers—because that was the problem—Henry would go home feeling overwhelmed. Here I am thinking everything is okay! Henry came up with this whole plan. We just sat there, and he ran the conference. I think we underestimate kids. We have to put them in a situation where they have to rise to the occasion, be responsible for themselves—and they do."

## SUMMARY

Tracey's classroom of students is a responsible, respectful, inquiring community. *Respect*, from her point of view, entails taking one another and oneself seriously. To do so means not allowing her students to shortchange themselves, for example, by not following through on projects or not engaging in productive learning. It means helping them to hold themselves to high standards and to understand that their experience can be the basis for valuable contributions to class knowledge construction. It means that students play a role in evaluating and reporting on their own progress and their difficulties.

Tracey is a constructivist thinker and a constructivist teacher (Fosnot, 1989; Keiny, 1994; Sutton, Lund, Schurdell, & Bichsel, 1996). She believes that important knowledge is complex, value-laden, and bound to life experiences, and she wants to hear what the children know. Students in her class are thus made aware of their own authority, which is expanded then through their independent and collaborative pursuit of different, but related, questions. The children's research on issues of social justice broadens this authority still further. Strategies such as holding a mock court to consider an issue of justice from a piece of children's literature lead to an understanding of the complexity of knowing as well as to an expansion of children's social imagination as they take on characters' ways of thinking that are not the same as their own. Multiple perspectives are assumed and differences valued. Good questions are valued as much as good answers.

Tracey facilitates the constructive and ubiquitous conversations that take place among students and form the basis of community in several ways. She chooses, or helps to choose, relatively accessible group and class reading material and arranges supporting material for students who cannot independently manage the level of complexity. She also arranges for children to read books that are at their level of competence, and she invites discussions of the similarities and differences across different authors and different works. In other words, Tracey arranges for children to engage in activities that are within their zone of proximal development (Vygotsky, 1978). She strikes a balance between supporting individual choice and competence, and building community collaboration. Thus, with her guidance, children spend time reading texts containing words to which they have access, and they engage in conversations that expand their thinking (McMahon et al., 1997; Langer, 1995).

Making literacy accessible also makes it possible for students to gain a sense of agency in their literate practice. Indeed, Tracey insists that they adopt this position by making clear in her interactions with them that learning, literacy, and classroom life are composed of intentional acts. When people write, it is for a purpose. When people do research, it is to answer questions they have generated. When people choose partners for learning, it is for a reason. Each choice and act, she shows them, has a consequence. She insists that they become inquirers. She emphasizes process language—"How did you . . . ?"—and routinely requires them to tell the story of their learning and literacy in a way that emphasizes their agency. She also shows her students what they have accomplished.

Tracey explicitly demonstrates literate processes—ways of thinking and structuring thought—that are grounded in students' experience with the genre being studied, and their own analytic examination of the writer's craft. She also helps children discover the strategies and structures of literate practice through careful questioning, thus expanding students' independence and sense of agency.

Because her students have a sense of the significance of diversity and the complexity involved in constructing knowledge and literate practice, they do not become caught up in disabling questions of who is smarter than whom. Their concern is with "how can I make this better." Because they share conferences about their reading and writing, they come to know, respect, and value one another; this interconnectedness reduces the likelihood of negative behavior and increases the level of caring and community in the classroom.

**John Cronin** is a doctoral student at the University at Albany–State University of New York. He works as a research assistant at the Center for English Learning and Achievement. He has a particular interest in studying motivational aspects of classrooms.

# PART III

## What Have We Learned about Good Fourth-Grade Teaching?

# 9

## Integrated Instruction in Exemplary Fourth-Grade Classrooms

The teachers in our study were selected not only because they are exemplary but also because they integrate their instruction. When we began our study, we were interested in integrated instruction for a number of reasons. First, our home state of New York has actively promoted integrated instruction, even providing models of integrated lessons and conducting state exams that require certain forms of curricular integration. Similarly, several professional teacher organizations have also supported integrated curricula (e.g., National Council for the Social Studies, 1989; International Reading Association and National Council of Teachers of English, 1996). Second, we found the principal ideas behind the concept of integration to be persuasive: that knowledge is interconnected in the "real world," that thematizing knowledge aids efficient learning, and that different ideas and methods crossing domains enrich each domain (Stember, 1991). Third, we found the idea of reading and writing as tools for real work in content areas to be a compelling one. Fourth, we were interested in the concept of integration as it relates to children's and teachers' understandings of themselves as literate individuals (Walmsley, 1994).

It is no surprise that our search for exemplary teachers led us to classrooms with more integrated instruction, since these two characteristics often coincide (see Chapter 2). Many advantages have been claimed for integrated instruction. In reviewing the literature on integrated instruction, Mathison and Freeman (1998, pp. 17–18) summarize the following advantages reported in the literature:

- An increase in understanding, retention, and application of general concepts.
- A better overall comprehension of global interdependencies, along with the development of multiple perspectives, points of view, and values.
- An increase in the ability to make decisions, think critically and creatively, and synthesize knowledge beyond the disciplines.
- The increased ability to identify, assess, and transfer significant information needed for solving novel problems.
- The promotion of cooperative learning, a better attitude towards self as a learner and as a meaningful member of a community.
- Increased motivation.

However, in the review of the literature on integrated literacy instruction, Gavelek and his colleagues (Gavelek, Raphael, Biondo, & Wang, 1999) observe that although there has been considerable proselytizing about the value of integrated instruction, there has been considerably less research on what actually constitutes integrated instruction and its value. There has been even less work towards formulating a productive theoretical framework.

Integration across the language arts, across disciplines, and across language arts and the disciplines are all of interest to us initially. But just as the construct *exemplary* turned out to be complex, in that there are more dimensions to achievement, and hence to teaching competence than we had expected, *integration* produced at least as much complexity. In our selection of teachers, we set no specific criteria for what would constitute "integrated instruction": rather, we used the study to examine what constituted integrated instruction in these exemplary classrooms so that we might understand its nature and significance.

As Gavelek and his colleagues found, basic distinctions regarding kinds of integration can be made quite quickly. Most commonly, the teachers we observed integrate reading and writing instruction, then oral language and literature study—integrated language arts.

Second, reading and writing are integrated across subject domains so that language skills are studied as tools in the practice of inquiry. Typically this integration involved social studies, probably because of the alignment in objectives between the two (Farivar, 1993) and the relatively easy topical alignment with children's literature. Third, home and school learning experiences are integrated. Although Gavelek and colleagues describe this dimension as independent of the other dimensions of integration, our observations suggest that people who integrate subject areas are more inclined to help students integrate home and school life.

In any case, this tripartite distinction only gets us so far. In this chapter we describe how we came to understand the characteristics of integrated instruction: the range of types of integration, the epistemological frames of integration, the dimensions of integration, the locations and vehicles of integration, and the ways in which integration is undermined. Finally, we will describe the significance of the integrated instruction we observed.

## RANGE OF INTEGRATION

The classrooms we studied provided a wide range of kinds of integration, each marked by issues of scheduling and the ways teachers talked. At the basic level, reading and writing are integrated in most classrooms. That is, writing is taught as a vehicle for understanding reading better, and vice versa. In such a class writing and reading might be scheduled together as language arts, or even scheduled separately (for example, on alternate days), but as a matter of emphasis only. Comments such as "What did the author *do* to make you giggle?" or "You're telling me what happened, not what the author did" were heard often. Commonly, reading/writing instruction include literature study. In these classrooms, literature is analyzed in terms of writers' intentions, forms, and tools. Teachers draw attention to authors' techniques and give noticeable examples; they ask their students to notice, for example, the things that "draw them" to a poem. Post-its are used in some classrooms for students to jot down their perceptions, and comments such as, "What would make you put a Post-it on that one?" were common.

Often teachers include other subject areas in reading and writing instruction by arranging for students to read, for example, historical fiction, such as the *Voyage of the Half Moon* (West, 1995), as we saw in Mary's classroom. Social studies is the most common subject thus integrated. For example, one teacher spent about one day on the social studies textbook chapter and then moved to trade books, usually on the same topic or set in the appropriate era, as in the study of California history. Within this arrangement students all could find books they were able to read, and the diversity produced lively conversations with a wide range of student contributions. Math is the least commonly integrated subject on the classrooms we observed. However, in some classrooms, writing is consistently integrated even into math by having students keep journals and document the strategies they are using to solve problems. Science is integrated most often through research projects. In both math and science, integration was more often a case of reading and writing being emphasized as a tool in the study of other subjects, as Gavelek and his colleagues also found.

However, curricular boundaries were barely visible in some classrooms. For example, in Joan Backer's research project on the ducklings (Chapter 3), even though she posted a daily lesson plan on the board, with some subject boundaries, she routinely ignored it as class sessions and projects evolved and sprawled across other subjects. Similarly, in Kim Duhamel's classroom (Chapter 4) children were immersed in researching prehistoric times through use of the trade book *Magic School Bus in the Time of the Dinosaurs* (Cole, 1995) and biographical sketches of their own "discovered" (designed) dinosaur. Some classrooms are organized for integration in a kind of block scheduling, studying three weeks of social studies, then three weeks of science, with reading and writing integrated throughout.

Not all of these integration efforts are equally productive, of course. There were times when even the most accomplished teachers' concern for integration did not lead to particularly rewarding experiences. For example, some teachers assigned children to write letters about their science projects that included their spelling words. However, such activities were relatively uncommon.

We found that there are not only multiple ways of conceptualizing integration and its significance but also multiple dimensions to implementing and evaluating it. We will begin with a brief exploration of the frameworks used by the teachers in our study.

## FRAMEWORKS OF INTEGRATION

Different teachers have different epistemological stances (Carlsen, 1997; Hoffer & Pintrich, 1997; Kardash & Scholes, 1996; Lyons, 1990; Nystrand, 1997). By *epistemology* we mean a theory of knowledge and knowing, including the implications for the individual as knower. As Palmer (1993) conceptualizes the process, a person's epistemology answers the questions: "What is the nature of the knower? What is the nature of the known? And what is the nature of the relations between the two?" (p. 20). Integration has different meanings within different epistemological stances. A classical distinction between epistemological stances is that of *received knowers* versus *constructed knowers* (Belenky et al., 1986).

Received knowers believe that knowledge is comprised of facts that are "out there," possessed by people in authority. Facts are viewed as the central aspect of schooling, and as independent of feelings or politics. Teachers with this framework do not feel comfortable addressing controversial issues or dealing with ambiguous or complex situations. Single sources of information are preferable in these classrooms: multiple perspectives would be problematic. For these teachers language is essentially a conduit through which facts are conveyed, and teaching is primarily a matter of delivering stacks of knowledge to students and checking to see whether they have received and stored it correctly. There is less student talk in such classrooms, and the talk that does occur does not develop or engage the topics being studied. Instead, recitation, summarization, and paraphrasing dominate both spoken and written responses. Students do not initiate academic talk in such instructional arrangements. Integration is not viewed as essential and is seen primarily as a straightforward matter of making connections across domains of knowledge. The value of integration is seen as a means of increasing memory of the facts.

This epistemology, in its pure form, was rare in our group of teachers, but examples did exist. Pam, one of the teachers presented elsewhere (Johnston et al., 2001), observed:

> Even in the social studies or any content area, I've never really had them insist that the answer was correct. . . . I'm more concerned with writing it and correcting it and making sure I explain it to them. . . .

> They tend to be very accepting of problems or explanations ... they don't question too often [with discussion]. So few ... actually stay engaged ... with the conversation, that I don't use it too often. ... They're very good if I'm leading the discussion. (p. 229)

Constructed knowers, in contrast, have a very different perspective on teaching and learning. They believe that knowledge is constructed in an active, subjective process, using language and always connected to feelings; that it is *never* value-free. People have the responsibility of utilizing the available sources of information to make sense of, make meaning out of, the information; ambiguity and complexity are expected and even enjoyed. For constructed knowers, language is one of many forms of representation; it is a tool for thinking rather than a conduit for information. These teachers' instruction is dialogical, and student-initiated academic talk is central. For example, Stacey's goal is that her students become "thinkers," and she views reading "as an opportunity to think ... a commitment to themselves as thinkers." She wants her students to respect one another and to expect and value differences of opinion. She and her students thrive on complexity and controversy, and she insists that her students "question every single thing." Within this framework, integration is taken for granted; reading and writing must be examined as part of knowing, since meaning is central, and knowledge does not come in subject stacks.

Applebee (1996), in analyzing English language arts curricula, refers to these two epistemological stances as different conceptions of curriculum: "one that treats curriculum as specific content and information, and the other that emphasizes issues and ideas" (p. 25). Nystrand (1997) refers to the distinction in terms of the nature of classroom discourse—monologic or dialogic. The former produces classroom discourse and activities that are "closed" (Turner, 1995), in that there is no space for a student ownership or exploration. Dialogic instruction, in contrast, uses "open" activities and conversations. There are times in dialogic instruction when facts and agreed-upon "right" answers are the focus, sometimes approached through teacher-directed question–answer sessions. However, these segments are usually a way to get everybody "on the same page" and refresh their memories, so that they are ready for the more open inquiry.

These epistemological frames can be influenced by the context (e.g., high-stakes testing) and the individual's experience with a particular academic domain. For example, a teacher might not think of math as a meaning-making representational system in the way she thinks about language, music, or art. Or, a teacher might think of science as limited to a comprehension of *the* scientific method rather than as a means of studying something systematically in order to understand it. Consequently, some teachers value integration, viewing social studies and literature as automatically part of the same whole, but must consciously work to integrate math. This finding echoes teachers' differential use of textbooks across subjects and teaching contexts (Sosniak & Stodolsky, 1993).

Teachers committed to integrated instruction often carefully plan surprising locations for lessons. For example, in one "science" lesson Jan Sun, a teacher working in an urban school, integrated science, math, and the current book being read, *Maggie among the Seneca* (Moore, 1990), which also integrated social studies. The exercise involved predicting the *carrying capacity* of a natural habitat for a particular animal, in this case deer. Some students were selected to be deer, and some to be the resources the deer needed to survive. The "deer students" picked from the resource pool. The students had to make a prediction for the number of deer in the fourth year. At one point a student observed that "there's still not going to be enough food, and some will die." This prediction was not something found in a textbook, and if it had been, it is unlikely that the same end would be realized. In this activity the students had to construct the database and explain the logic they used in arriving at their predictions.

## DIMENSIONS OF INTEGRATION

When integration is approached from a received-knower perspective, it is reduced to making connections across subject areas. However, in our observations, we found that integration occurs on many different dimensions and in many different ways, as we next explain.

### Interdomain Connections

Interdomain connections are the "factual" connections across subject domains, as, for example, when Mary Ellen introduced her students to a Native American stick number game as part of math. A second example is that of Joan's students wishing to name the ducklings born as part of science class—which led to a discussion of the power issues involved in who has the right to name people and things. Joan drew their attention to the book *Sign of the Beaver* (Speare, 1984) and how the Native Americans named children, which led them to observe and document the distinctive behaviors of the ducklings.

Other connections made across domains are metaphorical. For example, in Joan's class, looking for metaphors is habitual. An example of this practice is when Aja noticed Clive "step into" the duckling while explaining an observation about its behavior. She also noticed that they had been "stepping into" the characters in a book during their discussions. Metaphorical connections across areas of study are particularly important because they serve as a powerful tool for children that draws them into integrative thinking. We are inclined to think of metaphor as a higher order of cognition. Others disagree. Cynthia Ozick views metaphor as the "enemy of abstraction" because "it inhabits language at its most concrete" (quoted in Greene, 1997, p. 282). Wells (2001, p. 86) gives examples of metaphorical gesture, such as "closing the fist to represent 'contraction.' "

## Intertextual References

Intertextual references were commonly encouraged by all of the teachers. For example, while discussing a character in a book they were reading, Mary asked her class, "Do any of the characters in the books you've read remind you of Alan Brewster?" Responses included *Sheila the Great, Fudge*, and *Sarah Ida*. Mary asked each respondent why. Other examples include: Kim connecting *The Jolly Postman, Snow White*, and *Cinderella*; one of her students connecting the evil stepmothers in *Cinderella* and *Yeh Shen*; one of Sandy's students noting the similarity between the "runt" in *Charlotte's Web*—Wilbur—and *Where the Red Fern Grows*—Little Ann; and Joan's student pointing out the similarity between another student's comment during science/language arts, and a line in a Sid Fleischman book. These references sometimes crossed disciplinary boundaries and sometimes did not. Keene and Zimmerman (1997; see also Johnston, 1997) refer to these text-to-text connections as an important aspect of comprehension, along with text-to-self and text-to-world connections, the more general forms of which we address below as aspects of intrasubjectivity.

## Intersubjectivity

By *intersubjectivity* we mean the connections that form among the literate individuals in the classroom and beyond. These connections include the integration of knowledge resources, knowers, and perspective providers into a shared community of practice. In one classroom, for example, children took turns doing the morning roll call and tally; calling the roll here required each student to express an opinion on the issue of the day. Thus the child in charge got to do survey research and math; at the same time, all the students got to know one another and make connections in ways they might not have. These roll calls often led to engaging discussions in which new ways of thinking evolved in much the same way as they did they did in other kinds of dialogue in the classroom. In such classrooms, students learn to conceive of *thinking* as happening as much between individuals as within them, so that there is some awareness of the significance of others for one's own development. It could be said that minds become integrated in the process of ongoing interactions, particularly those that build on one another, as Joan's extended discussion demonstrates (Chapter 3). We describe this phenomenon in the next chapter as "distributed thinking."

Another means of facilitating the development of intersubjectivity is through the use of a flip chart, as teachers wrote down the students' ideas and theories, and these then became the basis for further discussion and modification. Hume (2001) has written about this collaborative knowledge-building in her science class: "Written discourse is particularly powerful . . . because it both represents current understanding and, simultaneously, can be reworked to allow for greater intersubjectivity—the ability of all participants to recognize each other's understanding and intentions and to work toward insuring that mutual understanding is maintained" (p. 101).

## Intrasubjectivity

In the standard Western view of science, feelings are seen as impediments to rational thought; therefore, feelings and thought are purposefully split apart—*un*integrated. so to speak. More recent thinking on this matter, however, has made it clear that this split between feeling and thought is not a productive end (Keller, 1985; Knoblauch & Brannon, 1988). A more productive approach is to learn to understand the relationships between these integral aspects of oneself—an intrasubjective literacy. An effective example of how this understanding can be facilitated was the discussion that arose around the dissection of the unhatched duck eggs in Joan Backer's classroom. That discussion involved careful interweaving of feelings, rationality, and ethical values in a way that kept them linked in a productive tension.

A second aspect of intrasubjective literacy is the integration of personal experience, in and outside of school, with school knowledge and literate engagements. We saw a good example of this in Sandy Knisely's (Chapter 6) class when, as part of their research writing in social studies, they studied family traditions by researching their own families. Historically, school and outside knowledge have been segregated, particularly for students at the lower end of the achievement distribution and those from lower socioeconomic groups (Anyon, 1981; Page, 1991; Bryson, 1993). Students who have consistently experienced this schism come to believe that it is appropriate and actively resist teachers who attempt to integrate their personal experience and school knowledge (Jones, 1991; McNeil, 2000).

## INTERREPRESENTATIONAL SYSTEMS

Language, spoken or written, is only one of the representational systems through which we experience and organize the world. Others include music, dance, visual arts, mathematics, and theater. Classrooms can foster children's exploration of the symbolic power of language and other representational systems as tools for thought—be this thought in the form of reflection or as a means of systematizing knowledge. Alternatively, these representational systems can be kept completely separate. Representational systems were not fully integrated in any of the classrooms we observed. However, there were places in which this sort of integration commonly did take place. For example, math problems were sometimes represented in numbers, words, and diagrams. Visual art and writing, such as poetry, were often combined. Many of the teachers discussed (and children sometimes produced) illustrated books in ways that integrated visual and verbal representation. Sometimes these representations also combined with theatrical representation as, for example, in the mock trial following the reading of *Shiloh* (Naylor, 2000), or the readers' theater in Sandy Kniseley's room.

## INTEGRATION ACROSS TIME

In almost all of the classrooms we observed, efforts were made to integrate material across time. For example, Joan's class maintained a historical record of discussions on a flip chart, which was referred to with some frequency. It was also common to hear "Remember when we . . . " In some ways this temporal interweaving created a kind of "narrativization" of class knowledge construction. In many classrooms this narrative component was part of the children's participation in planning what they learned. For example, children were asked what they had learned and what they wished to learn. The journals in which they chronicled this process served as tools that bestowed agency in their integration of all that they learned. The mediating factor in achieving this integration over time is children's perceived sense of agency in their own learning. For example, if they come to view themselves and each other as authors, as they did in many of these classrooms, then that identity makes it likely that they will seek continuity between their reading and writing experiences.

## POINTS AND VEHICLES OF INTEGRATION

Next we explore some of the points at which this integration revealed itself and the vehicles that produced it, followed by a consideration of the points where this integration broke down—and the factors that contributed to it.

### Teacher–Student Interests/Agendas

Interests and agendas that teachers brought to the classroom often demanded an integrated perspective. For example, one teacher had an interest in gender issues. This interest meant that many things that came up in the classroom—books read, forms of interaction, comments made—prompted the teacher to raise a question around gender. The same was true for students. Once students hooked into a class or individual interest, connections, examples, and metaphors kept revealing themselves. Teachers who were interested learners, and who assumed that students would have interests to pursue, created integrated classrooms.

Similarly, when a teacher took seriously the impending state science test, many topics in a range of subjects provided springboards to discussion of, and reading and writing about, science concepts to be covered on the test.

## Common Process

One vehicle for integration was similar kinds of talk across domains—in particular, strategic talk such as, "How can you find that out?" "How did you do that?" "How else?" "What's the problem?" "What makes you think that?" "How could you check?" This type of question is generalizable across subject domains and facilitates integration at the level of strategies. In addition, this sort of talk contains intentionality—which has its own way of producing an integrated perspective towards achieving a goal or solving a problem.

Some less explicit types of integration were equally common in these classrooms. For example, the skills of *learning how to contextualize actions* and *learning how to take the perspective of others* are applicable in literature, reading and writing, and are also central to historical thinking when applied to events of the past (Brophy & VanSledright, 1997). Recall how in Joan's room, while studying ducklings, one of the children observed another student "stepping into the ducklings"—imagining duckling thought processes as a way to generate scientific theories. Joan connected this "stepping into" to the strategy used while reading, to understand characters' thoughts, feelings, and behavior and writers' motives. In another example, a teacher pointed out to her students, "One of the things people do when they start a story is think of what they know. Mathematicians do this too. . . . Let's try it."

## Real Problems/Projects

Some forms of integration appeared to occur "naturally," particularly when children were involved in "authentic" projects. For example, recall how in Joan's classroom the children were involved in running an ice-cream stand. Ice-cream sales necessarily involved math, reading, writing, oral communication, and much more. These activities required not only an integration of various processes and domains but also the formation of integrative relationships among the children. Authentic projects produced issue-oriented engagements in which there were technical or human (rights, needs, perspectives, relationship) problems to solve. This approach to integration was quite different from the "themed" approach, which simply brought together different disciplines around a topic. The ownership, or intentionality, associated with this type of reality-based activity produced a seamless, apparently natural, integration.

## Inquiry

Inquiry is probably a specialized example of the "real problems/projects" category in that, if the inquiry is owned by the students, then it constitutes a "real" problem. As children learn to adopt an inquiring stance toward learning, they cannot help but notice things and ask questions. Teachers fostered this inquiring stance even in the area of "basic skills." Recall the example in Chapter 3 when Joan asked the students to help design a program of handwriting instruction that stemmed from the real problem of their having difficulty reading each others' drafts. When asked which letters to begin with, her students suggested options based on shape and frequency (among other things), which led a group of students to take on a homework assignment that would answer their question. Similarly, when the word *quagmire* came up as the word of the day, Joan asked the children to look for patterns in their attempts to spell the word, saying, "What are you noticing?" The overall pattern fostered is one of noticing, questioning, theorizing, and testing. Again the primary integrator is intention or ownership of a question without the feeling of being bound by a particular domain.

## Dialogue

Nystrand (1997) point out that dialogical instruction develops the coherence of discourse and works to "thematize" knowledge. By saying to students, "What are you thinking now?—share it," and encouraging them to respond to each other's thoughts, diverse perspectives are elicited with the linguistic constraint of relevance to each other. This approach was maximized, of course, in issue- or inquiry-oriented classrooms more than in the theme-based ones. In some classes the use of "quickwrites" produced similar energy, with the added benefit that more students easily participated in the conversations because they had time to think and a record to work from. Most of these classrooms were very conversational for much of the day because there were genuinely interesting things to converse around, collaborative activities, and genuine interest in what other members of the classroom community had to say.

## POINTS OF DIS-INTEGRATION

Although the classrooms we studied were chosen, in part, because the teachers integrated their instruction, we found various structural barriers to the nature and extent of the integration they were able to implement.

### Departmentalization

By fourth grade, already a great deal of the curriculum in some schools has been departmentalized. Consequently, some of the classrooms we studied were entirely self-contained, whereas others had varying degrees of departmentalized instruction, depending on the organization of the school. A study contrasting self-contained classrooms in the group with those that were more departmentalized found important differences (Allington, Block, Morrow, & Day, 1999). Self-contained classrooms were distinguished by the following:

- Multiple source use more common.
- More trade books and fewer commercial materials.
- More collaborative work and less seat work.
- More self-management.
- Less process talk.
- More careful listening to students.
- More student-centered activities.
- More unprompted discussion of books.
- More books read by students.
- More books read aloud by the teacher.
- More open writing activities versus structured assignments.

Although these distinctions were present, the common tendencies remained consistent. For example, although there was less process talk in the self-contained classrooms, there was still a lot of this kind of talk, and although fewer books were read in departmentalized classrooms, it was still a lot of books. Furthermore, those teachers whose classes were more departmentalized were concerned about the effect of departmentalization on the integration they valued, and on their relationships with the students. They were reluctant to give them up for part of the day. The teachers in self-contained situations also felt that a departmentalized schedule would disrupt their ability to be flexible and to accommodate the students' interests. The only real argument for departmentalization that any of the teachers made was that it reduced the necessary preparation.

Although departmentalization almost guarantees less integration, some teachers actively worked to counteract this trend. For example, in Joan's school, her students had separate instruction in science, Spanish, and dance. Joan counteracted the divisive effect of this scheduling by often going with the students to the other classes, primarily to observe, and by inviting those teachers into the classroom when relevant topics arose. In addition, the openness of the school and administration, and the amicable personal relationships among the teachers made an enormous difference in this regard. In some schools, teachers routinely "dropped in" for a friendly visit, picking up topics and themes with which to connect their subjects. For example, Dana's class was taught different subjects by different teachers in a team approach with lots of joint planning. When she was approached to become involved in the study, Dana said she would not do so unless we considered her planning partners exemplary and included them. So, although departmentalization did hinder integration, productive planning partnerships were possible.

## Class/School Schedule

Some schools enforced set schedules that created boundaries among subject areas even in self-contained classrooms. This style was basically a management decision. When the time was flexibly available to teachers, more inquiry-oriented and authentic projects were possible, and teachers could capitalize on a direction of study to shift attention to the same topic through a different subject domain. As one of the teachers said so succinctly, "I can't teach by a fixed schedule." Although there were curricular and time constraints in all of the schools, none of the teachers in this study worked in a school where time in various specific curriculum materials is tightly controlled, as might be seen, for example, in Success for All schools.

## State/District Testing Pressure

In some schools state mandates or testing pressures disrupted the integration of instruction, especially as the end of the year rolled around, when time pressure narrowed the classroom conversations and the consequent integration. Nevertheless, teacher determination produced some degree of integration. For example, when Mary Ellen was teaching social studies with the impending science test in the back of her mind, she could not help but use any opportunity to make the connection and remind students of an aspect of the science curriculum.

## Multiple Integrative Themes

Paradoxically, integrative themes were sometimes the enemy of integration for a similar reason to state/district testing pressure. For example, where the district basal reader specified one theme, the state social studies or science standards specified another; teacher and/or students had still other interests; and sometimes the district had add-on themes. Instead of facilitating integration, this mixed bag of integrative themes exacerbated the time–depth–breadth tensions and the tendency towards fragmentation.

## Monological Epistemology + Competition

At the start of this chapter we described the epistemology of the classroom as a framework that determined the fate of integration. A monological framework substantially reduces the likelihood of a range of integrative practices such as dialogue and inquiry. Furthermore, a monological framework is easily aligned with a competitive environment rather than a collaborative one. In such environments it is possible to hear students resist discussion because "you might give someone else the answer" (Thorkildsen, 1998). The reduction in collaborative interactions also reduces incidental forms of integration wherein students exchange experiences and ideas.

## Textbook/Basal

The very presence of 30 copies of a textbook implies a district-approved model of instruction that runs counter to integration, personalization, and a process-oriented focus. Furthermore, textbooks are often oriented around a delivery (monological) view of teaching and learning, which is usually accompanied by an emphasis on facts over meaning, splitting content from reading and writing, and splitting reading from writing as well. These divisions are particularly the case when there are separate textbooks for separate areas of instruction—social studies, reading, spelling, language arts, and so forth. The teachers in our study handled this mandate, depending on their circumstances, by supplementing the textbook(s) with trade books, research projects, and use of the Internet. They viewed the textbook(s) as *a* curriculum source, not *the* curriculum.

## INTEGRATING INTEGRATION

Applebee (1996), in referring to his work on effective secondary English classes, points out that "all elements are interrelated; discussion draws upon and reexamines previous ideas; conversation becomes self-sustaining" (p. 29). In spite of the obstacles we have described, the teachers we studied also produced this kind of coherence—and across many more curricular boundaries. However, the classrooms varied considerably in the nature and extent of integrated instruction. Often a single teacher took multiple stances on these matters in the course of a day, perhaps keeping math completely separate, while tightly integrating reading, writing, and art. Sometimes integration seemed forced, and sometimes so seamless as to appear "natural." But even in the most tightly integrated classrooms, there was still time scheduled for math, science, and other disciplines—and even if the integrative focus of the day absorbed these time slots, they were markers to help remind teachers to draw children's attention to important matters of disciplinary content and process.

It seemed to us that benefits accrued every time a child made a connection between something known in one domain and something being learned in another, as with the cognates of second-language learning. The word *like* was a marker of these interconnections. Whenever a student or teacher said "Oh, that's like . . . " mileage was gained in terms of knowledge consolidation through stronger connections, and the generalization of new knowledge (or strategy) beyond its immediate context. Fourth-grade academic subjects cover less familiar topics and more abstract concepts; linking the new to what is already known and to personal experience serves to ease the problem of acquisition and understanding. Furthermore, such connections, particularly those that are experiential, heighten the relevance of the subject matter.

The teachers' epistemological stances formed frameworks within which they interacted with students about reading, writing, math, science, and social studies, and in which students came to understand what it means to know and the significance of what they were learning. These teachers did not view themselves as specialists in subject matter. Although they taught the skills, information, and problem-solving strategies of the different disciplines, they were clear about the limits of their own knowledge, just as they were clear about the range of possible knowledge sources and the intrigue of novelty and complexity. They had confidence that the students' questions and problems would lead to engaging opportunities for disciplinary thinking. They did not abdicate their responsibility for orchestrating and initiating instruction, but they had a sense that children's time in school should be stimulating, that their learning should be relevant and meaningful, and that their job was teaching students to be independent and interdependent thinkers and citizens. Although they taught disciplinary thinking, they viewed it as subservient to these ends more than as an end in itself.

These teachers were, in fact, interested learners themselves; they were used to asking interesting questions and expected their students to do the same. They also listened to and respected their students. Doing so meant taking their ideas seriously, which naturally led to questions and issues that often exceeded disciplinary boundaries. At the same time, each of these teachers was very conscious of the official curriculum within which he or she was working. Overall, their commitment to integration and to this externally divided curriculum led to inventive ways to bring domains and disciplines together with efficiency and relevance.

The efficiency was necessary as an increasingly packed official curriculum left little time for the student-generated curriculum. And some of these efficiencies came with trade-offs. For example, bringing together the social studies and English curricula often meant that most of the works (novels, biographies, historical fiction, nonfiction) read in English language arts were selected to address social studies themes, reducing the range of works read in English. But such dilemmas are common in these teachers' lives. They live with constant tensions, suspended between their own and their students' controlling interests in the curriculum, between disciplinary thinking and the messiness of authentic questions and problems, between time spent building connections across domains and students, and time spent mastering individual domains. Just as Hargreaves and Moore (2000) found, integrated instruction is not easy and depends on a number of factors to be successful. At the same time, much about the design of modern schooling (schedules, textbooks, report cards, tests, state curriculum frameworks, licensure, preservice education methods courses, and so on), works against the achievement of integration. That it was so common in these rooms is primarily a statement about the remarkable efforts these teachers make to create intellectually demanding, but also engaging and rewarding, classroom experiences.

# 10

## Literate Achievements in Fourth Grade

In selecting the teachers we observed in this study, we used recommendations from multiple, informed sources, and observations. Test scores later provided additional support for the selection procedure. Although in seeking recommendations, we requested teachers who were successful in improving children's literacy performance, *literacy* was viewed quite broadly by those making the recommendations. The sentiment "I would like to have my child in this teacher's classroom" often accompanied the recommendations. Observing in these classrooms, we were often struck by this same feeling. We were also moved by the significance of what these teachers were accomplishing. Nevertheless, having watched in awe as teachers worked magic all day, it was common to hear them then express serious guilt over what they had *not* accomplished that day. In part because it seemed critical for the teachers to be aware of exactly what they *are* accomplishing, we turned some of our attention to describing the breadth of literate achievement in these classrooms.

That literate achievement is commonly—and solely—evaluated by standardized test performances has become an increasingly popular political stance. Observing the teachers and students in these classrooms, however, made us very aware of the inadequacy of these instruments for representing what students can learn in the process of acquiring literacy. What if children perform well enough on tests but never read a book of their own volition, or are unable or unwilling to generate productive conversations about what they do read? What if they learn to answer questions about texts they have read but have no sense of their own authority in their learning from these texts. What if, in the process of teaching children to become literate and perform well on tests, we diminish the development of curiosity? We documented the extent and variety of children's reading and writing in these classrooms through reading logs and writing folders; does sheer volume of reading and writing only count if it leads to improved test performance? Do the *habits* of literacy count as outcomes of schooling in addition to normative test performance? Must we trade one type of literate achievement for another?

Yevette Wanlass (2000) recently raised these questions in an article entitled "Broadening of the Concept of Learning and School Competence," where she pointed out that we should not value solely the "academic outcomes" and that a sense of competence is a basic psychological need. Our experience in this study leads us to agree with this view and to argue further that what is achieved in these classrooms is not simply a matter of valuing "nonacademic" outcomes and building a sense of competence. Observing in these classrooms and interviewing the students, we became increasingly aware of the significance of Vygotsky's (1978) claim that children grow into the intellectual environment of those around them.

This claim, now widely recognized in a range of disciplines, asserts the importance of the discursive classroom environment and argues that, in the process of becoming literate, children are learning not just ways of doing but *ways of being*. They are building literate identities and relationships and acquiring sets of values, beliefs, and epistemologies (Collins, 1995; Egan-Robertson, 1998; Ferdman, 1990; Gee, 1996; Johnston et al., 2001; Mahiri & Godley, 1998). In this chapter we explore a variety of literate achievements that are central to what we observed being accomplished in these classrooms but that are routinely ignored in discussions of outcomes—especially outcomes that are used to typify "effective" schools, classrooms, and teachers.

## ANALYTIC STRATEGY

The achievements we identify here are the result of an exploratory analysis of our data in which we sought patterns in a manner consistent with grounded theory (Glaser & Strauss, 1967), yet clearly influenced by our reading on democracy (e.g., Barber, 1984; Nicholls, 1989), discursive psychology (Harre & Gillett, 1994), communities of practice (Wenger, 1998), and a range of related topics such as dialogue (Burbules, 1993; Nystrand, 1997), caring (Noddings, 1984), and discourse analysis (Gee, 1996). Because of our interest in helping teachers understand and acquire a language for describing their classroom accomplishments, we focused our attention on productive examples. Nonetheless, the less positive examples that occur in almost every classroom, albeit substantially less in these classrooms, often provided the necessary contrast to reveal the significance of the productive ones.

In our analysis we tried to capitalize on moments of surprise or tension documented in the data—what Fairclough (1995) calls "cruces." For example, observing a group of urban fourth graders engage in a respectful and philosophical conversation for over an hour, with little intervention from the teacher, was a surprise that prompted us to consider its significance. A second example: When one student was asked, "Who are the good writers in the class?," she rejected the question as being an unreasonable way to talk about writers. Assuming this perspective to be a part of her literate socialization, we were prompted to contemplate what were regarded as "normal" conceptions and in this classroom. We documented these taken-for-granted aspects of classroom literate life as important, in part, because of their very invisibility to learners. It is this invisibility that makes it possible for teachers doing remarkable work in their classrooms to feel guilty at the end of the day for what they had *not* accomplished, rather than noticing what they *had* accomplished.

The case studies presented in this book reveal some of the range of possible productive learning environments teachers construct. Our initial selection of teachers who were successful in producing literate achievement opened the possibility of examining other differences in what was achieved through the classroom discourse. Furthermore, our selection of students who were more and less academically successful in those classrooms made it possible for us to examine the effects of discourse practices across different levels of normative competence.

In our analysis we attempt to expand the indicators and conceptions of children's literate development. Table 10.1 lists the important but neglected categories of literate achievement that arose in our

TABLE 10.1. Literate Achievements

---

*What it means to know (epistemology)*

- Self as knower
- Relationship to other knowers
- Relationship to object/subject of study
- Knowing/feeling/morality relationship
- What counts as an academic discipline, who does it, what counts as acceptable questions and evidence, theory versus data
- Habit of mind of observation/noticing

*What it means to be literate*

- Competence and its significance
- Agency

*Participation structures*

- Significance of, and relationships among, participants
- Distributed thinking
- Tolerance for, and ability to maintain, openness
- Sense of concrete practice of conducting scientific work

*Language*

- Valuing
- Inquiry into language
- Genre range and function
- Complexity of reasoning/argument

*Social imagination*

- Stepping outside one's own world
- Imagining characters and audiences
- Empathizing

---

analysis, and upon which we will now elaborate. These categories are not discrete but rather working emphases.

## THE RANGE OF LITERATE ACHIEVEMENTS

Every day another layer of "sediment" is laid down in children's minds around conceptions of literacy, identity, and literate relationships. Interaction by interaction, they learn what counts as a normal literate conversation, who has the right to an opinion about a piece of writing, whose experience counts, what it means to be a reader or writer, and so forth. Some of this learning can be observed as students talk about their reading and writing and pursue their daily literate practices. For example, a student who, when asked, "Are there different kinds of readers in your class?," notes that "some people like fiction, nonfiction, mysteries . . . challenging books, easy books . . . " has learned different things from a student who answers, "Some kids are at a little higher level than I am." What has been learned is (1) a conception of what it means to be literate, and (2) a conception of self and others as literate beings—in essence, a conception of personal competence and its interpersonal significance. Like the sense of masculinity or femininity (Gilbert, 1989; Malinowitz, 1995), these complex learnings are acquired as unstated presuppositions that form the infrastructure of literate development. The fact that they are often not stated directly makes them transparent and easy to assimilate (Todorov, 1996). However there is no question that these often subtle understandings are brought to children's interactions with print, and with each other around print, in ways that influence their meaning making.

## What It Means to Know

In the process of becoming literate, students learn what it means to know, who they are as knowers, and about the relationship between knowers and what is known. This is the province of epistemology. As Kelly (1995) notes "Reading and writing per se are not just essential forms of communicative action. . . . [but are] fused with questions of power and control in the structuring of knowledge itself" (p. 101). Consider Carlos's evaluation of himself as a writer: "Umm, bad. I never think of nothing to write about." This statement could be interpreted as indicating as a simple lack of skill or as suggesting a deeper epistemological concern. Carlos is certainly not alone in thinking that, in writing, he has nothing to say—but in most of the classrooms we observed, he would have been an anomaly. Students in these classrooms made and recorded careful observations and engaged in extended conversations with each other in which they routinely hypothesized explanations supported by a range of warrants, including their own experience—whose validity they assumed. These students expected to be taken seriously, took each other seriously, took seriously the particular subject of discussion or study, empathized with the object of study, followed up on their own initiative, and engaged in passionate exchange about it. They had developed a sense of the kinds of questions that are useful to ask, they routinely generated theories, and many knew what would count as evidence to justify or falsify their logic. Furthermore, they were not defensive about the possibility of having their theories countered by evidence from others. Indeed, students would offer half-formulated ideas for group consideration, with the expectation that they would be picked up and advanced by the group (a point we will return to presently).

At the same time, these students were learning about their relationship with their subject of study and with others involved in the study. Some developed a close relationship to their subject of study. Students learned that science involves observing and theorizing (orally and in print) as well as recording and representing. They learned what counts as science and social studies, who does it, what types of questions and evidence are acceptable as theory and as data—all indispensable for developing critical reading and writing. A good example of this process occurred in Joan's classroom (Chapter 3), when the children began to learn that doing science, such as dissecting duck eggs, involves inescapable ethical decisions.

In order to study exemplary literacy instruction, we chose classrooms in which there was some integration in the teaching. Children learned literacy in their subject areas, such as science and social studies, and vice versa. Indeed, our argument is that in science, for example, students are learning more about literacy as they read, take notes, write reports, and engage in discussions. In the process they learn what it means to conduct scientific work, who gets to do the conducting, who gets to ask the questions, theorize, manipulate, and document. They also learn where knowledge comes from—be it from authorless books, teachers, or their own research. When students construct their own experiments to answer their own questions, and document and report the results, as they did in some of our classrooms, they learn significantly more than the answer to the question. Similarly, when a proposed handwriting lesson is turned into an inquiry into how letters can be grouped by similarities, and which letters occur more frequently, in general, something more than handwriting knowledge is being acquired.

It is clear from our observations in these classrooms that these children developed theories of knowledge—epistemologies—and that their theories have more or less desirable implications. These theories are gleaned from daily literacy instruction in relation to literature, science, math, and social studies, and a year of such experience is unlikely to be discarded at the end of the grade. Parker Palmer (1993) points out that "the way a teacher plays the mediator role conveys both an epistemology and an ethic to the student, both an approach to knowing and an approach to living" (p. 29).

## What It Means to Be Literate: Conceptions of Literate Competence and Agency

There were substantial differences among students in their understandings of "normal" literate practice and the nature and significance of literate competence, in their sense of who they were as literate people and their sense of agency in their literate practice. Consider the conceptions of literacy and competence that underlie these comments students provided during our interviews.

- "When [good readers] read, they don't stutter or they don't mess up on words as much."
- "Good readers are the people who read the most books . . . who really enjoy it."
- "I'm a little better at it. . . . Last year I got a C, this year, a B+ on my report card."
- "I love to read mystery, adventure, suspense, and I like to read books about animals doing everyday things that we do."

These comments, though merely the tips of very large and complex conceptual icebergs, nevertheless reveal very different conceptions of literate practice—what literate people do and how and why they do it—and of what it means to be considered competent.

### Competence and Its Significance

For some students the central feature of being literate is saying or spelling the words correctly and quickly. Within this framework students are likely to be evaluated as either "good" or "not good." Satisfaction must be derived from successes (usually comparative) in convention, accuracy, and speed. There is little room in this conception for collaborative literate engagements.

Other students, such as the one who declined to engage in a conversation about "good" and "bad" writers, reject such simplistic categories as neither normal nor sensible. Indeed, that particular student essentially said to an adult authority, "That is a foolish line of conversation that I will not be party to," in much the same way as she might reject an invitation to engage in racist talk. For this student, and others like her, engagement or meaning making is the central feature of literate practice. Within this framework, differences in students' interests and experiences are regarded as normal and useful because they introduce new and interesting ways of thinking and are not easily pitted against one another. To be competent is to create interesting stories or interesting interpretations, or simply to be fully engaged (even if the product is of interest only to the student creating it). This conceptual understanding is an important literate achievement that contains space for different relationships among the students and different constructions of identity than would occur in a more normative framework.

In distinguishing the good authors in his class, one student described them by their strengths. For example, "For the funny part, Jessie is really funny. He writes a lot about fantasy stuff." Then there's Ron, who's "a pretty good writer . . . and he's a little better at drawing than writing . . . [and] Emilia gave details [in her mystery], as she described the characters. It was a really good mystery because it had a point and it had something that the reader had to figure out." This is a conception of competence that has much more room for others—unlike a competitive conception, which is inherently hierarchical and insists on some having more capacity than others, resulting in asymmetrical power relationships. Such competitive conceptions were not associated solely with the normatively more capable students. We encountered children who did well on tests but whose conceptions of literate competence, particularly their own, were more like those of the lowest performing students in other classes, and vice versa (Johnston et al., 2001). Furthermore, it is not that in some classes students were simply unaware of their normative competence with conventional spelling and word recognition. On the contrary, students always noticed such things. Rather, they knew this information but found it generally irrelevant, for most practical purposes. More relevant was the sphere of interest and expertise, and the persistent engagement. However, they did use their knowledge of relative differences in word recognition competence when they recommended books to each other.

In other words, differences in the ways students came to understand both their own competence as literate individuals and the significance of that competence in relation to others were acquired, along with other "skills." Some children came to believe that being competent means technical efficiency and that the significance of their competence is that they have power over others to give or withhold information or to demean. Other children learned that the significance of their competence is the pleasure they get from it and that they are able to contribute different dimensions to the meaning-making enterprise and to other students' developing competence.

## Sense of Agency

Part of students' understanding of themselves as literate individuals lies in their sense of agency—the extent to which they feel a sense of control and responsibility in their literate practices. We saw in June's classroom (Chapter 5) how students, having studied the topic of war, wrote letters to politicians expressing opinions about what should be done. These students learn a literacy that is used as a tool to implement action in relation to social causes. The absence of this sense of agency diminishes engagement as well as literacy learning. For example, one very capable writer in another classroom, when asked how he would describe himself as a writer, commented, "Very good and then not very good." When asked what made him say that, he noted, "Sometimes I get really good grades, and sometimes I get really bad grades." When choosing his best piece of writing, his logic was "I got a good grade on it." Asked what he had learned most recently as a writer, he could not think of anything, but after a very long pause, he noted that "If you're stuck, either keep on thinking or ask for help." In spite of this student's tested competence, he shows little sense of agency in either his writing or his literate learning. In contrast in another classroom, a student describes herself as a good writer because "I can write for a long time, and I like writing, and when I get a topic, I can flow on it and just keep writing and writing." When things do not go smoothly, she knows what to do: "With my Diana report, I got stuck in the beginning because there was, like, too much information. I just thought, well, what is the most interesting and what would the reader like to hear about."

In a similar vein, we asked students what they had learned most recently in reading and writing and what they would like to learn next. Some students, both high and low performing, could not comprehend the question we were asking. They had no sense of their own learning or of the possibility of exercising some control over it.

Others were able to answer such questions. For example, Justin observed: "I learned that I really do like books like *Hatchet* and that I know what kind . . . so when I go to the library, I know what kind of books I want to pick out." Students who gave such responses had a sense that ability is not a matter of capacity but of learning, as well as a sense of their own learning trajectory—which opens the possibility of agency in their own development.

Our data suggest that the sense of agency comes from three principle sources. First, students' attention is drawn to the process of how things get done. One of the important features of these classrooms is the regularity with which conversations about *how* something gets done are conducted. Others have found similar phenomena. For example, Hume (2001) reports an upper-grade elementary student observing, "Other years we focused on getting things done, but now we take things one step further, by processing how we do things while getting them done" (p. 103). Second, students are socialized to notice details of literate performance so that changes can be recognized and connected to the process. Third, there is an expectation that literacy and learning are goal-directed and consequential. These sources of agency were present in the classrooms we observed, to varying degrees. Students who have a sense of agency about their own literate development feel in control of their learning. They can answer the questions like "What would you like to learn next in writing (or reading)?" and "How are you going to learn about it?" They also view literacy as a tool they can use to accomplish their own goals. They see themselves as people who *do* read and write and will continue to do so.

## Participation Structures

It remains common to think of literacy as an individual act, carried out solely within the confines of one's own head. Indeed, posters designed to encourage children to read portray it as a solitary activity, and current testing practices insist upon this view. This, despite the fact that many have demonstrated (Dyson, 1993; McGill-Franzen & Lanford, 1994) literacy to be a social endeavor; and, outside of school, people use print in social ways and for social purposes. Furthermore, thinking (a central part of literacy) is often sharpened and refined through dialogue. For example, in several classrooms we saw intense discussions taking place around books and other texts over an extended period. In Sandy's classroom (Chapter 6), book discussions led to students "becoming" the characters in *Charlotte's Web* (White, 1974). In Joan's room (Chapter 3) the children bounced off each others' ideas, children hypothesizing about the ducklings' pecking behavior, with Art suggesting that it might be territorial and asking what would happen if the tank were larger; Aja adding the possibility that it is like gang behavior and signals exclusion; Clive proposing that it is like monkeys' grooming behavior. Others noted that:

> "All the ducklings did it at the beginning."
> "Maybe it's not that bad—you just don't know."
> "Maybe they like to peck, and they are bored with pecking the food."

Each added a new layer of possibility and a different way to make sense of what was being observed. Our teachers encouraged this kind of interplay through comments such as, "You need to listen to each other so you can help each other to refine your questions."

These literate thoughts are unlikely to have been thought without the conversational environment in which they arose. As noted, such social environments are called "dialogical" by Nystrand and his colleagues (1996), and contrasted with "monological" environments, which consist primarily of IRE (teacher initiates, student responds, teacher evaluates) interaction patterns. The learning potential of dialogical environments has been documented elsewhere. Lori Shepard (2000), in writing about productive curriculum, asked, "Could we create a learning culture where students and teachers would have a shared expectation that finding out what makes sense and what doesn't is a joint and worthwhile project, essential to taking the next steps in learning?" (p. 10). Based on our research, we can assert that such environments can be created, and that this experience of learning via dialogue is an acquisition that students take with them, and which contains strategies and expectations that constitute major achievements.

In some classrooms we saw evidence of another important achievement: Children appeared to be developing the ability to take control of this intellectual tool—knowing how to ask "big" questions and how to respond productively to others—enabling them to structure literate social contexts to scaffold their own thinking. Ultimately, this ability enables children to take control of their own intellectual development, a particularly important achievement because, in learning how to do this, children also have to learn to value differences—since it is differences in thinking that tend to lead to more interesting literate conversations, and associated thoughts. Such a conceptual achievement has the added advantage of producing a more powerful stance toward diversity than mere tolerance of differences.

Other researchers have documented this important aspect of literate development, referring to it as "distributed cognition" (Salomon, 1993), and making it clear that it is not merely a context for literate thinking but a kind of literate thinking in itself (Resnick, 1991). The central feature of distributed thinking is the cooperation of multiple minds, through talk, to produce more complex thought than any one of the minds could produce independently. It requires setting up trusting relationships such that participants can feel comfortable extending half-baked or barely formulated ideas into the public arena, knowing that they will not be judged but, rather, that someone else will pick up the idea and extend it. This sort of conversation requires a tolerance for and ability to maintain openness, and a set of normalized or expected attributes that includes trust, respect, and distributed authority. These conditions, expectations, and competencies were clearly evident in many classrooms, though not recorded on the standard assessments of literacy instruction outcomes.

Distributed thought, and the strategic refinement of it is a literate achievement, should be valued not only as a fundamental competence in a democratic citizen but as equally for productive business organizations. One student asked whether she had writing conferences with other students, replied matter-of-factly, "Yes. I read my story and if they really like it, they say so, and if they don't like it, they try to give me some ideas that they think could make it better. And I try to do the same for them."

## Language

One of Sandy's students (Chapter 6) noticed that Wilbur in *Charlotte's Web* (White, 1952) and Little Ann in *Where the Red Fern Grows* (Rawls, 1989), are both described as *runts*; Aja, a student in Joan's class (Chapter 3), created the word *cutified*. Both students are demonstrating that they value literate language (in the latter case, valuing language so much that it is worth savoring certain words and playing with them). This propensity is important for the ongoing expansion of literate competence. Similarly, the student in June's class

(Chapter 5) who wrote, "I'm as slow as a rock that sat on a glacier . . . I'm as fast as electricity." was not just learning to write interesting similes but to think metaphorically, an important cognitive tool. The effects of such linguistic acquisitions might well show up on tests. However, the noticing and treasuring of language that is acquired is an important literate achievement *in and of itself.*

Beyond noticing and valuing language, we found that in some classes children were learning to notice and inquire into authors' particular use of language. For example, there were discussions of the gendered use of language and the appropriateness of particular terms for minority groups. Discussions in classrooms where children are asked to "talk about the story in terms of what the writer did" and to examine carefully their word choice in their own writing, take on greater significance as children come to understand their agency in both reading and writing. Johnston et al. (2001) report a student's comments about his writing: "But then I said to myself, well, where's a place that gets the reader in good suspense so they want to read on, but it's a good stopping place?" and, "how can I make it . . . make that word 'trophy' be more symbolized in the statue" (p. 229). Word usage is an important and relevant achievement, particularly in the current media environment in which children are bombarded by carefully manipulated language, and by language whose history gives it peculiar power over us. Although word usage can be taught as a skill, potentially measurable on a standardized test, as a propensity it is even more valuable.

Not normally screened in standardized tests is children's knowledge of the kinds of texts that are available for use, and their functions. For example, in one class children wrote fantasies, research reports, realistic fiction, essays, poetry (two forms), biography, mystery, journals, goal statements, reflective analysis of their own writing, friendly letter, formal letter requesting information, thank-you letter, and various Internet forms. Other classrooms explored only three or four forms. This knowledge is not likely to be tapped by most standardized tests, which sample from a smaller range of genres, but the broader understanding of social, communicative, and functional possibilities to be explored through writing is nonetheless important.

We observed children using language that was more complex than we would expect of fourth graders—partly as a result of dialogical instruction, we believe. For example, in one discussion in

Joan's class (Chapter 3), Shirley proposed a pecking order theory to explain the ducklings' pecking behavior. Her proposal drew disagreement from Jack and Gordon, who believed that the older ducks were aware of other ducklings' ages and infirmities and would therefore make suitable accommodations. The discussion continued until Laura made the following statement, which synthesized many of the points so far: "I disagree with Shirley because [evidence], and I agree with Jack and Gordon because [observation] and . . . [observation] . . . So . . . [hypothesis] . . . because . . . [observation]. . . . But . . . [observation]" (Johnston, 1998, p. 96). The complexity of this thought is unusual for a fourth grader and we believe it is unlikely to have occurred without the scaffolding of dialogical interactions. Indeed, we saw this as a wonderful example of distributed cognition (Salomon, 1993): students of varying competence collaborated conversationally to produce thought and language that was more complex than any one of them could have produced independently.

## Social Imagination

Some of the children we observed developed what we and others (Dyson, 1993; Johnston, 1993) call a "social imagination"—the ability, and propensity, to imagine the thinking and experiences that lie behind people's actions: why an author chose a particular word or setting, what motivated a character to do certain things, what would persuade a particular reader or audience. Activities like theater and role playing book characters, as occurred in Sandy's class (Chapter 6), were commonly associated with the display of this competence. Even classroom management practices that required students to understand others' motives and responses seemed productive in this regard.

We gathered clues to this kind of development in the book discussions and in our interviews. For example, when we asked children who else in the class would like a particular book, they offered observations such as:

- "Probably Patrick. He's not the kind of guy who laughs, and he doesn't smile too much. And in this book, he might smile."
- "Ryan kind of likes challenging books, and that's kind of a challenging book, [and] he kind of likes adventure, and that's pretty much adventure."

Other ways in which the students showed us they had developed a social imagination came in their observations about characters' motives and their writerly recognition of an audience's needs. Another poignant indicator appeared: When a student classified as emotionally disturbed was quietly perseverating on his torn page during reading group and his neighbor noticed and simply traded books.

Some aspects of a social imagination such as imagining a character's motives, an author's intent, or what would persuade an audience, might well show up on a sophisticated test. However, the underlying empathic competence, central to caring and democratic living, particularly in a diverse society (Giroux, 1991), might easily pass unnoticed and not be counted as a critical achievement of exemplary teaching practice.

## NOT JUST SKILLS, NOT JUST FRILLS

The accomplishments we have documented in this chapter are not merely processes that lead to "real achievement" on tests. Some of them almost certainly do so, of course, but not all. We argue, instead, that they are important achievements in themselves. Genuinely collaborative learning practices might be justified on the basis of their effectiveness in producing testable learning. We argue, instead, that within such forms of participation, students acquire values, beliefs, practices, and norms that become part of who they are as literate people and shape how they participate in literate activities. They become part of the sedimentary base of students' identities as literate citizens. Consequently, understanding the nature of these outcomes is critical to any effort to improve literacy instruction. Finding out "what works" requires also asking "works to achieve which end?"

These accomplishments, however subtle, cannot be viewed as mere icing on the test-score cake. We believe that, rather than frills to be added after other "basics" have been learned, these accomplishments are themselves equally basic. Not only do they form the foundation for the acquisition of other competencies, but they are also central qualities in a democratic citizenry. Palmer (1993) makes it clear that "deliberation . . . is the basic labor of strong democracy—the labor necessary to create, deepen, and extend democracy in an ongoing manner" (p. 204). Such deliberation was common in the classrooms we studied and was relatively (and uncommonly) free of counterproductive exclusions and power dynamics. These class-rooms were socializing children in a way that enables them to form caring, literate relationships and participate in civic engagement, through and in literacy—a socialization that is central to a demo-cratic society (Powell, 1999). In order for children to be able to bal-ance their own interests against those of others, towards the greater good, they must stand in their own shoes and, at the same time, in those of others. They must develop social imaginations and the pro-pensity to use them. Developing such "democratic minds" (Reichen-bach, 1998, p. 233) requires a democratic intellectual life into which the minds can grow. Many of the classrooms we observed provided exactly this sort of literate environment. Not only are such accom-plishments often not recognized, but the complexity of accomplish-ing them for every student, while managing 25–35 students in a class, is also often not recognized.

Remember, too, that not all classrooms offered students quite such an ideal set of circumstances. Some of the teachers who were perfectly capable, as indicated by classroom standardized test scores, were less productive in terms of these other aspects of literate achievement (Johnston et al., 2001). Our data indicate that providing such an intellectual experience *does not compromise* the achievement of good test scores. In this sense, it is possible to have most of our cake and eat it, too.

Failure to recognize these important aspects of literate develop-ment leaves teachers unaware of the full importance of their work as they apprentice children into a literate democracy. This lack of awareness leads to the wearing and distracting guilt we heard de-scribed by many of the teachers, who were unable to fully recognize and name the fruits of their own instruction. Indeed, in spite of our arguments about the discursive nature of learning, we are aware that some of those who agree with the importance of what we have docu-mented will nonetheless argue that though it is important, it is not literacy. The problem with this stance is where it is likely to lead: If these unrecognized aspects are not part of literacy, and also do not fall into the other subject areas, they can easily become devalued and even squeezed out of the curriculum in the press to accomplish those aspects that are named as being a legitimate part of the curriculum.

# 11

---

# The Nature of Good
# Fourth-Grade Teaching

The six case studies in this volume typify the good fourth-grade teaching we observed. While working in school and classroom contexts that varied one from another, each of these teachers created a rich, engaging learning environment. The case studies were prepared from the field notes members of the research team composed during the 10 days spent in each teacher's classroom (the field note methodology was designed to capture both the structure of classroom activity and the essence of the language environment) along with audio and video recordings of classroom activities, which allowed closer analysis of some lessons. Additional data were gathered in (1) two semistructured and multiple spontaneous interviews with each teacher, (2) structured interviews with target children from each classroom, and (3) samples of student writing and reading logs provided by children. In our overview here of the cross-case instructional methods and processes, we draw upon two independent cross-case analyses of these data, both designed to locate common features of good fourth-grade teaching (Allington & Johnston, 2000; Boothroyd, Day, Johnston, & Cedeno, 1999). Twelve teachers from the larger sample of exemplary fourth-grade teachers, including the six teachers featured in this volume, provided the primary data for these analyses. We documented four common features of the instruction offered by the exemplary fourth-grade teachers, each of which is detailed below:

- The nature of classroom talk.
- The nature of the organization and use of curriculum materials.
- The nature and organization of instruction.
- The nature of evaluation.

Although we attempt to discuss these four features independently, for practical purposes, there is a substantial degree of interdependence.

## THE NATURE OF CLASSROOM TALK

Perhaps the single most striking feature of these classrooms was the nature of the conversations that flowed therein. The observers routinely noted that students in these classrooms talked with the teacher and with each other much more often than has been reported previously in the research literature (e.g., Cazden, 1988; Dillon, 1988; Mehan, 1979; Nystrand, 1997). The talk was respectful, supportive, and productive, and not only was it modeled by the teacher in her interactions with students, but it was also deliberately taught, nurtured, and expected. Creating such conversational communities was the focus of lessons across the year, but especially at the beginning of the year, and required building trusting relationships. Talk between teacher and student was often personalized, focused on the student's personal knowledge of various topics, his or her strengths and interests—and included conversations about homelife and out-of-school events.

Classroom talk was process-oriented; these teachers used conversations—*authentic* conversations—to learn about their students. Even the instructional talk was often conversational, as these teachers engaged students in discussions of their understandings, responses, and puzzlements. These teachers routinely encouraged students to engage each other's ideas, and authority was more distributed than centralized. While Knapp (1995) noted that discussion was a central feature of the higher-achievement classrooms he studied, we also noted that, in the case-study classrooms, discussions included a considerable amount of what we call "tentative talk"— open-ended talk that made it possible for others to complete incomplete ideas or otherwise contribute to the group thinking and understanding. When Kim Duhamel says "I don't know, let's look on the Internet," or when Joan Backer says "Tell me what you are think-ing," the interaction conveys a spirit of exploration and a valuing of multiple responses to a text or a question and leave the conversa-tional floor open for further discussion. Such conversations clearly involve an element of trust and a nonjudgmental context. It is proba-bly no coincidence that both Ruddell's (1997) and Ladson-Billing's (1994) teachers ranked establishing trust through personal contact with students as a critically important feature of their teaching.

We describe the teacher talk as tentative in that all answers were treated as having potential; rarely was *no* or *wrong* uttered by the teachers (except in response to gross social transgressions, which oc-curred very rarely in these classrooms). Rather, they identified what was productive about a response or behavior, supported the partially correct, turned attention to the process, and encouraged further thinking or reflection, even about a "correct" answer. The teachers readily admitted (1) their limited knowledge of various topics (nota-bly those raised by their students), (2) their mistakes, and (3) their own interests. Tracey Bennett's confession to her students that she was responsible for confusing them, and Joan Backer's admission of error, for example, made the teachers "real," distributed authority, turned error-making into a source of learning and strategy refine-ment, and opened a space for authentic dialogue. As with Haber-man's (1995a) successful teachers, those in our sample routinely demonstrated the limits of their own knowledge and expertise—their fallibility. Their natural demonstrations of *how* literate people think as they read and write—including making errors and self-correcting—made their own and their students' thinking available as models and for discussion.

This flowing and productive classroom talk also made genuine in-quiry possible—indeed, common—and inquiry about underlying pro-cesses were a normal topic of conversation ("How could we find that out?"). The emphasis was clearly on making meaning and the means for doing so. Normalizing conversations about the process of making meaning and accomplishing meaningful ends also meant that strategies were regularly modeled and articulated by both teacher and students. By identifying the process they used for solving problems, students lo-cated themselves in a position of agency with respect to learning. Sev-eral of the teachers actively encouraged students to build identities around this agency, with comments such as, "As writers, how can you solve this problem?" (Ivey, Johnston, & Cronin, 1998).

The observed instruction was more conversational than interrogational. Conversation involves verbal interactions that invite individual participation and contributions. When teachers ask, " What are *you* thinking?" or "Where would *you* prefer to live?" or "Say more about that," they are inviting students into a conversation and not into a recall competition. The dominance of the IRE sequence was replaced in these classrooms, as noted earlier, by the IRRRR sequence. And, as also noted earlier, instructional conversations between students were common (not just between teachers and students). As researchers, we pondered over various strategies that would allow us to capture multiple, simultaneous instructional conversations that we observed occurring throughout these classrooms. We never did identify or construct a procedure that suited the complexity of this task. We believe that work on this problem should top the agenda of those interested in studying the impact of teachers and their teaching.

The talk in these classrooms was also connective. That is, these teachers routinely connected (1) topics under study to earlier topics and to students' experiences and background knowledge, (2) authors to other works by the same author and to other authors' works, (3) strategies from one subject to another, (4) lessons from one week or month to the next, and so on. When the teachers weren't making such connections explicitly, they were asking students to consider connections. Again, however, as researchers, we lack even a basic scheme for describing this connecting language.

## THE NATURE OF THE ORGANIZATION
## AND USE OF CURRICULUM MATERIALS

The curriculum in these classrooms was commonly multisourced. These teachers typically organized their instruction around multiple curricular materials rather than relying on a single text or curricular material. Although many teachers often dipped into textbooks on science, social studies, and reading, they hardly ever followed the traditional curriculum plan for these subjects. For instance, they might use the social studies basal on Mondays to introduce the chapter topic and then use supplementary texts on the remaining days of the week. Or they might complete three chapters in a social studies text during a single week and then, for the following 2 weeks, have students read supplementary texts, research, and write on that topic or theme.

A strong literary emphasis pervaded these classrooms, each of which had substantial libraries. The teachers used historical fiction, biography, and informational books in social studies, for instance. They drew reading materials from, or had their students locate them on, the Internet, in magazines, and in other nontraditional curricular sources. These texts and trade books were used to model strategies in thinking and composing, to enrich and extend understandings of content, and to promote high-volume, engaged reading. These teachers, then, were more inclined to fill students' days with reading and writing beyond the textbooks, as earlier studies of effective teaching have well documented (e.g., Knapp, 1995; Ruddell, 1997; Pressley et al., 1998). This more extensive use "beyond the textbook" materials provided not only substantially greater opportunities to read but also introduced substantially more content. Thus we typically observed a "win–win" situation as students developed improved reading proficiency and expanded knowledge of core academic content through this use of more varied reading.

Materials in these classrooms commonly reflected a diversity of genres, of human cultural, gender, and class experience. We saw studies of different cultures strongly supported through children's literature. Concentrations of African American, Asian American, or Native American works (less often Hispanic) occurred not just in schools with higher proportions of these students but in classes that had almost none of them.

The organization of a multisourced curriculum also led to a multilevel curriculum—texts that varied in their range of difficulty. This variation resulted in texts students could actually read and understand—*all* the students. The combination of these two features appeared to be central to the high levels of engagement in academic work that we observed across the classrooms of these teachers (and which, again, has been well documented previously in more effective classrooms). The multisourced and multilevel curriculum also fostered independence and a sense of ownership of the topic, and instruction was more easily and often personalized. These features, in turn, made it possible for teachers to work with small groups and individuals without constant distraction.

Sometimes curricular goals and materials involved fundraising and planning for a class trip, participating in a local history project, conducting class and community surveys, or running a class business. In other words, difficulty, relevance, and meaning were important aspects of the curricular materials teachers selected to use.

Far too often, however, these teachers worked with limited organizational support in these matters, receiving from their school districts multiple copies of the same basal text. As has been demonstrated (Budiansky, 2001; Chall & Conard,1991; Ciborowski, 1994), these textbooks are neither well written nor interesting and, additionally, are too difficult for many students to read. To craft the sorts of curriculum that we typically observed, these teachers had to locate the supplementary texts (or have students do so) and often then purchase selected materials with their own funds. Good teaching should not be so difficult.

Language itself was a curriculum material—a topic of meaningful study in the materials teachers read to students, the materials students read themselves, and the texts the students composed. In these classrooms, even word study (a standard feature) emphasized a search for meaningful patterns, meaning acquisition, interest in words and turns of phrase, and the strategic, purposeful selection of words. We observed wall charts where students posted interesting words they encountered in their reading. Periodically, words served as the focus of group or class discussions. In some classrooms, students "captured" phrases or sentences from the texts they read, language bits that they felt demonstrated an interesting, skillful, or powerful use of words, as in Joan's "I wish I had written . . . " assignments. These teachers drew attention to and praised the skillful use of language in students' writing and during class discussions, and would interrupt their read-alouds to marvel over the turn of a phrase in literature. Skillful use of language was noticed and celebrated.

In this managed-choice model, teachers set out multiple curriculum materials within a framework that honored student interests and, at the same time, accommodated required curriculum topics. For instance, when students were studying the Iroquois confederacy or the California mission period as part of the mandated study of state history, teachers might use a social studies textbook that presented coverage of the topic but supplement this with a collection of 20–60 books of various levels of complexity from which students could choose three to read. Thus teachers managed the range of text choices and, at times, were even more direct in steering certain students toward reading particular texts. In science class each student might select a local insect to study—to observe, sketch, and gather data to be organized and presented to the class. The teacher might very well provide a framework for the sorts of data to be gathered and the general format for the presentation, but students still were given broad leeway in both selection and preparation of their reports.

All these features, in our view, worked to ensure that more kids were engaged in productive academic work more minutes of the day. The available supply of appropriately difficult texts, the options that allowed students more control over the texts to be read and the work to be accomplished, the collaborative nature of much of the work, the opportunity to discuss what was read and written, and the meaningfulness of the activities are previously established features of high-engagement learning environments (Almasi & McKeown, 1996; Pressley, 2002; Turner, 1995; Wigfield, 1997). Unfortunately, researchers often narrow their focus to one or two factors because of their interactive complexity. Rarely are these factors treated as part of a larger interacting cluster of classrooms characteristics. In fact, we know of no observational system capable of tracking the impact of these factors in the complex learning environment of the classroom.

## THE NATURE AND ORGANIZATION OF INSTRUCTION

The exemplary teachers we observed planned their instruction, but, at the same time, remained prepared to depart from and revise their plans to capitalize on the "teaching moment." Indeed, we might think of them as planful opportunists, because their plans tended to foster instructional opportunities. In their planning, these teachers sought learner engagement first and situated their concern for curriculum coverage somewhere lower on the agenda. Their instruction was a sort of problem setting. They strove to focus student attention on problems to address rather than simply "facts" to be learned. Although the instruction was not "individualized" in the traditional sense, it was "personalized" in that these teachers knew their students' interests and needs, strengths and weaknesses.

We observed frequent use of managed choice in these classrooms. Although students did not exercise full control over the instructional decisions, these teachers presented choices to students and made sure they either chose productively or learned from their errors. Choice in conjunction with the use of *open tasks*—tasks for which there are multiple "correct" answers and multiple routes for demonstrating knowledge and skill acquisition—are clearly linked to the high levels of engagement we observed (Turner, 1995). Open tasks also provide multiple opportunities for making thinking visible. As students explain their responses, and as their teachers probe to clarify and extend, other students get a window into the thinking of their peers. And when their teachers ask how else the problem might be solved, students learn to be flexible in their use of strategy.

In the format of open tasks, students selected the sort of project they would complete while working with a novel; they invented their own dinosaurs after reading *Miss Rumphius* (Cooney, 1982); they often selected the texts they would read to complete a unit of study; they shared narratives of their own design. All this, when coupled with the invitations to participate in discussions—to supply one's two-cents worth—fostered high levels of engagement throughout the school day and personalized the teaching.

Although the teachers were in front of the class only occasionally, constant instruction took place in these classrooms—a finding recently reported by Taylor and colleagues (2000) as more characteristic of effective primary classrooms than less effective ones. That is, more often we observed these teachers working alongside students, individually and in small groups, than working from the front of the room. Each teacher used a range of interactional formats. However, a great deal of instruction was done not by the teacher but by the students, who had learned to consult one another and to make their thinking available to one another. Collaborative learning was common; students were not only learning how to learn but how to teach and how to interact in ways that fostered mutual learning. Students were expected to manage group work, and when it broke down, the problem was dealt with not as misbehavior but as an important interactional event to be solved strategically.

Tailored, collaborative, meaningful problem-solving work dominated the instructional day. The teachers focused on developing students' personal responsibility for learning, with a focus on choice, goal setting, and collaborative independence. Working together was valued as a source of important learning skills. So, too, was self-regulation; students learned to manage inquiry, projects, and composing as well as their role in group work. Self-regulation was essential to the work that was longer-term in nature. Assignments that lasted for a week or more were more common than the use of many small and unrelated tasks to be completed each day. Integration across subjects, topics, and time was common (see Chapter 9 for a fuller discussion of curricular integration in these classrooms). For instance, often we found it difficult to determine whether the classroom focus was science or language arts. This integration not only worked to foster student motivation and engagement (Guthrie, Wigfield, & VonSecker, 2000; Walmsley & Walp, 1990) but also to add instructional coherence to the day. This orientation towards lesson planning was likely to produce longer instructional blocks where productive and complicated student work could be achieved.

## THE NATURE OF EVALUATION

As was the case with Haberman's (1995b) effective teachers, the teachers we studied evaluated student work more on improvement, progress, qualities, and effort than on the achievement of a single a priori standard. As June Williamson (Chapter 5) explained to her students, "Your effort is what counts the most." This emphasis produced an instructional environment in which all students worked hard—unlike many classrooms where effort and improvement are not heavily weighted in evaluation. When achievement is the primary criterion for evaluating student work, and effort and improvement are largely disregarded, higher-achieving students do not have to put forth much effort to attain high grades. On the other hand, lower-achieving students may work hard and improve considerably but still lag behind the development of their higher-achieving peers. When neither effort nor improvement is considered in grading, there is less (external) motive for sustained effort.

Evaluations made by the teachers we observed were personalized, as they necessarily attended to individual students' development and goals. The evaluations were often holistic—rubrics designed for teachers and adapted for student use—and focused on complex achievements (thinking like a biographer, for instance).

We observed many examples of performance assessment and routinely observed these teachers providing focused feedback; they often led the student to the evaluation target rather than spelling it out explicitly. Self-evaluation was also widely encouraged, shaped, and supported. As one teacher told us, in relation to developing students' writing, "My job is to develop their abilities to edit their own work. If I did the 'red pen' corrections, I'd be doing all the work and they wouldn't be able to see how *they* were improving a piece."

This focus on self-evaluation and self-regulation mirrors that described by Joan Servis (1999) in her autobiographical discussion of good fourth-grade teaching; "I want every student to have the confidence, self-discipline, and skills to function without constant direction from me. Over the years I've come to the conclusion that fourth-graders are capable of doing more than adults—including me—permit. By working in groups and searching out answers for themselves, my students gradually become more independent" (p. 30). The teachers we observed approached evaluation more often from the stance "How do *you* feel about this work? What have *you* done to improve it?" All students were expected to demonstrate improvement over time, towards a standard informed by state guidelines and frameworks. The emphasis on "How can I make it better?"—rather than "Whose is better?"—fostered an environment that was less likely to provoke counterproductive views of individual competence (Nicholls, 1989).

The focus on personal improvement, however, required high levels of knowledge about each student's literacy development and how it was changing across the year. Such a focus also seemed central to the high levels of engagement in academic work that characterized these classrooms. Goals were attainable and personal—attributes critical to the level of engagement experienced (Pressley, 2002; Guthrie & Wigfield, 2000).

## THE FIT WITH PREVIOUS STUDIES

There is a substantial convergence between earlier studies (see Chapter 2) and this study. Indeed, there are few items on the combined list (see Table 11.1; compare with Table 11.2) that we did not find to be important, one way or another. There are, of course, some differences in the weighting of the constructs, but the collective studies are clearly not at odds with one another—though there is room for negotiation. For example, unlike other studies, Snow and her colleagues (1991) situate "explicit instruction" in the foreground. Our observations fit more with Haberman's (1995) and Taylor and her colleagues' (2000) analyses, which use the construct "coaching" as opposed to "directive teaching." The notion of *coaching* offers a range

**TABLE 11.1. Cross-Case Analyses of Features Associated with Exemplary Teachers**

Personal characteristics

- Warm, caring, supportive, encouraging, friendly, genuinely likes people (trusting, respectful, nonjudgmental).
- Enthusiastic, enjoys work.
- Sense of agency, confidence.
- Accurate self-assessment.

Beliefs, attitudes, expectations

- Expects diversity.
- Assumes potential.
- Learning is social.
- Learning requires ownership, relevance, choice.
- Error is important.
- Modeling is important.

Practice

*Classroom talk*

- Students talk to each other publicly; respectful, supportive, and productive talk is expected, modeled, and taught.
- Talk between teacher and student is personalized; teachers actively learn about students.
- Teachers encourage students to engage each other's ideas, thereby distributing authority.
- Discussion is common, including "tentative" talk, making it possible for others to complete incomplete ideas or otherwise contribute to the group thinking.
- "No" or "wrong" rarely heard. Teachers support the partially correct, turn attention to the process, and encourage further thinking or reflection, even about a "correct" answer.
- Teachers admit their limited knowledge of various topics (especially those raised by students), their mistakes, and their own interests.
- Inquiry and problem-solving processes are normal topics of conversation, such as "How could we find that out?" Emphasis is on making meaning and finding the means for doing so.

*Curriculum materials*

- Instruction is multisourced (e.g., in social studies: historical fiction, biography, informational books).
- Multisourced curriculum is also multilevel, with texts varying in difficulty.
- Utilize the Internet, magazines, and other atypical materials as informational sources.
- Relevance and meaning are important aspects of curriculum materials selected (e.g., materials from projects such as fundraising, planning a class trip, or running a class business).
- Language itself treated as a curriculum material; even word study emphasizes a search for meaningful patterns, meaning acquisition, interest in words and turns of a phrase, and the strategic, purposeful selection of words.
- Strong literary emphasis.
- Instruction often guided by an awareness of state or district standards but not driven by them.

TABLE 11.1 *(continued)*

*The organization of instruction*

- Plan open instructional opportunities on which to capitalize.
- Curriculum coverage is lower on agenda than curricular engagement.
- Instruction is personalized (versus "individualized"); teachers know students' interests, strengths, and needs.
- Utilize managed choice: Strategically arrange for students to have choices and make them productively, or learn from their errors.
- More individual and small-group than whole-class instruction; students learn to consult with one another.
- Collaborative, meaningful problem-solving is common; students learn how to learn, to teach, and to interact in ways that foster mutual learning.
- Students are expected to manage group work; breakdowns are dealt with not as misbehavior but as interactional problems to be solved strategically.
- Foster personal responsibility for learning by providing choice, goal setting guidelines, and collaborative independence.
- Much of the schoolwork is longer-term in nature rather than a series of small and unrelated tasks.
- Integration across subjects, topics, and time fosters engagement and curricular coherence.

*Evaluation*

- Improvement, progress, and effort are valued more than achievement of a single a priori standard.
- Personalized attention is given to individual development and goals.
- Rubrics designed for teachers are adapted for student use and focused on complex achievements (e.g., thinking like a biographer).
- Feedback is focused.
- Self-evaluation is widely encouraged, shaped, and supported.

of instructional possibilities. For example, Cazden (1992) distinguishes between "revealing" and "telling" as tools of instruction. We encountered both. Teachers were not explicit all the time about everything. Rather, they were explicit when they needed to be explicit, with whom they needed to be explicit, and in the context of ongoing literate engagement. Indeed, part of what we found impressive is this very ability to know when to be explicit (Duffy, 2002), which entails knowing roughly what students know, what they need to know at a particular point, and what they can figure out for themselves. The difference is important, because if a teacher delivers all of the knowledge or is overly "directive," then students do not get to experience independence or gain a sense of agency in their knowledge construction. Clay (1993) argues similarly with regard to strategy instruction; she supports teaching *for* strategies more than simply teaching strategies. The former entails confronting students with problems that they can solve, or partially solve, and highlighting for them exactly how they solved them. This strategy leads students to think strategically rather than merely implement strategies already learned.

Similarly, although Spencer and Spencer (1993) argue that exemplary teachers are comfortable saying no, they also point out that such teachers set boundaries so well that they do not have to spend their time telling students what not to do. We would add that, in our research, "saying no" is not used much for academic matters but might be used for serious social transgressions. However, generally these teachers turn those few observed transgressions into opportunities for learning rather than simply correcting inappropriate behaviors.

Not only do the characteristics identified in the studies have considerable commonality, but some of the constructs form *clusters*: that is, given some items, one would expect other items. There are doubtless reasons for this. For example, to arrive at these constructs, personal characteristics were inferred from teachers' behaviors. *Caring* is likely to be inferred from teachers' personal attention to, and flexible accommodation of, students' interests, needs, and concerns. It might also be inferred from supportive, encouraging, and friendly verbal interactions, rather than judgmental ones. Students, too, probably infer these characteristics from similar indicators.

These clusters of beliefs, attributes, and personal characteristics are important to consider in relation to the clusters of instructional practices and classroom talk (Table 11.2). Considering the potential links between these might ultimately lead us to a more unified theory. For example, a teacher who genuinely likes children is likely to be interested in their experiences, is unlikely to be judgmental, may have more confidence in children's ability to make good choices, and is likely to view error as an opportunity for learning rather than for correction.

Similarly, Spencer and Spencer's (1993) report that effective teachers tailor presentations to their audience and give flexible responses to individual interests and needs, implies that these teachers listen to, observe, and assess their students; *careful listening, observation*, and *assessment* are additional descriptors identified by Spencer and Spencer. Other researchers also point out that good teachers are sensitive to and accommodate individuals' interests, needs, and motivations (Falk, 2000; Ladson-Billings, 1994), which is perhaps why their classrooms offer a wide range of difficulty and high engagement

TABLE 11.2. Documented Characteristics and Beliefs in Relation to Instructional Practices

| | Practice |
|---|---|
| **Characteristics** | |
| Warm, caring, supportive, encouraging, friendly, genuinely likes people (trusting, respectful, and nonjudgmental). | Draws attention to the positive and personalizes instruction. Shows an interest in children's lives and their way of thinking. Organizes to prevent negative and authoritarian interactions by engaging students, teaching and encouraging self-management, and focusing on the partially correct. |
| Enthusiastic (can be quietly) and enjoys work. | Models own learning, shows genuine interest in students and their ideas and arranges for interesting things to happen in the classroom. |
| Sense of agency, confidence. | Reflects on and actively changes practice when the need arises; uses multicultural materials. |
| Accurate self-assessment. | Reflects on and changes practice, consults others as necessary, and admits own limited knowledge and errors. |
| **Beliefs** | |
| Expects diversity. | Often has students engaged in a variety of tasks and in diverse groupings. When everyone is included in the same activity, it is porous enough for all to participate. Emphasizes respectful, supportive talk, distributes authority, and values different ideas. |
| Assumes potential. | Makes tasks accessible, engaging, and relevant so students apply themselves optimally and display maximal competence and own it. Uses process–agency talk so students recognize potential and build personal responsibility. Students not allowed to opt out or put themselves down. Improvement and effort valued. |
| Learning is social. | Helps students learn to manage group activities and collaborative projects. Fosters discussion, tentative talk, distributed authority, respectful student–student talk. Multisource curriculum encourages discussion and collaboration. |
| Learning requires ownership, relevance, choice. | Fosters managed choice, responsibility, performance and publication, personal goal setting, and distributed authority. Multisourced curriculum forces personal decision making. Organized opportunistic teaching, inquiry-oriented curriculum, and emphasis on meaning making and relevance predominate. Multicultural materials used. |

(continued on next page)

**TABLE 11.2.** (*continued*)

| | Practice |
|---|---|
| Beliefs (*continued*) | |
| Error is important. | Admit own errors. Challenging curriculum (in zone of proximal development). Emphasize the problem-solving, self-monitoring, and self-correction – independence. |
| Modeling is important. | Demonstrates self as a learner, reader, writer, inquirer, and reveals process-thinking explicitly. Talks about own mistakes and treats students with respect and fairness. |

in academic materials. Furthermore, it may be the careful listening and observation that make it possible for these teachers to successfully challenge their students (often reported as "having high expectations") in ways that students can actually meet and are prepared to pick up. At the same time, the "engrossment" of these teachers in learning about each student has been emphasized by Noddings (1995) and others (Goldstein, 1999; Tappan, 1998) as a central part of caring relationships, teaching–learning relationships, and productive relationship development itself.

Consider another potential cluster. In each of the studies we reviewed, there is a focus on making meaning and how to go about it. Knapp (1995) and Cantrell, Lang, and Mathews (1999) also reported that more meaning-centered upper-grade elementary teachers produced students who were more successful on a range of reading and writing measures. These teachers engage children in discussion, ask inferential questions (which can lead to discussion), and integrate subjects with one another and with children's experience, making instruction personally relevant—in other words, meaningful. In the process, these practices probably go a long way towards establishing trust and respect in the classroom. Doubtless it goes the other way, too, in that listening to students' discussion and experiences requires a measure of respect in the first place.

The focus on meaning making, distributed authority, and inquiry also means that differences in relative competence are of limited significance. When students worry about having less capacity than their peers, they easily reduce their own worth and view themselves as having little to contribute, particularly in competitive contexts (Nicholls,

1989)—contexts that were rare in our study. The use of collaborative tasks, open and challenging enough for maximal participation, reduces interest in more ego-based goals, such as differences in competence and relative performance. In these contexts, students also are likely to be more strategic (Greene, 1997).

Such theoretically consistent clusters of descriptors are exactly what we sought in our research efforts—constructs that are coherent but at the same time practical for they provide the focusing intention, the stance, and the means for improving instruction. In our efforts to study these clusters of beliefs, attributes, and practices, we have examined teachers' epistemologies (Johnston et al., 2001) and have reason to believe that the position of *constructed knowing* (Belenky et al., 1986) provides a framework that integrates a great many of the characteristics and practices of these exemplary teachers (see Chapters 9 and 10 for more on this point).

## THE WEIGHT OF EVIDENCE AND THE WAY FORWARD

In one sense, our observations and interviews with exemplary teachers simply confirm and refine a body of research, much of which already "rings true."

Through studies such as ours, we move closer to identifying and cultivating the best of instructional practice. However, we must qualify our findings in several ways. We studied a relatively small number of teachers, opting for greater detail on those we did study in order to recognize the full complexity of their work. In creating research designs, there is always a balance to be negotiated between individual detail and the generalizability that comes with larger numbers. There are certainly differences among the practices of good teachers (e.g., Johnston et al., 2001) and the contexts in which they work. By studying teachers in a wide range of states and situations, and applying cross-case analyses, we tried to strike a balance, preserving both individual detail and generalizability across individuals and contexts.

None of the teachers we studied would argue that their classrooms are the best that is possible. Neither should we. Even in exceptional classrooms there is more to be done, particularly in expanding aspects that were present but not as strong or widespread as other themes. For example, the use of multicultural literature was uneven. Also, although we encountered a substantial degree of critical literacy in the classrooms we observed, we might hope for more, given other recently documented cases (e.g., Comber et al., 2001; Powell, Cantrell et al., 2001). It was certainly present, for example, in the study of *The Story of Ruby Bridges* in Mary Ellen's room (Chapter 7), and in their project on fair housing. When one of Tracey's students researched the difficulties of African Americans becoming airline pilots, he, too, was using critical literacy in the service of social justice. In his reading and interviewing, he asked questions about privilege. When he brought his project to class discussion, the class studied issues of inequity and expanded their social imagination in ways that cannot help but serve a multicultural democracy. When, during a read-aloud, Joan (Chapter 3) encouraged and extended her students' conversation about gender roles and their inequities, they, too, were learning critical literacy around issues of social justice.

We must also reiterate that we studied teachers identified as exemplary, whose students turned out to be doing well on standardized tests. We did not study teachers whose students simply scored highest on tests. Perhaps if we had, our results would have been different. Perhaps there are ways, such as through intensive test preparation, to produce even higher test performance than our teachers' students garnered, but we seriously doubt it, and others have shown the costs of such a strategy (e.g., Smith, 1991). What we have described produces particular kinds of *literate individuals*. Reading and writing are not merely ways of communicating; they are inescapably attached to relationships of power and control, and conceptions of knowing and literate identity (Gee, 1996; Collins & Blot, in press).

The students in these classrooms came to expect particular ways of interacting with others through literacy. They expected trusting, respectful conversations about important issues; they expected to manage their literacy learning, to be taken seriously, and to be recognized for their contributions rather than for their limitations. They expected to encounter problems and to solve them strategically, to make mistakes and learn from them, to struggle sometimes for extended periods in the search for meaning and their best work. They expected to think about literacy in terms of social intentions and consequences. These are high expectations, indeed, but anything less would not feel right to them.

These normalized ways of developing and practicing literacy are not just features of classroom life that make literacy learning possible, though they do that. We believe that these teachers prepared students not merely to do well on tests but to participate actively in a literate democratic society. As Kerr (1996) points out, "recognition, mutual respect, and trust" are not only the "basis for moral lives and democracy [but also] constituents of both nurture and the social fabric that supports it" (p. 41). Without these attributes and their consequences for literate identities, true democracy is probably not possible (Barber, 1984; Pradl, 1996; Reichenbach, 1998). These literate achievements must become more concretely recognized and valued, not only because of their social implications, but because it would reduce the strain on exemplary teachers who do what they know to be right but spend so much time feeling guilty about what they might not be achieving. We sincerely hope that the rich descriptions provided by our case studies offer models that inspire and support teachers in their efforts.

We also hope that these cases inform and inspire administrators and policymakers to support the efforts of teachers such as the ones we have profiled. Indeed, administrators might look to these teachers' classrooms for demonstrations of how professional learning communities, such as schools, can operate. The fact that policymakers and administrators often work to minimize the likelihood of these classroom characteristics (through scripted instructional materials, pacing schedules for materials coverage, mandates for whole-class lessons and standard lesson plans, increased use of group achievement tests, underfunded teacher education programs, and so on) reduces the numbers of exemplary teachers in our schools by constraining teachers to engage in trivial ends and limited practices, and by forcing teachers who know better to behave in ways inconsistent with their deeper commitments. Such friction makes joyful teaching more difficult and retirement more attractive.

We hope that administrators, politicians, and members of the general public reading these cases gain an understanding that teaching is incredibly complex work. When it looks easy, it is because it is being done so well and because it is carefully planned and orchestrated. Even those who are close supporters of teachers, including spouses, may not comprehend the effort it takes to teach. As one of our teachers put it:

"If you're a teacher, you have to plan on spending time outside the classroom correcting, evaluating, planning. You really need time to sit and think about what you're going to do. You know, it's hours outside of school, yeah. My husband wonders if I just can't get it. I mean, he keeps saying, 'What are you doing?' Really, 'How do you do this every year, and, you know, sit and tell me you have to plan for 2 hours?' "

If our book reduces some of this misunderstanding and its consequences for these and other teachers, the effort will have been worth it.

# Shifting the Focus
# of the Reading Debate
## *A Cautionary Afterword*

GERALD G. DUFFY

First and foremost, this book is a political statement designed to blunt the current move toward high-stakes testing and "proven" commercial programs. As the authors put it, the book's purpose is to use exemplary teaching to "shift the focus" away from trivial forms of literacy and regulatory constraints on teachers and toward literacy instruction that emphasizes "acquiring values, beliefs, practices and norms that become part of who . . . [students] . . . are as literate people, and how they participate in literate activities" (p. 202). I have little to add to this central premise. We need to shift the focus. Tests fail to measure literacy's real contribution of humanizing and empowering individuals, and instructional mandates ignore the reality of both student individual differences and the adaptive nature of effective teaching. In short, the research findings reported in this book add to our growing understanding that good literacy teaching is complex and multidimensional, with complex and multidimensional outcomes. One can only hope policymakers and politicians learn from it.

But even if policymakers and politicians do attend to this book, the job will be far from over. Shifting the focus is a complex, evolutionary endeavor. We do not accomplish it with a single report of research. Consequently, in this chapter I raise three issues we must come to terms with as we continue to "shift the focus." One elaborates on the so-called high stakes involved in literacy instruction. The second focuses on our need to balance the ideal of literacy instruction with the pragmatic dilemmas teachers face when teaching struggling readers. The third examines the fundamental issue of how to prepare more exemplary teachers like the six who are profiled in this volume.

## WHAT'S REALLY AT STAKE HERE?

Shifting the focus requires changing the general public's culturally-embedded view of literacy. According to that view, reading is a simple matter of learning "basic skills." Hence, there is a lot of talk about "systematic phonics instruction" and, among the more enlightened, some fragmentary mention of "comprehension." Overall, the sense one gets from the public debate is that reading is pretty basic and routine, and that the stakes are primarily economic in that citizens must possess reading (and writing) skills to make them employable in the Information Age.

This book raises the stakes by featuring six teachers who embed reading instruction in larger contexts. For instance, Joan Backer (Chapter 3) teaches reading within a framework of inquiry and mutual respect; Kim Duhamel (Chapter 4) teaches reading within a framework of pride in self and respect for others; June Williamson (Chapter 5) chooses reading content that develops the ability to deal with controversial issues; Sandy Kniseley (Chapter 6) develops reading and writing within the framework of collaborative work; Mary Ellen Quinlan (Chapter 7) builds a learning community that rescues students from the margins; and Tracey Bennett (Chapter 8) teaches reading as an integral part authorship and thinking.

Decoding and comprehension are important for all these teachers, as evidenced by the fact that they produce better than average achievement test scores. But their teaching goes well beyond basic skills. Reading instruction for them includes developing "invisible" learnings, learnings that are not specified in the curriculum guide or tested on the annual state assessment test. They include understandings such as who has a right to an opinion, how to pursue a topic, how to respond to dissent, how to work out conflicts, how to respect divergent opinions, and other values and beliefs central to survival of a democratic society. Hence, literate development is, in the words of Johnston and Backer, fundamental to "the survival of democracy."

In policymakers' zeal to guarantee the teaching of trivial knowledge measured by tests, they are blocking development of these larger understandings. Thus, what's really at stake is more than developing employable citizens; what's at stake is the preservation of our society's way of life.

To attain these larger goals, teachers need to be free to pursue enlightened instruction, characterized in this book as "laying down layers of sediment" by utilizing constructivist techniques. That is, students are immersed in genuine literate experiences and, within that environment, given "a controlling interest in their learning" that encourages them to construct understandings about how to live in the world. The teacher's job is two-fold: (1) to ensure that integration of learning (Chapter 9) and a variety of literate activities (Chapter 10) give students opportunities to construct intended understandings about power, control, self, and democratic participation; and (2) to respond to children with dialogical conversations and coaching that respect their efforts to discern understandings. This kind of instruction stands in stark contrast to the general public's prevalent perception of teaching as comprised of directive telling, lecture, recitation, and compliant students.

Sadly, however, it is directive teaching that tests and restrictive mandates promote. Teacher autonomy in making instructional decisions is being curtailed. Teachers are less and less free to embed reading instruction in experiences that encourage students to build schemata regarding who has the right to an opinion, how to pursue a topic, how to deal with diversity, and so on. Instead, teachers are forced to follow narrow, prescriptive directives that encourage students to be submissive and compliant rather than self-reliant and flexible.

We pay a steep price for this. We lose good teachers because they leave the field when they discover that they cannot be creative in making professional decisions. And we lose the benefit of "invisible" values, beliefs, and attitudes associated with meaningful integration and literary experiences.

Hence, there's a lot more at stake than just basic skills "stan-

dards." Shifting to higher stakes, however, requires changing culturally engrained beliefs about what it means to teach reading. The task
is huge.

## BALANCING CONSTRUCTIVIST AND PRAGMATIC CONCERNS

Obviously, constructivist instructional techniques are essential in
raising the stakes. But we cannot confine ourselves to constructivist
instruction. We must also honor the role of other kinds of instruction, particularly as these relate to the pragmatic problems teachers
face when teaching struggling readers.

This book emphasizes constructivism because politicians and
policymakers are unaware of the crucial importance of "invisible"
learning and the roles played by integration, literate experiences, and
the constructivist nature of learning. However, taking this tack leaves
the reader unclear about how these fourth-grade teachers assess and
teach students who read well below grade level.

Struggling readers are a pragmatic concern of both teachers and
policymakers. Fourth grade is where most of the mandated testing
begins, and it is where teachers encounter students who may range
from first-grade reading level to 10th-grade reading level. Everyone is
happy about the children reading at fourth-grade level, and above.
But a pressing and persistent reality, both in teachers' lives and in the
minds of the policymakers we are trying to influence, is how to help
those who currently do not meet fourth-grade standards.

Although this book does not provide us with specific evidence,
the implication is that the six featured teachers were successful with
struggling readers because they produced good achievement test
scores. What we do *not* know is how they did it. Were "coaching"
and "dialogue" and abundant opportunities to read authentic material sufficient to get struggling students to a level of success? One
must conclude that they were *not*, since the authors report that these
exemplary teachers sometimes *were* directive. In Chapter 11, for instance, it is stated that exemplary teachers were "explicit when they
needed to be explicit, with whom they needed to be explicit, and in
the context of ongoing literate engagement." However, any reference
to "explicit" or "directive teaching" is avoided.

This reluctance to specify the explicit techniques teachers integrate into their instructional tapestry is puzzling, especially given the research findings documenting that explicit techniques help struggling readers (to name just a few such studies, see Baumann, 1984; Brown, Pressley, Van Meter, & Schuder, 1996; Dewitz, Carr, & Patberg, 1987; Dole, Brown, & Trathen, 1996; Duffy, 1993; Duffy et al., 1987; Winne, Graham, & Prock, 1993). The result is that we get no conceptually substantive descriptions of what the six teachers did when "they needed to be explicit."

Consider the example of modeling. In Chapter 3, for instance, Joan Backer engages in "think-aloud modeling," but we have no description of exactly what constitutes a "think-aloud model" or whether such a form of modeling is different in any important way from "dialogue" or "coaching" or "conversation" or other forms of classroom talk. In fact, one gets the feeling that whatever "think-aloud modeling" might be, it is not as valued as Joan's "commitment to dialogue, particularly the dialogue of inquiry-response." In Chapter 4, Kim Duhamel is described as providing a "good role model," meaning that she herself is a "voracious reader." We know from Chapter 5 that June Williamson teaches strategies explicitly, but the only example we get is that she "paused long enough for a discussion about the definition and purposes of using brainstorming as a strategy" and, later, that she provided her students with a mnemonic aid. Similarly, in Chapter 6 Sandy Kniseley is said to balance "modeling and presenting strategies and providing purposeful opportunities to practice and use those strategies." However, we get no precise description of *how* Sandy models these behaviors.

Did these teachers' modeling include explanation of the mental processing involved in using reading strategies? If so, what kinds of specific information did the explanations include? Did these teachers provide scaffolds to assist students, as they attempted to implement strategies and skills? If so, what form did these scaffolds take, and how were they structured for students? Following modeling, did teachers make systematic attempts to ensure that skills and strategies were used in real reading? In their work with struggling readers, did these teachers avoid mindless "skill-and-drill" exercises in favor of explanations designed to develop metacognitive understandings? How did these teachers integrate explicit modeling into the larger constructivist framework operating in their classrooms?

The feeling one gets is that these teachers accomplish situationally appropriate modifications of constructivist instructional patterns in response to the pragmatic needs of struggling readers (that is, they are explicit when they need to be). But we are left on our own to imagine what exactly they did. My guess is that they used techniques of (dare I say it out loud?) . . . direct instruction. That is, they assessed, they took charge of the learning for a brief period, they specified what the student(s) needed to learn, they explained (that is, modeled) how one thinks one's way through the task, they scaffolded the students' attempts to emulate the teacher's model, and then they integrated the new learning into the ongoing constructivist activity in the classroom.

If, indeed, they employed such actions, we should celebrate this usage, not omit it. True, constructivist techniques must be highlighted. But to complete the tapestry, we must go beyond saying that they "were explicit when they needed to be explicit." We must also describe how assessment and more direct forms of instruction are woven into the constructivist framework. After all, it is the blending of instructional techniques that truly distinguishes exemplary teaching. *Within* an overall environment that promotes the highest forms of literacy, good teachers use a variety of directive and nondirective instructional techniques to meet the needs of all students. They preserve constructivist ideals *and* deal with the pragmatics of how to serve struggling readers who need more structured assistance.

Masking the role of more direct forms of teaching implies that constructivist techniques are better than direct teaching methods. That is not the point. The point is that teachers must have pedagogical freedom to move. To obtain that kind of freedom for teachers, we must document that good instruction is a matter of mixing and matching method to student within an overall constructivist perspective. We cannot do so if we mask the pragmatics teachers face when teaching struggling readers.

## DEVELOPING EXEMPLARY TEACHERS

While this book is not about teacher education, the implication is that we should prepare more teachers like the six presented here. As the editors themselves state, these six teachers are presented to us to "better articulate the nature and qualities of the instruction crafted by good upper-elementary teachers." But preparing such teachers is a daunting task. This is partly because of the "dizzying array of features that might characterize good fourth-grade teachers," and partly because we know so little about how to develop certain characteristics associated with expertise.

Consider, for instance, three characteristics of the six teachers featured in this book. First, all six possess personal visions that are the genesis of the themes dominating their daily classroom activity. Joan Backer's vision is that her students will be inquirers; Kim Duhamal's vision is that students will take pride in themselves and others; Sandy Kniseley's vision is that students will be collaborative; Mary Ellen Quinlan's vision is of a caring, responsible community of learners; June Williamson's vision is that students will learn to deal with controversy in effective ways; and Tracey Bennett's vision is that her students will become thinkers. The editors describe this characteristic as "The crucial question . . . [of] . . . what the 'something' is that they are trying to do—what conception of literacy teaching and learning guides these teachers' practice." But I think it is more accurate to say that, first, these teachers have visions of what they want their kids to become. Their visions translate into classroom themes. Those themes, in turn, provide contexts for developing certain kinds of literacy teaching and learning (i.e., the "invisible" learnings). So their passion is not rooted in a "conception of literacy" as much as in a larger moral conviction regarding what they want their students to become. That vision causes literacy to be used in service of a theme that embraces the vision. Consequently, a personal vision for why one is teaching is a crucial part of expertise. Teachers with a vision possess both a thematic framework for their constructivist instruction and the passion that sustains them through the difficulties of daily teaching. But as teacher educators, we know little about how to help prospective teachers get in touch with their personal morality.

Of equal concern, all six teachers deal effectively with the ambiguity of teaching. For instance, they are all comfortable teaching in relation to several goals simultaneously. That is, they develop high forms of literacy while, at the same time, developing the trivial aspects featured on assessment tests. Doing both doesn't bother them. Similarly, they deal with the inherent ambiguity that comes with being responsive to kids. Seldom do children's needs fit neatly into the prescribed curriculum or the expectations of superiors. Consequently, good teachers do not "follow" a curriculum in an orderly and sequential way. This is illustrated in Chapter 3, where Joan

Backer is described as "planning her curriculum around the children's concerns, dragging the formal curriculum along behind." Dealing with such ambiguity is a requirement of exemplary teaching. But how do we teach teachers to deal with ambiguity?

Similarly, teaching takes courage, particularly given the conditions under which today's teachers work. Most elementary teachers now face the specter of state or district standards and the high-stakes testing that accompany them. Given the pressures, it is tempting to simply allow one's teaching to be driven by instructional mandates from outside authority. But all six of these teachers resist doing so. They teach kids first, and they do not let the public pressure associated with high-stakes testing stifle their professionalism. It takes courage to do so. But how do we develop courage in teachers?

But even if we learn how to develop such characteristics, teacher education still will be constrained by three institutional problems. Consider, for instance, the above discussion of the clash between maintaining constructivist ideals while simultaneously meeting the pragmatic demands of bringing struggling readers "up to standard." Teachers must be eclectic to meet this challenge. Teacher educators, however, work in an academic setting that often views eclecticism as sloppy thinking. Hence, teacher educators are encouraged to adhere to one or another philosophy, theory, or ideology. When preparing teachers, they often emphasize their favored positions without teaching how to deal with the pragmatic simultaneously and honorably. Yet the reality of classroom life dictates that teachers must do both. They must create classroom environments that cause children to construct large understandings while simultaneously providing direct assistance for certain children at certain times. When teachers are taught only one perspective during their teacher education and are then confronted, on the job, with the pressures of high-stakes testing, it appears to them to be an irreconcilable conflict. They don't know how to employ eclectic combinations as a means for dealing with the conflict, so they become bitter and cynical about their teacher education and submit compliantly to the directives of the mandate. To effectively combat policy mandates, we must teach teachers how to make situationally appropriate modifications of constructivist instructional patterns in response to the pragmatic needs of struggling readers. This means that teacher educators must teach within an eclectic framework so that prospective teachers understand how to use a variety of instructional techniques to meet students' particular needs. But the institutional culture discourages this.

Another institutional problem is the university itself, where most pre-service teacher education occurs. To survive as a university professor, teacher educators must prioritize research and publication; improving teacher education requires this very research undertaken by teacher educators to investigate such questions as how to teach teachers to have a vision, deal with ambiguity, and have the courage of their convictions in the face of high-stakes testing. But excellence in teacher education also demands an additional priority. Unlike most university programs, successful teacher education requires that faculty energy be devoted to the ongoing task of ensuring programmatic cohesion among all participants. That is, all professors teaching courses in the program must be coordinated and "on the same page"; field-based cooperating teachers must likewise be "on the same page" so that teacher candidates can construct a coherent model of how to teach school. But programmatic cohesion doesn't just happen. It takes faculty time and energy. We currently have no system for meshing the need to generate scholarship with the need to sustain programmatic coherence. Consequently, teacher educators who want to commit themselves to quality teacher preparation are caught between the proverbial "rock and a hard place." Teacher education institutions must find ways for teacher educators to engage in scholarship in the traditional academic sense while also cultivating and preserving program coherence.

Finally, there is no institutional way to meet the reality that teacher expertise is a career-long process. Teachers do not become experts as a result of teacher education programs. Expertise comes with years of continued growth. But we have no system for promoting long-term professional growth. New teachers are usually thrown into the classroom; seldom are they given a structure to support their early efforts. Continued professional growth is limited either to graduate programs where professors, once again, promote their favored theories; or to fragmented and occasional in-service programs conducted on a "one-shot" basis in individual schools or at professional conferences. Longitudinal and conceptually integrated staff development is rare. In short, becoming an exemplary teacher is often an individual, "catch-as-catch-can" proposition. To develop exemplary teachers on a larger scale, this situation must change. We need coordinated, collaborative efforts involving the university, public school, and political stakeholders in a long-term and conceptually congruent process. However, no such system is in view.

Obviously, these teacher education issues are well beyond the scope of this book. However, we must be able to develop exemplary teachers if we are to continue shifting the focus of the reading debate. The challenge is immense.

## CONCLUSION

As a "cautionary afterword," it may sound like I am pessimistic about our chances of shifting the focus. Not so. To the contrary, instruction in reading has been shifting for over 50 years. Thanks to the last half century of research on reading and on the teaching of reading, today's classroom reading instruction, as well as today's teacher preparation, is better than it has ever been. While this book's immediate concern is to respond to the current political debate, it also continues an evolutionary move towards a broader view of literacy learning that has been going on for decades.

I believe this evolutionary move will continue despite the current pressures of the politics of reading. However, there is no sense being naïve. To ensure that it does, we must do two things. We must continue to battle the public's long-held belief that literacy is a trivial matter of learning to decode the squiggles on the page, and that teaching itself is a relatively routine and one-dimensional task that any intelligent college graduate can do. At the same time, we must battle our own reluctance to confront the fact that exemplary teaching involves a mix of constructivist and more direct techniques and that preparing exemplary teachers requires more than teaching a good course.

The task is huge. The stakes are high. This book keeps us on the evolutionary road. To stay on that road, we must embrace the complexities associated both with exemplary teaching and with preparation of exemplary teachers.

---

**Gerald G. Duffy, EdD,** is Professor Emeritus from Michigan State University where he served for 25 years as a teacher educator and researcher. He now resides in Deer Park, Washington where he continues to consult and write.

# APPENDIX

---

# Achievement Growth
# on Standardized Reading Tests

We estimated the effects of the reading instruction offered by the teachers nominated as exemplary fourth-grade teachers using the following post hoc procedure:

- After the observation year was completed, we contacted the principals of the schools where these teachers worked to discover which ones participated in a nationally normed standardized testing for both third and fourth grades.
- We asked these principals to provide us with both the third- and fourth-grade test scores for all students enrolled in exemplary teachers' classrooms (scores were sent to us without student identification). We received complete test data for 19 classrooms. The fact that many schools do not test at every grade level accounts for the missing data.
- We converted both the third- and fourth-grade test scores to normal curve equivalents (NCEs) and then tested whether the mean NCE for fourth grade was significantly different from the third-grade NCE. It was ($t_{243}$, $p < .000$), with the fourth-grade mean 6.4 points higher than the third-grade NCE.

This result indicates that students in these exemplary fourth-grade classrooms made better than average reading progress during their year in fourth grade. In other words, if children make average progress—typically, 1 year's growth on a standardized achievement test—the NCE would remain unchanged from year to year. When the reading NCE increases, we can infer that greater than expected reading growth occurred.

However, as noted in Chapter 10, standardized reading achievement tests measure only a portion of the literate achievements of the students in the classrooms we studied.

# References

Adams, E. L. (1995). *A descriptive study of second graders' conversations about books.* Unpublished doctoral dissertation, State University of New York at Albany, Albany, NY.

Allington, R. L. (1991). The legacy of "slow it down and make it more concrete." In J. Zutell & S. McCormick (Eds.), *Learner factors/teacher factors: Issues in literacy research and instruction* (Vol. 40, Yearbook of the National Reading Conference, pp. 19–30). Chicago: National Reading Conference.

Allington, R. L. (2000). How to improve high-stakes test scores without really improving. *Issues in education: Contributions from educational psychology, 6,* 115–124.

Allington, R. L., Block, C. C., Morrow, L. M., & Day, J. P. (1999, April). *Departmentalization and curriculum interaction: Contradictions teachers confront in instruction.* Paper presented at the American Educational Research Association meeting, Montreal.

Allington, R. L., & Cunningham, P. (2002). *Schools that work: All children readers and writers.* Boston: Allyn & Bacon.

Allington, R. L., & Johnston, P. H. (2000, April). *Exemplary fourth grade teachers.* Paper presented at the annual meeting of the American Educational Research Association, New Orleans, LA.

Allington, R. L., & Johnston, P. H. (2001). What do we know about exemplary fourth-grade teachers and their classrooms? In C. M. Roller (Ed.), *Learning to teach reading: Setting the research agenda* (pp. 150–165). Newark, DE: International Reading Association.

Allington, R. L., & McGill-Franzen, A. (1992). Unintended effects of educational reform in New York State. *Educational Policy, 6,* 396–413.

Almasi, J., & McKeown, M. (1996). The nature of engaged reading in classroom discussions of literature. *Journal of Literacy Research, 28,* 107–146.

235

Anyon, J. (1981). Social class and school knowledge. *Curriculum Inquiry, 11*, 3–41.

Applebee, A. N. (1996). *Curriculum as conversation: Transforming traditions of teaching and learning.* Chicago: University of Chicago Press.

Atwell, N. (1998). *In the middle: New understandings about writing, reading, and learning* (2nd ed.). Portsmouth, NH: Heinemann.

Barber, B. (1984). *Strong democracy: Participatory politics for a new age.* Berkeley: University of California Press.

Battistich, V., Watson, M., Solomon, L., Lewis, R., & Schaps, R. (1999). "Beyond the three R's: A broader agenda for school reform." *Elementary School Journal, 99*(5), 415–432.

Baumann, J. (1984). Effectiveness of direct instruction paradigm for teaching main idea comprehension. *Reading Research Quarterly, 20*, 93–108.

Bear, D., Invernizzi, M., Templeton, S., & Johnston, F. (2000). *Words their way: Word Study for phonics, vocabulary, and spelling instruction* (2nd edition). Upper Saddle River, NJ: Prentice Hall.

Belenky, M. F., Clinchy, B. M., Goldberger, N., & Tarule, J. M. (1986). *Women's ways of knowing: The development of self, voice, and mind.* New York: Basic Books.

Bereiter, C., & Scardamalia, M. (1993). *Surpassing ourselves: An inquiry into the nature and implications of expertise.* Chicago: Open Court.

Bond, G. L., & Dykstra, R. (1967). The cooperative research program in first-grade reading instruction. *Reading Research Quarterly, 2*, 5–142.

Boothroyd, K., Day, J. P., Johnston, P. H., & Cedeno, M. (1999, May). *Individuality and commonality in exemplary teaching practice.* Paper presented at the annual meeting of the International Reading Association, San Diego, CA.

Brophy, J. (1997). *Motivating students to learn.* New York: HarperCollins.

Brophy, J., & Van Sledright, B. (1997). *Teaching and learning history in elementary school.* New York: Teachers College Press.

Brown, R., Pressley, M., Van Meter, P., & Schuder, T. (1996). A quasi-experimental validation of transactional strategies instruction with low-achieving second-grade readers. *Journal of Educational Psychology, 88*, 18–37.

Bryson, M. (1993). School-based epistemologies?: Exploring conceptions of how, what, and why students know. *Learning Disabilities Quarterly 16*(4), 299–316.

Budiansky, S. (2001, February). The trouble with textbooks. *Prism*, 24–27.

Burbules, N. (1993). *Dialogue in teaching: Theory and practice.* New York: Teachers College Press.

Cantrell, S., Lang, C., & Mathews, S. (1999). *Raising readers and writers: Approaches to school-wide literacy initiatives in conservative times.* Paper presented at the National Reading Conference, Orlando, FL.

Carlsen, W. S. (1997). Never ask a question if you don't know the answer: The tension in teaching between modeling and scientific argument and maintaining law and order. *Journal of Classroom Interaction, 32*(2), 14–23.

Cazden, C. B. (1992). *Whole language plus: Essays on literacy in the United States and New Zealand.* New York: Teachers College Press.

Cazden, C. B. (1988). *Classroom discourse: The language of teaching and learning*. Portsmouth, NH: Heinemann.

Chall, J. S. (1983). *Stages of reading development*. New York: McGraw-Hill.

Chall, J. S., & Conard, S. S. (1991). *Should textbooks challenge students?* New York: Teachers College Press.

Chi, M. T. H., Glaser, R., & Farr, M. J. (1988). *The nature of expertise*. Hillsdale, NJ: Erlbaum.

Ciborowski, J. (1994). *Textbooks and the students who can't read them: A guide to teaching content*. Cambridge, MA: Brookline.

Clay, M. M. (1993). *Reading recovery: A guidebook for teachers in training*. Portsmouth, NH: Heinemann.

Clement, J. (1991). Nonformal reasoning in experts and in science students: The use of analogies, extreme cases, and physical intuition. In J. F. Voss, D. N. Perkins, & J. W. Segal (Eds.), *Informal reasoning and education* (pp. 345–362). Hillsdale, NJ: Erlbaum.

Coles, G. (2000). *Misreading reading: The bad science that hurts children*. Portsmouth, NH: Heinemann.

Collins, J. (1995). Literacy and literacies. *Annual Review of Anthropology, 24,* 75–93.

Collins, J., & Blot, R. (in press). *Literacy and literacies: Texts, power and identities*. New York: Cambridge University Press.

Comber, B., Thompson, P., & Wells, M. (2001). Critical literacy finds a place: Writing and social-action in low-income Australian grade 2/3 classroom. *Elementary School Journal, 101,* 451–464.

Compton-Lilly (2000). "Staying on children": Challenging stereotypes about urban parents. *Language Arts, 77*(5), 420–427.

Council, N. R. (1996). *National science education standards*. Washington, DC: National Academy Press.

Crook, C. (1994). *Computers and the collaborative experience of learning*. London: Routledge.

Cruickshank, D. R., & Haefele, D. (2001). Good teachers, plural. *Educational Leadership, 58*(5), 26–30.

Csikszentmihalyi, M. (1990). *Flow: The psychology of optimal experience*. New York: Harper Perennial.

Daniels, H. (1994). *Literature circles: Voice and choice in the student-centered classroom*. York, ME: Stenhouse.

Darling-Hammond, L. (1997). *The right to learn: A blueprint for creating schools that work*. San Francisco: Jossey-Bass.

Darling-Hammond, L. (1999). *Teacher quality and student achievement: A review of state policy evidence*. Center for Teaching Policy, University of Washington, Seattle.

Datnow, A., & Castellano, M. (2000). Teachers' responses to Success for All: How beliefs, experiences, and adaptations shape implementation. *American Educational Research Journal, 37,* 775–799.

Day, J. P. (2000). The acquisition of exemplary teaching capacity: Teacher voices on teacher learning. Manuscript submitted for publication.

Dewitz, P., Carr, E., & Patberg, J. (1987). Effects of inference training on comprehension and comprehension monitoring. *Reading Research Quarterly,* 22, 99–121.

Dillon, J. T. (1988). The remedial status of student questioning. *Curriculum Studies, 20,* 197–210.

Dole, J., Brown, K., & Trathen, W. (1996). The effects of strategy instruction on the comprehension performance of at-risk students. *Reading Research Quarterly, 31,* 62–89.

Dozier, T., & Bertotti, C. (2000). *Eliminating barriers to improving teaching..* Washington, DC: U.S. Department of Education.

Driver, R., Leach, J., Millar, R., & Scott, P. (1996). *Young people's images of science.* Buckingham, UK: Open University Press.

Duffy, G. G. (1993). Re-thinking strategy instruction: Teacher development and low achievers' understandings. *Elementary School Journal, 93,* 231–247.

Duffy, G. G. (1997). Powerful models or powerful teachers? An argument for teacher-as-entrepreneur. In S. Stahl & D. Hayes (Eds.), *Instructional models in reading* (pp. 351–365). Mahwah, NJ: Erlbaum.

Duffy, G. G. (2002). The case for direct explanation of strategies. In C. C. Block & M. Pressley (Eds.), *Reading instruction: Research-based best practices* (pp. 28–41). New York: Guilford Press.

Duffy, G. G., & Hoffman, J. V. (1999). In pursuit of an illusion: The search for a perfect method. *Reading Teacher, 53,* 10–16.

Duffy, G. G., Roehler, L., & Herrmann, B. A. (1988). Modeling mental processes helps poor readers become strategic readers. *The Reading Teacher, 41,* 762–767.

Duffy, G. G., Roehler, L., Sivan, E., Rackliffe, G., Book, C., Meloth, M., Vavrus, L., Wesselman, R., Putnam, J., & Bassiri, D. (1987). Effects of explaining the reasoning associated with using reading strategies. *Reading Research Quarterly, 22,* 347–368.

Duke, N. K. (2000). For the rich it's richer: Print experiences and environments offered to children in very low and very high socioeconomic status first-grade classrooms. *American Educational Research Journal, 37,* 441–478.

Dyson, A. H. (1993). *Social worlds of children learning to write in an urban primary school.* New York: Teachers College Press.

Edmonds, R. (1979). *A discussion of the literature and issues related to effective schooling.* St. Louis, MO: CEMREL.

Egan-Robertson, A. (1998). Learning about culture, language, and power: Understanding relationships among personhood, literacy practices, and intertextuality. *Journal of Literacy Research, 30*(4), 449–487.

Fairclough, N. (1992). *Discourse and social change.* London: Longman.

Fairclough, N. (1995). *Critical discourse analysis: The critical study of language.* London: Longman.

Falk, B. (2000). *The heart of the matter.* Portsmouth, NH: Heinemann.

Falk, B., MacMurdy, S., & Darling-Hammond, L. (1995). *Taking a different look: How the Primary Language Record supports teaching diverse learners.* National Research Center for Restructuring Education, Schools, Teaching, NY: Columbia University.

Farivar, S. (1993). Continuity and change: Planning an integrated history-social science/English-language arts unit. *Social Studies Review, 32*(2), 17–24.

Ferdman, B. M. (1990). Literacy and cultural identity. *Harvard Educational Review, 60,* 181–203.

Ferguson, R. F., & Ladd, H. (1996). How and why money matters: An analysis of Alabama schools. In H. Ladd (Ed.), *Holding schools accountable.* Washington, DC: Brookings.

Ferguson, R. F. (1991). Paying for public education: New evidence on how and why money matters. *Harvard Journal on Legislation, 28,* 465–491.

Fosnot, C. T. (1989). *Enquiring teachers, enquiring learners: A constructivist approach for teaching.* New York: Teachers College Press.

Freire, P., & Macedo, D. (1987). *Literacy: Reading the word and the world.* Hadley, MA: Bergin and Garvey.

Gambrell, L. (1996). Creating classroom cultures that foster reading motivation. *The Reading Teacher, 50,* 14–25.

Gavelek, J. R., Raphael, T. E., Biondo, S. M., & Wang, D. (1999). *Integrated literacy instruction: A review of the literature.* Technical Report #2–001, Center for the Improvement of Early Reading Achievement, East Lansing, MI.

Gee, J. P. (1996). *Social linguistics and literacies: Ideology in discourses* (2nd ed.). London: Falmer Press.

Gilbert, P. (1989). Personally (and passively) yours: Girls, literacy and education. *Oxford Review of Education, 15*(3), 257–265.

Giroux, H. (1991). Democracy and the discourse of cultural differences: Towards a politics of border pedagogy. *British Journal of the Sociology of Education, 22,* 501–520.

Glaser, R., & Strauss, A. (1969). *The discovery of grounded theory.* Chicago: Aldine.

Goldstein, L. S. (1999). The relational zone: The role of caring relationships in the co-construction of mind. *American Educational Research Journal, 36*(3), 647–673.

Goodlad, J. (1984). *A place called school: Prospects for the future.* New York: McGraw-Hill.

Greene, B. A., & Miller, R. B. (1996). Influences on achievement: Goals, perceived ability, and cognitive engagement. *Contemporary Educational Psychology, 21,* 181–192.

Greene, M. (1997). Metaphors and multiples: Representation, the arts, and history. *Phi Delta Kappan, 78*(5), 387–394.

Guthrie, J. T., Van Meter, P., McCann, A., Wigfield, A., Bennett, I., Poundstone, C., Rice, M., Faibisch, F., Hunt, B., & Mitchell, A. (1996). Growth of literacy engagement: Changes in motivations and strategies during concept-oriented reading instruction. *Reading Research Quarterly, 31,* 306–322.

Guthrie, J. T., & Wigfield, A. (2000). Engagement and motivation in reading. In P. Mosenthal, M. Kamil, P. D. Pearson, & R. Barr (Eds.), *Handbook of reading research* (Vol. III, pp. 403–422). Mahwah, NJ: Erlbaum.

Guthrie, J. T., Wigfield, A., & VonSecker, C. (2000). Effects of integrated instruction on motivation and strategy use in reading. *Journal of Educational Psychology, 92,* 331–341.

Haberman, M. (1995a). Selecting "Star" teachers for children and youth in urban poverty. *Phi Delta Kappan, 76,* 777–781.

Haberman, M. (1995b). *Star teachers of children of poverty.* West Lafayette, IN: Kappa Delta Pi.

Hargreaves, A., & Moore, S. (2000). Educational outcomes, modern and postmodern interpretations: Response to Smyth and Dow. *British Journal of the Sociology of Education, 21,* 27–43.

Harre, R., & Gillet, G. (1994). *The discursive mind.* Thousand Oaks, CA: Sage.

Heath, S. B. (1990). The sense of being literate: Historical and cross-cultural features. In R. Barr, M. Kamil, P. Mosenthal, & P. D. Pearson (Eds.), *Handbook of reading research* (Vol. 2). White Plains, NY: Longman.

Heubert, J. P., & Hauser, R. M. (1999). *High stakes: Testing for tracking, promotion and graduation.* Washington, DC: National Academy Press.

Hoffer, B. K., & Pintrich, P. R. (1997). The development of epistemological theories: Beliefs about knowledge and knowing and their relation to learning. *Review of Educational Research, 67*(1), 88–140.

House, E. R., Glass, G. V., McLean, L., & Walker, D. (1978). No simple answers: Critique of the Follow Through evaluations. *Harvard Educational Review, 48,* 128–160.

Hume, K. (2001). Seeing shades of gray: Developing knowledge-building communities through science. In G. Wells (Ed.), *The care for dialogic inquiry* (pp. 99–117). New York: Teachers College Press.

International Reading Association and National Council of Teachers of English. (1996). *Standards for the English language arts.* Urbana, IL: Author.

Ivey, G., Johnston, P. H., & Cronin, J. (1998, April). *Process talk and children's sense of literate competence and agency.* Paper presented at the annual meeting of the American Educational Research Association, Montreal, Canada.

Johnson, D. W., & Johnson, R. T. (1989). *Cooperation and competition: Theory and research.* Edina, MN: Interaction.

Johnston, P. H. (1992). *Constructive evaluation of literate activity.* White Plains, NY: Longman.

Johnston, P. H. (1993). Assessment and literate "development." *The Reading Teacher, 46*(5), 428–429.

Johnston, P. H. (1997). *Knowing literacy: Constructive literacy assessment.* York, ME: Stenhouse.

Johnston, P. H. (1998). The consequences of the use of standardized tests. In S. Murphy (Ed.), *Fragile evidence: A critique of reading assessment* (pp. 89–101). Mahwah, NJ: Erlbaum.

Johnston, P. H. (1999). Unpacking literate achievement. In J. Gaffney & B. Askew (Eds.), *Stirring the waters: A tribute to Marie Clay* (pp. 27–46). Portsmouth, NH: Heinemann.

Johnston, P. H., Allington, R. L., Guice, S., & Brooks, G. W. (1998). Small change: A multi-level study of the implementation of literature-based instruction. *Peabody Journal of Education, 73,* 81–103.

Johnston, P. H., Woodside-Jiron, H., & Day, J. (2001). Teaching and learning literate epistemologies. *Journal of Educational Psychology, 93*(1), 223–233.

Johnston, R. C. (2001, January 24). Dropout studies target "pocket of problems." *Education Week*, p. 3.

Jones, A. (1991). *"At school I've got a chance." Culture/privilege: Pacific Islands and Pakeha girls at school*. Palmerston North, New Zealand: Dunmore Press.

Kardash, C. M., & Scholes, R. J. (1996). Effects of preexisting beliefs, epistemological beliefs, and need for cognition on interpretation of controversial issues. *Journal of Educational Psychology, 88*(2), 260–271.

Keene, E. L., & Zimmerman, S. (1997). *Mosaic of thought: Teaching comprehension in a Reader's Workshop*. Portsmouth, NH: Heinemann.

Keiny, S. (1994). Constructivism and teachers' professional development. *Teaching and Teacher Education, 10*(2), 157–167.

Keller, E. F. (1985). *Reflections on gender and science*. New Haven, CT: Yale University Press.

Kelly, E. E. (1995). *Education, democracy, and public knowledge*. San Francisco, CA: Westview Press.

Kerr, D. H. (1996). Democracy, nurturance, and community. In R. Soder (Ed.), *Democracy, education, and the schools* (pp. 37–68). San Francisco: Jossey-Bass.

Knapp, M. S. (1995). *Teaching for meaning in high-poverty classrooms*. New York: Teachers College Press.

Knoblauch, C., & Brannon, L. (1988). knowing our knowledge: A phenomenological basis for teacher research. In L. Z. Smith (Eds.), *Audits of meaning: A festschrift in honor of Ann E. Berthoff*. Portsmouth, NH: Heinemann—Boynton/Cook.

Knoblauch, C., & Brannon, L. (1993). *Critical teaching and the idea of literacy*. Portsmouth, NH: Boynton/Cook.

Kuhn, D., Garcia-Mila, M., Zohar, A., & Anderson, C. (1995). Strategies of knowledge acquisition. *Monographs of the Society for Research in Child Development, 60*(4), .

Ladson-Billings, G. (1994). *The Dreamkeepers: Successful teachers of African-American children*. San Francisco: Jossey-Bass.

Lampert, M. (1985). How do teachers manage to teach? *Harvard Educational Review, 55*(2), 178–194.

Lampert, M., & Clark, C. M. (1990). Expert knowledge and expert thinking in teaching: A response to Floden and Klinzing. *Educational Researcher, 19*(5), 21–23.

Langer, J. A. (1995a). Literature and learning to think. *Journal of Curriculum and Supervision, 10*, 207–226.

Langer, J. A. (1995b). *Envisioning literature: Literary understanding and literature instruction*. New York: Teachers College Press.

Lawrence, J. A. (1991). Informal reasoning in the judicial system. In J. F. Voss, D. N. Perkins, & J. W. Segal (Eds.), *Informal reasoning and education* (pp. 59–81). Hillsdale, NJ: Erlbaum.

Light, P., & Glachan, M. (1994). Facilitation of individual problem solving through peer interaction. *Educational Psychology, 5*, 217–225.

Lindfors, J. W. (1999). *Children's inquiry: Using language to make sense of the world*. New York: Teachers College Press.

Linn, R. L. (2000). Assessments and accountability. *Educational Researcher, 29,* 4–16.

Lyons, C. (1990). *Belief systems and instructional decisions: Comparisons between more and less effective Reading Recovery teachers.* Technical report, Ohio State University, Columbus, OH.

Mahiri, J., & Godley, A. J. (1998). Rewriting identity: Social meanings of literacy and "re-visions" of self. *Reading Research Quarterly, 33*(4), 416–433.

Malinowitz, H. (1995). *Textual orientations: Lesbian and gay students and the making of discourse communities.* Portsmouth, NH: Heinemann–Boynton/Cook.

Mathison, S., & Freeman, M. (1998). *The logic of interdisciplinary studies.* Technical Report #11004, National Research Center on English Learning and Achievement, Albany, NY.

Matthews, G. (1984). *Dialogues with children.* Cambridge, MA: Harvard University Press.

McGill-Franzen, A. (2000). Policy and instruction: What is the relationship? In M. Kamil, P. Mosenthal, P. D. Pearson, & R. Barr (Eds.), *Handbook of reading research* (Vol. III, pp. 891–908). Mahwah, NJ: Erlbaum.

McGill-Franzen, A., Allington, R. L., Yokoi, L., & Brooks, G. (1999). Putting books in the room seems necessary but not sufficient. *Journal of Educational Research, 93,* 67–74.

McGill-Franzen, A., & Lanford, C. (1994). Exposing the edge of the preschool curriculum: Teachers' talk about text and children's literary understandings. *Language Arts, 71,* 264–273.

McGill-Franzen, A., Ward, N., Goatley, V., & Machado, V. (in press). Teachers' use of new standards frameworks and assessments for English language arts and social studies: Local cases of New York State elementary grade teachers. *Reading Research and Instruction.*

McKenna, M., & Robinson, R. (1990). Content literacy: A definition and implications. *Journal of Reading, 34,* 184–186.

McMahon, S. I., Raphael, T. E., Goatley, V., & Pardo, L. (1997). *The book club connection: Literacy learning and classroom talk.* New York: Teachers College Press.

McNeil, L. M. (2000). *Contradictions of school reform: Educational costs of standardized testing.* New York: Routledge.

Mehan, H. (1979). *Learning lessons: Social organization in the classroom.* Cambridge, MA: Harvard University Press.

Murphy, S. (Ed.). (1998). *Fragile evidence: A critique of reading assessment.* Mahwah, NJ: Erlbaum.

National Commission on Teaching and America's Future. (1997). *Doing what matters most: Investing in quality teaching.* New York: Author.

National Council for the Social Studies Bulletin. (1989). *Curriculum standards for social studies.* Washington, DC: Author.

National Reading Panel. (2000). *Teaching children to read: An evidence-based assessment of the scientific research literature on reading and its implications for reading instruction: Reports of the subgroups.* Washington, DC: National Institute of Child Health and Development.

Newkirk, T., & McLure, P. (1992). *Listening in: Children talk about books (and other things)*. Portsmouth, NH: Heinemann.

Nicholls, J. G. (1989). *The competitive ethos and democratic education*. Cambridge, MA: Harvard University Press.

Noddings, N. (1984). *Caring: A feminine approach to ethics and moral education*. Berkeley: University of California Press.

Noddings, N. (1995). Teaching themes of care. *Phi Delta Kappan, 76*, 675–679.

Nystrand, M. (1997). *Opening dialogue: Understanding the dynamics of language and learning in the English classroom*. New York: Teachers College Press.

Page, R. N. (1991). *Lower track classrooms: A curricular and cultural perspective*. New York: Teachers College Press.

Paige, R. (2001, April 27). *Remarks as prepared for delivery by U.S. Secretary of Education Rod Paige*. Paper presented at the Education Writers Association, Phoenix, AZ.

Palmer, P. J. (1993). *To know as we are known: Education as a spiritual journey*. San Francisco: HarperCollins.

Perkins, D. N. (1993). Person-plus: A distributed view of thinking and learning. In G. Salomon (Ed.), *Distributed cognitions: Psychological and educational considerations* (pp. 88–110). New York: Cambridge University Press.

Pogrow, S. (2000). "Success For All" does not produce success for students. *Phi Delta Kappan, 82*, 67–80.

Postlethwaite, T. N., & Ross, K. N. (1992). *Effective schools in reading: Implications for educational planners*. The Hague, Netherlands: International Association for the Evaluation of Educational Achievement.

Powell, R. (1999). *Literacy as a moral imperative*. New York: Rowman & Littlefield.

Powell, R., & Cantrell, S. C. (2001). Saving Black Mountain: The promise of critical literacy in a multicultural democracy. *Reading Teacher, 54*, 772–795.

Pradl, G. M. (1996). Reading and democracy: The enduring influence of Louise Rosenblatt. *The New Advocate, 9*(1), 9–22.

Pressley, M. (2002). *Reading instruction that works: The case for balanced teaching* (2nd ed.). New York: Guilford Press.

Pressley, M. (in press). Effective beginning reading instruction: A paper commissioned by the National Reading Conference. *Journal of Literacy Research*.

Pressley, M., Allington, R. L., Wharton-McDonald, R., Block, C. C., & Morrow, L. M. (2001). *Learning to read: Lessons from exemplary first-grade classrooms*. New York: Guilford Press.

Pressley, M., Wharton-McDonald, R., Allington, R., Block, C. C., Morrow, L. M., Tracey, D., Baker, K., Brooks, G., Cronin, J., Nelson, E., & Woo, D. (2001). A study of effective grade-1 literacy instruction. *Scientific Studies of Reading, 5*, 35–58.

Pressley, M., Wharton-McDonald, R., Mistretta-Hampston, J., & Echevarria, M. (1998). Literacy instruction in 10 grade fourth- and fifth-grade classrooms in upstate New York. *Scientific Study of Reading, 2*, 159–194.

Pressley, M., Yokoi, L., Rankin, J., Wharton-McDonald, R., & Mistretta, J. (1997). A survey of the instructional practices of grade 5 teachers nominated as effective in promoting literacy. *Scientific Studies of Reading, 1,* 145–160.

Public Agenda. (2000). *A sense of calling: Who teaches and why.* www.public agenda.org/specials/teachers/teachers/htm [accessed on 6/7/00].

Raspberry, W. (2000, May 12). They never learn. *Washington Post,* p. A47.

Reichenbach, R. (1998). The postmodern self and the problem of developing a democratic mind. *Theory and Research in Social Education, 26,* 226–237.

Resnick, L. B. (1991). Shared cognition: Thinking as social practice. In L. Resnick, J. Levine, & S. Behrend (Eds.), *Socially shared cognitions* (pp. 1–19). Hillsdale, NJ: Erlbaum.

Rogoff, B., & Toma, C. (1997). Shared thinking: Community and institutional variations. *Discourse Processes,* 471–497.

Rose, L. C., & Gallup, A. M. (2000). The 32nd annual Phi Delta Kappa/Gallup poll of the public's attitudes toward the public schools. *Phi Delta Kappan, 82,* 41–58.

Routman, R. (1996). *Literacy at the crossroads.* Portsmouth, NH: Heinemann.

Ruddell, R. (1997). Researching the influential literacy teacher: Characteristics, beliefs, strategies, and new research directions. In C. Kinzer, K. Hinchman, & D. Leu (Eds.), *Inquiries in literacy theory and practice* (Vol. 46, *Yearbook of the National Reading Conference,* pp. 37–53). Chicago: National Reading Conference.

Sacks, P. (2000). *Standardized minds: The high price of America's testing culture and what we can do to change it.* Cambridge, MA: Perseus.

Salomon, G. (1993). No distribution without individuals' cognition: A dynamic interactional view. In G. Salomon (Ed.), *Distributed cognitions: Psychological and educational considerations* (pp. 111–138). New York: Cambridge University Press.

Sanders, W. L. (1998, December). Value-added assessment. *School Administrator, 55,* 101–113.

Schweinhart, L. J., & Weikart, D. P. (1997). The High/Scope preschool curriculum comparison study through age 23. *Early Childhood Research Quarterly, 12,* 117–143.

Sergiovanni, T. J. (2000). *The lifeworld of leadership: Creating culture, community, and personal meaning in our schools.* San Francisco: Jossey-Bass.

Servis, J. (1999). *Celebrating the fourth: Ideas and inspirations for teachers of grade four.* Portsmouth, NH: Heinemann.

Shepard, L. (2000). The role of assessment in learning. *Educational Researcher, 99,* 4–14.

Shepard, L. A., & Bliem, C. L. (1995). Parents' thinking about standardized tests and performance assessments. *Educational Researcher, 24*(8, Nov.), 25–32.

Smith, M. L. (1991). Put to the test: The effects of external testing on teachers. *Educational Researcher, 20*(5), 8–11.

Snow, C., Barnes, W., Chandler, J., Goodman, I. F., & Hemphill, L. (1991). *Unfulfilled expectations: Home and school influences on literacy.* Cambridge, MA: Harvard University Press.

Sosniak, L. A., & Stodolsky, S. S. (1993). Teachers and textbooks: Materials use in four fourth-grade classrooms. *Elementary School Journal, 93,* 249–275.

Sowell, T. (2000, June 20). A reply to teachers. *Tampa Tribune,* p. A9.

Spencer, L. M., & Spencer, S. M. (1993). *Competence at work: Models for superior performance.* New York: Wiley.

Stember, M. (1991). Advancing the social sciences through the interdisciplinary enterprise. *Social Science Journal, 28*(1), 1–14.

Sutton, R. E., Cafarelli, A., Lund, R., Schurdell, D., & Bischel, S. (1996). A developmental constructivist approach to pre-service teachers' ways of knowing. *Teaching and Teacher Education, 12,* 413–427.

Tappan, M. B. (1998). Sociocultural psychology and caring pedagogy: Exploring Vygotsky's "hidden curriculum." *Educational Psychologist, 33*(1), 23–33.

Taylor, B. M., Pearson, P. D., Clark, K., & Walpole, S. (2000). Effective Schools and accomplished teachers: Lessons about primary-grade reading instruction in low-income schools. *Elementary School Journal, 101,* 121–165.

Taylor, D. (1998). *Beginning to read and the spin doctors of science: The political campaign to change America's mind about how children learn to read.* Urbana, IL: National Council of Teachers of English.

Thomas, K. F., & Barksdale-Ladd, M. A. (1995). Effective literacy classrooms: Teachers and students exploring literacy together. In K. A. Hinchman, D. J. Leu, & C. Kinzer (Eds.), *Perspectives on literacy research and practice* (pp. 169–179). Chicago: National Reading Conference.

Thorkildsen, T. A. (1998). The way tests teach: Children's theories of how much testing is fair in school. In M. Leicester, C. Modgil, & S. Modgil (Eds.), *Classroom issues: Practice, pedagogy and curriculum.* Philadelphia: Falmor.

Todorov, T. (1996). Living alone together. *New Literary History, 27*(1), 1–14.

Turner, J. C. (1995). The influence of classroom contexts on young children's motivation for literacy. *Reading Research Quarterly, 30,* 410–441.

Tweney, R. D. (1991). Informal reasoning in science. In J. F. Voss, D. N. Perkins, & J. W. Segal (Eds.), *Informal reasoning and education* (pp. 3–16). Hillsdale, NJ: Erlbaum.

Vacca, R. T., & Vacca, J. L. (1999). *Content area reading: Literacy and learning across the curriculum* (6th ed.). New York: Longman.

Venezky, R. L. (1998). An alternate perspective on Success For All. In K. K. Wong (Ed.), *Advances in educational policy* (Vol. 4, pp. 145–165). Greenwich, CT: JAI Press.

Vygotsky, L. S. (1978). *Mind in society: The development of higher psychological processes.* Cambridge, MA: Harvard University Press.

Vygotsky, L. S. (1979). *Thought and language* (rev. ed.). (A. Kozulin, translator and editor). Cambridge, MA: MIT Press.

Walmsley, S. A. (1994). *Children exploring their world: Theme teaching in elementary school.* Portsmouth, NH: Heinemann.

Walmsley, S. A., & Allington, R. L. (1995). Redefining and reforming instructional support programs for at-risk students. In R. L. Allington & S. A. Walmsley (Eds.), *No quick fix: Rethinking literacy programs in America's elementary schools* (pp. 19–41). New York: Teachers College Press.

Walmsley, S. A., & Walp, T. P. (1990). Integrating literature and composing into the language arts curriculum: Philosophy and practice. *Elementary School Journal, 90,* 251–274.

Wanlass, Y. (2000). Broadening the concept of learning and school competence. *Elementary School Journal, 100,* 513–528.

Wells, G. (2001). *The case for dialogic inquiry.* New York: Teachers College Press.

Wells, G., & Chang-Wells, G. L. (1992). *Constructing knowledge together: Classrooms as centers of inquiry and literacy.* Portsmouth, NH: Heinemann.

Wenger, E. (1998). *Communities of practice: Learning, meaning, and identity.* Cambridge, UK: Cambridge University Press

Wigfield, A. (1997). Children's motivations for reading and reading engagement. In J. T. Guthrie & A. Wigfield (Eds.), *Reading engagement: Motivating readers through integrated instruction* (pp. 14–33). Newark, DE: International Reading Association.

Wilkinson, L. C., & Silliman, E. R. (2000). Classroom language and literacy learning. In M. L. Kamil, P. B. Mosenthal, P. D. Pearson, & R. Barr (Eds.), *Handbook of Reading Research* (Vol. 3, pp. 337–360). Mahwah, NJ: Erlbaum.

Winne, P., Graham, L., & Prock, L. (1993). A model of poor readers' text-based inferencing: Effects of explanatory feedback. *Reading Research Quarterly, 28,* 52–69.

# Children's Publications Cited

Aardema, V. (1975). *Why do mosquitoes buzz in people's ears?* New York: Dial.

Ahlberg, J., & Ahlberg, A. (1995). *The jolly postman.* New York: Little, Brown.

Allard, H. (1988). *Miss Nelson has a field day.* Boston: Houghton-Mifflin.

Amos, J. (1992). *Animals in danger.* Chatham, NJ: Raintree Steck.

Babbit, N. (1986). *Tuck everlasting.* New York: Farrar, Strauss & Giroux.

Boyd, W. (1984). *Ice cream war.* New York: Viking Penguin.

Burns, M. (1995). *The greedy triangle.* New York: Scholastic.

Calmenson, S. (1989). *The principal's new clothes.* New York: Scholastic.

Cole, J. (1995). *Magic school bus in the time of the dinosaurs.* New York: Scholastic.

Cole, J. (1997). *Magic school bus and the electronic field trip.* New York: Scholastic.

Cooney, B. (1982). *Miss Rumphius.* New York: Puffin Books.

Corbalis, J. (1988). *The ice cream heroes.* Boston, MA: Little Brown.

Coville, B. (1989). *My teacher is an alien.* Madison, WI: Demco.

Dahl, R. (1996). *James and the giant peach.* New York: Penguin.

Dahl, R. (1996). *Charlie and the chocolate factory.* New York: Penguin.

Fleischman, S. (1986). *The whipping boy.* New York: Greenwillow.

George, J. C. (1995). *There's an owl in the shower.* New York: HarperTrophy.

Heide, F. P. (1995). *The day of Ahmed's secret.* New York: Morrow.

Hest, A. (1997). *When Jesse came across the sea.* Cambridge, MA: Candlewick Press.

Hoff, S. (1958). *Danny and the dinosaur.* New York: HarperCollins.

Keene, C. M. (1998). *Operation Titanic.* Somerset, NJ: Peanut Butter Publishing.

Kemper, D. (1995). *Writer's express: A handbook for young writers, thinkers, and learners.* Wilmington, MA: Great Source.

Lansky, B. (Ed.). (1997). *No more homework, no more tests: Kids' favorite school poems.* New York: Simon & Schuster.

Leitner, I. (1992). *The big lie: A true story.* New York: Scholastic.

Lawlor, V. (1995). *I was dreaming to come to America: Memories from the Ellis Island oral history project.* New York: Viking.

Levine, E. (1993). *If your name was changed at Ellis Island.* New York: Scholastic.

Levitin, S. (1987). *Journey to America.* New York: Aladdin.

Louie, A. (1982). *Yeh-Shen: A Cinderella story from China.* New York: Putnam.

Manes, S. (1996). *Be a perfect person in just three days!* New York: Bantam Doubleday.

Martin, A. M. (1993). *Maid Mary Ann: Babysitter's club no. 66.* New York: Apple.

Metaxas, E. (1992). *King Midas and the golden touch.* Old Tappan, NJ: S & S Children's.

Mieder, W. (1997). *As strong as a moose.* Shelburne, VT: New England Press.

Moore, B. (1990). *Maggie among the Senecas.* New York: Harper Row.

Moore, R. (1987). *Words that taste good.* Toronto: Pembroke Publishers.

Moss, J. (1989). *Butterfly jar.* New York: Bantam.

Naylor, P. (1999). *Saving Shiloh.* New York: Simon & Schuster.

Naylor, P. (1999). *Shiloh's Season.* New York: Simon & Schuster.

Naylor, P. (2000). *Shiloh.* New York: Simon & Schuster.

Numeroff, L. (1985). *If you give a mouse a cookie.* New York: HarperCollins.

Prelutsky, J. (1984). *New kid on the block.* New York: Greenwillow.

Rathmann, P. (1995). *Officer Buckle and Gloria.* New York: Putnam.

Rawls, W. (1989). *Where the red fern grows.* New York: Bantam Books.

Reiss, J. (1987). *The upstairs room.* New York: HarperCollins.

Rylant, C. (1987). *Henry and Mudge under the yellow moon.* New York: Aladdin.

Say, A. (1993). *Grandfather's journey.* Boston: Houghton Mifflin.

Schwartz, A. (1991). *Scary stories 3.* New York: HarperCollins.

Scieszka, J. (1991). *The frog prince continued.* New York: Viking.

Scieszka, J. (1995). *Math curse.* New York: Viking.

Scieszka, J. (1996). *The stinky cheese man and other fairly stupid tales.* New York: Viking.

Seibold, J. O. (1997). *Olive, the other reindeer.* San Francisco: Chronicle Books.

Shreve, S. (1984). *The flunking of Joshua T. Bates.* New York: Knopf.

Silverstein, S. (1974). *Where the sidewalk ends.* New York: HarperCollins.

Smith, R. K. (1972). *Chocolate fever.* New York: Dell.

Smith, R. K. (1984). *The war with Grandpa* (R. Lauter, Illustrator). New York: Yearling Books.

Spinelli, J. (1990). *Maniac Magee.* Boston, MA: Little Brown.

Stine, R. L. (1995). *Welcome to dead house: Goosebumps no. 1.* New York: Apple.

Surat, M. M. (1989). *Angel child, dragon child.* New York: Scholastic.

Van Leeuwen, J. (1993). *Tales of Oliver Pig.* New York: Puffin.

Walsh, V., & Seibold, J. T. (1997). *Olive, the other reindeer.* San Francisco: Chronicle Books.

West, T. (1995). *Voyage of the Half Moon.* New York: Silver Moon Press.

White, E. B. (1952). *Charlotte's web.* New York: Harper & Rowe.

White, E. B. (1970). *Trumpet of the swan.* New York: HarperCollins.

Wood, A. (1989). *Quick as a cricket.* Auburn, ME: Child's Play.

# Index